WHEN
COURAGE
WAS
STRONGER
THAN FEAR

Remarkable Stories of
Christians and Muslims
Who Saved Jews from
the Holocaust

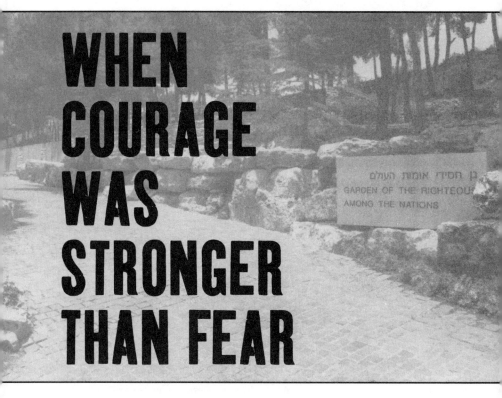

WHEN
COURAGE
WAS
STRONGER
THAN FEAR

ם חסידי אומות העולם
GARDEN OF THE RIGHTEOUS
AMONG THE NATIONS

PETER HELLMAN

[MARLOWE & COMPANY]
NEW YORK

WHEN COURAGE WAS STRONGER THAN FEAR:
Remarkable Stories of Christians and Muslims
Who Saved Jews from the Holocaust

COPYRIGHT © 1980, 1999, 2004 BY PETER HELLMAN

Published by
Marlowe & Company
An Imprint of Avalon Publishing Group Incorporated
245 West 17th Street • 11th Floor
New York, NY 10011-5300

AVALON
publishing group incorporated

Two earlier editions of this book were published—
first, in 1980, as *Avenue of the Righteous,* then, in 1999,
under the current title, by Marlowe & Company/Balliett & Fitzgerald.

Library of Congress Cataloging-in-Publication Data is available.

ISBN 1-56924-414-6

9 8 7 6 5 4 3 2 1

Designed by Pauline Neuwirth, Neuwirth & Associates, Inc.

Printed in the United States of America

Contents

Author's Note: Work on this book spans more than 25 years. Chapters 1, 3, 4, and 5, with their 1998 epilogues, are unaltered. The final chapter is new to this edition.

In memory of Violet Grace Hellman (1915–2002)

My mother was not given to pronouncements, but she did once say that if each person, instead of lecturing other people on what they should do, simply did the right thing in his or her own small space, all those personal acts would add up to a better world. She wasn't thinking of the people in this book, but she could have been.

[PHOTOGRAPHS]

Acknowledgments

From the hour that I came upon the Avenue of the Righteous at Yad Vashem in Jerusalem, I hoped to find a publisher who would commission a book on the subject. That hope was first fulfilled by Marc Jaffe, then head of Bantam Books. After *Avenue of the Righteous*, as that book was called, went out of print, I didn't expect it to get a new life. But thanks to Will Balliett of Balliett & Fitzgerald, and Matthew Lore of Marlowe & Company, a new, expanded edition was published in 1999 under the current title. Now that Will has moved on to head up Carroll & Graf Publishers, Matthew has given me the opportunity to once again expand the book in this third edition. I am grateful to have an editor who shares my belief in the importance of this subject.

I wish to acknowledge the work of the Jewish Foundation for the Righteous. Founded by Rabbi Harold Schulweis, the Foundation provides financial support to rescuers. Many of them pursued Righteousness at the cost of financial comfort. The Foundation provides confidential stipends ($1.3 million in 2003) thrice yearly to more than 1,600 needy rescuers in 30 countries, including at least one profiled here. The Shoah Foundation, founded by Steven Spielberg, has created an invaluable library of filmed interviews with rescuers, including one with Monsignor Schivo (Chapter 2).

For their assistance on this edition, I am grateful to Ivan Čerešnješ, Dr. Bodgan Denitch, and Ronit Greenwald. Dr. Mordecai Paldiel, Director of the Department of the Righteous at Yad Vashem, unfailingly responded to my queries with information and insight. Pauline Neuwirth brought clarity to the timeline. Belatedly, I thank Shlomit Landau for her translations of the piercingly beautiful letters of Leokadia Jaromirska.

—PETER HELLMAN

introduction

Until the age of twenty-five, I kept a wary distance from the subject of the Holocaust. It wasn't that I averted my eyes from those ghastly film clips of mounded corpses and walking skeletons in the death camps. I didn't. What seemed more fearful to me was what I couldn't see: all those people, presumably normal in other ways, who had done their part in bringing our world to that moment. Actually, one of those people can be seen in a grainy photo somewhere in the Holocaust archives—a soldier in a long khaki coat shooting a mother clasping an infant. At close range, no less. How did he not recoil from pulling the trigger?

Being an optimist, I much prefer to believe that otherwise normal people, by and large, want to do the right thing. And that each person's moral wiring has a fuse box. Asked to do certain awful things, the circuit is tripped. Did that circuitry not exist in the man in the khaki coat? Or had it been bypassed through Nazi indoctrination? For genocide to be carried out, one or the other has to be true. And it has to be so on a scale as massive as the murders. If there was not a speck of human good to think about, then I tried not to think about it at all.

In 1968, despite some misgivings, I visited Yad Vashem, Israel's national Holocaust place of memory, set in the rocky slope of Mount Herzl in Jerusalem. The Hebrew, plucked from a verse in

Isaiah, means "place and name." Most of what I saw at Yad Vashem was as expected: the grim history of the Nazi war against the Jews detailed in museum exhibits, anguished artwork, a Hall of Names, and a stark Hall of Remembrance whose recessed stone floor is etched with the names of the twenty-two largest death camps. Its dim interior is lit by a flame that rises over an urn containing ashes of the martyrs—a few handfuls to represent the Six Million. From time to time, birds darted into the grey light of the hall. They would swoop about briefly, then—as if sensing that this was not a happy place—quickly find their way out.

Yet, surprisingly, all was not grim at Yad Vashem. All along the path that led to the memorials grew rows of leathery-leaved carob trees. Under each tree was a small plaque inscribed with the name of a rescuer who had saved one or more hunted Jews from the Nazis. They came from Holland, Poland, France, Belgium, Denmark, Hungary, Russia, Italy, tiny Luxembourg, and even Germany—all the Nazi controlled countries where Jews desperately needed a saving hand. And a few others, too, ranging from England to Japan. Each rescuer, honored with a tree, had faced the evil head-on and struck back with courage and goodness. These were the rays of light in the otherwise total darkness of the Holocaust. To whatever extent they were able, they redeemed us.

The main intent of Yad Vashem is to give a "place and name" to the victims who went up as ash or down into mass graves. But Article 9 of the Martyrs and Heroes Remembrance Act of 1953, which created Yad Vashem, mandated that "a place and a name" also be given to those gentiles who acted to save their fellow humans. Since the Nazis made it clear in every nation conquered by them that those who acted to help the Jews would share the same fate, such aid was death defying.

The Hebrew title given to these heroes is *Hasidei Ummot ha-Olam*—the Righteous Among Nations. Rabbinic sages used the term at least as early as the tenth century to designate those gentiles who, by their merit, are as eligible as any member of the

House of Israel to share in the Hereafter—a dispensation that was not often reciprocated.

In English, "Righteous Among Nations" sounds a bit stilted. Usually, the honorees are just called the Righteous, or the Just. "Righteous Christians" is also heard, but as the first story in this book makes clear, that term is too narrow. Dozens of Muslims, mainly from Bosnia-Herzegovina in the former Yugoslavia, have been honored along with the Christian majority. The ground rule for recognition is activism that puts one's own body at risk. It is not enough to abstain from evil or to sympathize with the victim. One must do positive deeds. "Execute justice in the morning and deliver from the hand of the oppressor him who has been robbed" (Jeremiah 21:12). Robbed of the right to live, in this case.

Jeremiah's exhortation became most urgent in Nazi-ruled nations. It wasn't helpful to express sympathy for hunted persons or even to pray for them in their terminal misery. Action had to be the order of the day, however inconvenient or dangerous. Many of the Righteous, in fact, seem more adept at action than explanation. Asked why they risked all, often for a stranger, it is typical of them to shrug their shoulders and say, "I did nothing special. Anybody would have done it." Or they might not say anything at all, even to their children. Lamija Jaha, whose parents hid a young Jewish woman in their home during the Nazi occupation of Sarajevo in the former Yugoslavia, heard nothing about that deed while growing up after the war. Only when Yad Vashem honored her parents as a result of testimony from the rescued person did Lamija learn what they had done.

An articulate exception to the laconic attitude of the Righteous toward their own actions was a Belgian woman named Jeanne Daman Scaglione. As a young teacher in Brussels during the Occupation, she specialized in finding hiding places for Jewish children:

> I became persuaded that it was imperative for a non-Jew to concern herself with saving Jewish lives under

pain of indirect collaboration by default in the destruction of the Jewish community. To the extent that I could, I tried to come out of this war having refused, at least, to find refuge in an easy neutrality.

A more succinct explanation came from Herta Muller-Kuhlenthal, one of the Righteous from Holland: "What I did came naturally. It would have been unnatural not to do it." A Polish honoree, Eduard Fajks, said: "God gives us life as a precious loan. No one but God has the right to claim it. That's all I know. The rest is unimportant."

Thirty-five members sit on the committee on the Righteous Among Nations. Its director since 1982 has been Dr. Mordecai Paldiel. He is a man with direct knowledge of the Righteous. Thanks to Father Simon Gallay, a Catholic cleric, Paldiel's family was smuggled from occupied France into neutral Switzerland in 1943. Paldiel and his staff work out of an office where files bulge and desks are heaped with letters from many places—some of them in wobbly script that suggests the advanced age of the writers. Sixty years after the Holocaust, the number of new nominations holds steady at about six hundred annually. According to Paldiel, many who write in belatedly had previously found it too hard to summon up the painful past, even if that meant bringing honor to a rescuer. Approaching the end of life, they gather their strength and do what must be done.

The great Italian writer Primo Levi, who survived Auschwitz thanks to extra soup secretly brought to him daily by Lorenzo Perrone, a contract bricklayer at the death camp, never nominated his rescuer to be one of the Righteous. But Levi did write of Perrone's "pure and uncontaminated" humanity. He and his wife also honored the bricklayer by naming their son Renzo and giving their daughter the middle name Lorenza. After Levi's death in 1987, Carol Angier, who was writing a biography of the writer, wrote to Yad Vashem, urging that Perrone be honored. After testimony was received from Renzo Levi and a fellow slave laborer with Levi, Perrone was inscribed in the Garden of the Righteous in February, 1999.

Some applications come directly to Yad Vashem, while others arrive via an Israeli embassy abroad. Investigations are carried out along strict judicial lines. Testimony is taken, witnesses examined. A questionnaire is furnished to rescued persons to guide them in their testimony. Questions include: "How and when did you meet your rescuer?" "What, in your opinion, were the rescuer's motivations?" "Cover-up story: how was your presence explained to family members and neighbors?"

The motive must have been pure. It's okay for a hidden person or family to have given money to the rescuer to pay for food and other needs of life. But if payment was demanded as a condition of saving, the honor is not conferred. Even a gentile who saved a Jewish spouse is denied—though, more than once, savior and saved fell in love and married after the war. (Bojenna Rotman, an assistant in the Department of the Righteous, is the daughter of a Christian mother honored by Yad Vashem who married the man she saved. The couple moved to Israel.)

Even the very young can grasp the essence of the rescuer's impulse. "Suppose a Christian person had a Jewish girlfriend or boyfriend when the Nazis came," I proposed to a class of nine-year-olds in a San Diego school. "And you said to that person, 'Don't worry, I'm going to hide you even though I'm risking my life.' After the war, you are nominated by that person to be honored as one of the Righteous. Would the application be approved?"

"No," said a girl in the back row.

"Why not?"

"Because if you didn't love that person, you might not have agreed to save him."

Exactly. Love may be beautiful, but it compromises the standard of rescue for humane rather than romantic reasons.

The rigors of the committee's selection process can lead to bitterness. Dietrich Bonhoeffer, the revered German theologian, has been repeatedly rejected as one of the Righteous even though he was a vigorous anti-Nazi hung by order of Hitler in April, 1945, only a month before the defeat of the Third Reich. The reason given is that Bonhoeffer, a Lutheran, saved not one Jew, as required by Yad Vashem. Stephen Wise, a Connecticut attorney whose grandfather, a noted rabbi, knew Bonhoeffer, has assailed Yad Vashem for its "blackballing rules" and "procedural obstacles." Some years ago, a nomination was submitted on behalf of an SS officer who acted to save Jews as they were about to be shot in a slave labor camp during the last days of the war. He, too, was rejected. The reasoning was that an SS man, by dint of his membership in an elite Nazi terror force, couldn't be one of the Righteous. Late in the war, brutal SS men and other Nazis had an incentive to change their ways in hope of saving their skins.

Most such cases occur in the shadows. But not that of Wilm Hosenfeld, a German army officer and music lover who saved the Polish-Jewish pianist Wladyslaw Szpilman from almost certain death in the Warsaw Ghetto. The story was dramatized in Roman Polanski's Academy Award–winning film, *The Pianist*. Szpilman's son, Andrzej, demanded that Yad Vashem recognize Hosenfeld as one of the Righteous for having saved his father. The nomination was turned down. One reason is that the burden of proof for honoring a German officer is stricter for a person threatened by Germans. And the distinction made by the nine-year-old in San Diego also comes into play: Hosenfeld had saved a piano virtuoso who played only for him. But would he have been willing to save Szpilman if he couldn't play a note?

Though Germans in uniform face an uphill battle in being honored by Yad Vashem, German civilians are evaluated objectively. Oskar Schindler, the "hero" of the book and movie, *Schindler's List*, is buried in Jerusalem. His funeral procession was composed of Jews whom he saved. In 2003, 358 Germans had been honored as Righteous.

The Department of the Righteous Among Nations does not automatically reject candidates when it hears the word "Nazi." Dervis Korkut, the Muslim museum curator in Sarajevo who with his wife hid a young Jewish woman from the Germans, was himself later accused of being sympathetic to the Nazis and was imprisoned. In fact, he was framed. A copy of the certificate honoring Korkut and his wife became the "visa" allowing their daughter and her family to start a new life in Israel after they were driven out of Kosovo in 1999. Their story, spanning six decades, is new to this edition.

In the early years, the committee recognized three degrees of valor. Some candidates got a certificate of honor. Others also got the right to plant a tree, and still others were awarded not only a tree, but were also given a bronze medallion. That tier system proved to be onerous and also led to bitterness ("Why did my rescuer only get a certificate, while yours got to plant a tree?"). In the mid-1980s, the tiers were eliminated. One and all were treated the same.

Certificates and medals are standard expressions of honor in most nations. But for people living in a land where forests were long ago stripped away, asking the honorees to plant a tree was especially apt. In Israel, few official acts are without biblical connection. In the case of the tree plantings, Yad Vashem took its cue from the psalmist on the subject of the person who "walks not in the counsel of the wicked."

> He is like a tree planted by streams of water that yields
> its fruit in its season, and its leaf does not wither. In all
> that he does, it prospers. (Psalm 1:3)

In the beginning, only the carob tree honored the Righteous. The choice was a practical one. The carob's leathery leaves are neither withered by dry summer wind nor stripped by winter gales. Yad Vashem understood the carob's significance to Christians. According to the Book of Mark, John the Baptist was sustained during his sojourn in the wilderness by honey and locusts—not the plague insects but the chocolatey brown bean pods of the carob tree known as Saint John's bread. Yad Vashem actually overlooks Ein Karem, the narrow, verdant valley from which John the Baptist is said to have hailed.

In 1962, the first trees were planted in double rows on the broad path leading into Yad Vashem. Underlying the national importance of the dedication, it was attended by Prime Minister Golda Meir. That section, whose trees are gnarly with age, is the original Avenue of the Righteous. Then came plantings that extended the Avenue to a north-facing knoll at the rear of Yad Vashem. These trees command a particularly lovely and sweeping view of the worn Judean hills, through which the road from the coastal plain can be glimpsed wending up to the Heavenly City. With nearly a thousand trees planted by the 1980s, this site also filled up. The next extension was to a lower slope on the south side of Yad Vashem. For the first time, olive trees were substituted for carobs— a change suggested by staff gardeners, who felt that the carobs were getting too much water and ultimately would not survive.

The olive tree has its own roots in the New Testament. In Romans 16:11–24, the apostle Paul, discussing tensions between gentile and Jewish converts to early Christianity, compares the grafting of the "wild olive" branch to the "cultivated" one. Mordecai Paldiel says of the olive tree, "It may grow crooked, it suffers, but it never dies. It is a symbol of the Jews."

Over the years, Yad Vashem steadily expanded. So did the number of Righteous Among Nations. The trees became a forest, and finding a particular tree became daunting. In 1989, a decision was made to abandon tree-planting in favor of inscribing names of honorees on tablets in the Garden of the Righteous, located on a lower slope. Grouped by countries, names became easier to find. And while trees may die, names etched in stone do not.

As of January 2004, 20,205 persons from 35 countries had been designated. Early on, Holland held the lead in honorees. The tree most often visited by Christians was planted by Kory Ten Boom, the Dutch farm woman whose story of rescuing Jews is told in the film *The Hiding Place*. Thanks to another film, Steven Spielberg's *Schindler's List*, the tree of the German businessman

Oskar Schindler is as famous as Kory Ten Boom's. With the end of the Cold War and the thawing of relations between Israel and Eastern Europe, Polish honorees took the lead—currently about 5,700, compared with 4,500 from Holland. That these two countries share top honors is ironic and sad: Poland was severely anti-Semitic, and some Jews who survived the Germans were killed there by Poles in postwar pogroms. Holland, despite many res-cuers, was the deadliest killing ground during the Nazi Occupation. Eighty-five percent of Dutch Jews, including the best-known single victim, Anne Frank, were murdered. The only entire country to be honored with a tree is Denmark, which acted almost as one people to rescue its eight thousand Jews, nearly all of whom were rowed by night to safety in neutral Sweden.

One of the most sought-out trees is Raoul Wallenberg's. The Swedish diplomat, posted to Budapest, dispensed thousands of visas to Jews, saving them from arrest during a Nazi deportation blitz in 1944. Wallenberg himself was arrested when the Russian army occupied Budapest in the winter of 1945 and was never heard from again. Curiously, his tree long failed to thrive. Underneath it was "a rock as big as a meteor," according to Paldiel, and its roots could not find nourishment. Some Wallenberg stalwarts believed that Wallenberg's tree would never prosper until the truth was learned about his fate and his spirit could rest.

Out of more than twenty thousand documented cases of the Righteous, I have profiled seven, each representing a different country. Faced with such a multitude of life and death dramas, I chose with one exception only those in which the honored person was still living and cooperative. The most cooperative was Raul Laporterie, a dapper Frenchman who, along with being a serial rescuer, was an exceptional archivist. Almost up to the time of his death in his nineties, Laporterie regularly sent me and my wife, Susan, snapshots and documents from the wartime years kept in his private archive in a country village, all annotated in a flowing hand.

As I sifted through the departmental archives, three cases seared by injustice jumped out at me. In each one, the person honored by Israel had been treated shabbily by his own country for acting as a rescuer. They were noble exceptions to the rule that the Righteous must have risked their lives to be rescuers. These three—one police officer and two diplomats—only risked their careers. Although all three had died by the time I was ready to write, their courage deserves a brief recounting here.

One was Paul Grueninger, police chief of the Swiss border town of Saint Gallen. In August 1938, the Swiss closed their border to Jews forced out of Austria after its annexation by the Third Reich. Grueninger backdated the entry papers of 3,601 Jews seeking asylum, many of them children, so that their entry into Switzerland appeared legal even though it came after the deadline. His manner was gentle, and in a 1997 documentary film called *Grueninger's Fall*, a rescued man says, "I know that everything I was and later became in my life I basically owe to those five minutes I spent with him."

When Swiss authorities discovered what Grueninger had done, he was prosecuted for violating Swiss law. Convicted, he was dismissed and his pension was canceled. After the war, Grueninger barely eked out a living. He sought neither publicity nor redress. At age seventy-eight, he was honored as one of the Righteous in a ceremony in Bern. Two years later, newspaper stories embarrassed the Swiss government into "rehabilitating" Grueninger. He died soon after, and his widow traveled to Jerusalem to plant a tree in his honor.

Similar is the case of Aristedes de Sousa Mendes, Portuguese counsel in Bordeaux at the onset of the Nazi invasion of France, and Belgium in May 1940. After a rabbi who had fled from Belgium first explained the plight of the Jewish refugees, de Sousa Mendes and two of his sons worked around the clock for days issuing transit visas to thousands of other refugees gathered outside the consulate. All were desperate to flee to neutral Portugal, a few hours away by rail. As many refugees as could be fit in the counsel's house and offices were given refuge. De Sousa

Mendes issued so many visas that his government sent two officials to bring him back to Portugal. On the way back, he stopped for a day in Bayonne to stamp more visas because the local counsel refused to do so himself. Further along, at Handaye, he found a way for those with visas to pass through Spain on the way to Portugal, even though the Spanish border was closed.

Like Paul Grueninger, Mendes, father of fourteen children, lost his job and his property for his rescue efforts. Neither was ever restored, but until to his death in 1954, Mendes insisted that he would have acted the same way all over again, saying, "My desire is to be with God against man, rather than with man against God." He also said that if thousands of Jews had to suffer because of one Catholic (Hitler), then it was only right for one Catholic to suffer for thousands of Jews. A tree was planted at Yad Vashem in the name of Aristedes de Sousa Mendes in 1966. In 1987, his diplomatic rights and pension were posthumously restored by Portugal.

Third to be left out in the cold by his own country was Chiume Sugihara, a Japanese diplomat. At summer's end, 1940, Sugihara issued at least six thousand transit visas to desperate Jews crowding the gate of his consulate in Kovno, Lithuania—even though his government had cabled him three times to stop. Returning to Japan in 1947, Sugihara was curtly dismissed from the diplomatic corps. His colleagues whispered that he didn't need even his bare-bones pension since, in their eyes, he must have taken bribes for issuing all those visas. Locked in their own dreary mind-set, they couldn't imagine that Sugihara's motive was pure.

Sugihara was too ill to plant his tree on the Avenue of the Righteous when it was awarded in 1985. He died the next year. Eventually, his own country also recognized his moral valor. When a Sugihara memorial was dedicated in his mountain hometown of Yaotsu in 1992, his widow noticed a majestic red hawk circling overhead, as if watching. "It reminded me," she wrote later, "of my husband's spirit."

The wrongs that were done to Grueninger, de Sousa Mendes, and Sugihara might never have been righted if a tree had not been planted for each of them in Jerusalem. Though the ceremonies were modest, they resonated strongly in the honorees' own countries.

Digging into the details of the cases presented here, I was struck by the rescuers' mingling of humdrum daily duties, with, when the moment came, decisions that were, literally, death-defying. The humdrum included regular deliveries of food to hidden persons, daily pickup of slop buckets from attics, basements, pockets under stairwells or beneath kitchen floorboards, holes in the earth, and even cemetery vaults. Such routines could stretch from days into years.

In the moral realm, acts of rescuers could have a quiet power, as when the Postma family in a Dutch village informed Nurit Hegt, the Amsterdam teenager hidden by them, that they didn't want her to share in household chores. Their explanation: "We didn't take you into our home to be a maid." Another small act of kindness that counted large to the recipients was the 1943 Christmas Eve visit of Beniamino Schivo, an Italian priest, to a Jewish family he had hidden in a deserted hilltop convent in Umbria. The priest walked for seven hours to the convent, arriving at midnight. Before dawn, he walked back down. And all to bring the family holiday food and encouragement.

At the other extreme are acts at the outer limits courage. When Leokadia Jaromirska, a Polish Christian, was about to be executed with a Jewish child in her arms, she asked the German soldiers whose rifles were raised to grant her one last wish: "Shoot me first, so that I don't have to see the blood of the child."

It's easy to equate courage with heroism, yet they are not the same, and neither are all heroes. The firefighter who rushes into a burning building to save someone trapped within is unquestionably courageous, maybe even a hero. But that is what the firefighter is trained and equipped to do. The passerby who dashes into the flames, on the other hand, is the rarest kind of hero because he or she could have kept on walking rather than risking death. The Righteous Among Nations, too, could have "kept right on walking."

The question persists: Why did some people risk their lives to save humans who may have been strangers? Mordecai Paldiel, who has pondered this issue each work day since 1982, points to the research of the psychologists Samuel and Pearl Oliner. In their book, *The Altruistic Personality: Rescuers of Jews in Nazi Europe*, the Oliners divide the Righteous into groups of those who acted out of pure love for humanity and those who acted on stern ethical grounds—the latter of which may not have had a whit of love for their fellow humans. Some "ethicists," in fact, were outright anti-Semites, yet they drew the line between social discrimination and fatal cruelty. One was the Polish novelist Sophia Kossak-Szczucka, an organizer of the Council to Aid Jews, known by the Polish acronym Zegota. Kossak-Szczucka held anti-Semitic views, which she did not retract even after the war.

Pure love, with no strings attached, as the motive for rescue, was notably expressed by Pope John Paul II, also a Pole, who met with and blessed his would-be assassin. But idealism had to be harnessed to a vulpine cunning as the rescuers maneuvered for days, months, years to fool the Nazis and their henchmen. Even the smallest act had its effect, as when Raoul Laporterie, the dapper Frenchman, softened up the German guards at the border between Vichy France and the Occupied Zone by bringing them gifts of fresh oysters and items from his men's haberdashery. The result was a less closely inspected crossing when Laporterie passed refugees with false papers across the border.

Most of us pass through the days of our lives awaiting some drama, a chance to vault beyond the ordinary, even a way to be put physically at risk for the right reason. Along with the twenty thousand persons honored as Righteous Among Nations, uncounted others did the same without ever being proposed for official recognition. Summing up a career of deciding who merits the title and who falls short, Mordecai Paldiel says, "To the hunted Jew standing before you at your doorstep, you were irreplaceable. The Nazis had decided that this person must die.

Deep inside your mind, you decided that it was also a thrust at you. At that moment, in deciding to act, the Righteous were playing God. They were partners in Creation."

Leokadia Jaromirska

One evening early in January 1966, a twenty-five-year-old kibbutznik named Yoram Katzir sat down to write a letter to his wife's stepmother in Poland. Her name is Leokadia Jaromirska. Yoram had never met this woman, never been to Poland, rarely strayed much farther from this kibbutz in the Jordan Valley than the twenty-minute bike ride alongside fields of avocado, banana, and cotton to the blue oval of the Sea of Galilee. From late in childhood he and his wife had shared an identical life, right down to meals in the communal dining hall. It was the years before then that Yoram now asked Leokadia to tell him about, the years when, with an affection not always equaled by natural children, this infant had learned to call her "Mother."

Leokadia was at home when the letter arrived at her third-floor apartment in the grim old Teutonic building hard beside the main trolley line in the Silesian city which for six hundred years the Germans called Breslau and the Poles, reclaiming it after the war, now call Wroclaw. It was only by chance that Leokadia was at home when the mail came. Having hurt her foot in a fall at the bottle factory where she worked, she had been given ten days' sick leave by the doctor. Since no woman enjoyed burying herself in a book—novels, the Bible, travelogues, whatever—more than Leokadia, she normally would have spent the ten days doing just that. But now she used the time to write her first long letter to Yoram.

It could not be ruled out that Leokadia, who had no formal education, might have stumbled in her task, or not known where to begin, or forgotten too much, or managed only to turn out a few pages of dry facts. But none of these things happened. For ten days she wrote steadily the first of what was to be a long stream of such letters. This one arrived at the kibbutz early in February. A Polish-born nurse who had translated Yoram's letter into Polish now translated Leokadia's reply into Hebrew:

January 18, 1966

Dear Yoram,

I will try to fulfill your request by telling you the story of a little girl whose name was Bogusia and is now Shifra. For me she will ever be Bogusia because this name was engraved on my heart in love and suffering.

It might be that this story will not be written according to the rules of writing, because I don't have that talent. I also don't have a grosz's worth of imagination. It is difficult to sit down and write this—but especially today on the twenty-first anniversary of the day we were liberated [from the Germans]. Memories overtake me. It happens three times a year—on October 6th, January 18th, and May 16th. But now to the point . . .

So this story starts for Leokadia Jaromirska with the sound of not one but two infants crying in the night. The place is a tiny settlement a few miles north of Warsaw—just a place where the train stops, really—called Bialoleka. It is the evening of that first date she mentions to Yoram, October 6. The year is 1942, when the Nazis, though they didn't yet know it, were about to begin the downward curve of their reign over nearly all Europe. The only endeavor in which they would still surpass themselves was in killing Jews.

Killing Jews, in fact, was the prime topic of discussion when Leokadia went down the hall of her low-slung apartment building to have tea with neighbors that Sunday evening. For several days, the Germans had been busy "liquidating" the nearby ghetto of Legionowo. This meant, in practical terms, that the six thousand Jews who had been herded into a walled-up section of the town twenty months earlier were now scheduled to be loaded into boxcars for the trip to the killing center at Treblinka. The process was meant to be orderly. But not all the Jews in the ghetto were willing to take that ride. In the night some had bolted the ghetto walls. Now, like animals driven out of the forest by fire, they could be seen dashing haplessly about the surrounding area. The Germans did not hesitate to shoot or beat them to death on sight. This is what Leokadia and her friends discussed over tea. *We cursed the Krauts and felt pity for what they were doing to those poor people and the children.*★ As she returned to her apartment at about eleven o'clock, Leokadia heard two infants crying. *I thought it must be the children of a neighbor, who were always fighting. In quiet, I went to sleep.*

As usual on workdays, Leokadia left at ten minutes to six to catch the 6:05 train to Warsaw, where she worked at a German warehousing center. The morning was cool and damp. She had just said hello to another neighbor, Mrs. Koklinska, when again she heard the sound of infants crying. The two women followed the sound along the wall of a convent set in a forest beside the road. There, in the tall grass, they found two baby girls. One, perhaps nine months old, lay on her back. The other, a bit over a year

---

★Note: Throughout her story, passages extracted from Leokadia's letters are italicized. Passages from conversations with her are quoted.

old, sat up. Their voices were hoarse and their cheeks swollen from so much crying. Both women knew that illegitimate newborn babies were sometimes abandoned to the mercies of a convent like this one. But, as Mrs. Koklinska pointed out, these children were too old for that. They would surely have to be Jewish children, probably given up by hunted parents from Legionowo.

"Jewish children or not, they are abandoned, and it is a pity," said Leokadia. She picked up the older girl while Mrs. Koklinska held the other. They stood there, two women with their morning routine disrupted, not knowing what to do.

"Take them home with you for the morning," said Leokadia. "I'll try to get off work at noon. Then we'll decide what to do."

Leokadia's situation, as of that morning, begins with the facts that she was thirty-four years old, handsome in a forthright way, and alone. Bolek, her husband of eight years, had been arrested one day in April 1940, by the Gestapo at the Gdansk station in Warsaw for possession of an illegal newspaper—that is, one which the occupiers had not approved for publication. Leokadia went to the station that afternoon to wait for him. She waited and waited. Finally the stationmaster asked who she was waiting for. "My husband," she answered.

"Oh, don't wait for him. He won't come back. He was arrested."

That night Leokadia dashed to the Gestapo headquarters in Warsaw, hoping to find Bolek. She took with her some tomatoes and dry bread—all that she had in the house. But it was too late. Bolek had the unhappy distinction of being one of the first Poles shipped off as a political prisoner—and new slave—to the concentration camp at Oswiecim, better known to the world by its German name, Auschwitz.

Until the war, life hadn't been bad for this couple. Bolek owned a modestly profitable metal-galvanizing shop on Stawicki Street, in what would become the Warsaw ghetto. In 1938, Leokadia contracted what she calls a "throat disease" for which the doctor recommended "country air." They moved to Bialoleka, a two-hour commute to the central city. Life continued on the edge of comfort until the German assault on Warsaw in September 1939, when a bomb destroyed the shop and killed a worker. "Bolek wanted to rebuild the place," she says, "but I was against it because it was sickening to have lost our worker. I didn't want any more to do with the place." On the day he was arrested, Bolek had been on his way to scout out a new location to rebuild the business.

With Bolek and the business both gone, Leokadia grasped for whatever work she could find—as a washerwoman, cleaning woman, full-fledged maid, then as a quality-control checker in a vodka bottle factory. This last job paid the best, but much of the work was outdoors. In the winter of 1941 she was sick again, this time with malaria, back in bed in Bialoleka, and out of a job. In the summer she found indoor work with the German warehousing authority in Warsaw. The pay was not as good but, besides being indoors, the job had one matchless advantage. She was issued an ID card emblazoned with the eagle of the Third Reich. It was her guarantee—as much as a Pole could be guaranteed—that, unlike her husband and so many others, she would not be detained, arrested, or deported as a result of one of the frequent but unpredictable roundups carried out by the Gestapo. If she was to survive, Leokadia's instincts told her, she could do it best in the midst of the enemy. So now, each morning, she took the 6:05 to work and, each afternoon, the 5:08 home. After months during which she heard nothing, she was allowed to write a postcard to Bolek once a week. He was allowed to write a postcard back at the same intervals. He always said he was well, but Leokadia wondered. The prescribed format of the cards, allowing only for bare and mechanical language, was certainly no solace.

Being a good worker, well liked by her German employers, Leokadia managed to get permission to go home at noon, as she had hoped. The trickier problem was that on Mondays the potato ration was given out. "It took some maneuvering to reserve a place in line," says Leokadia, "so that I could get back to old Koklinska. On the train I still had no idea what would await me or what I would do."

A crowd of women had gathered in a knot in front of the tiny store where Leokadia shopped. At the center was the older child. *She was holding a roll in one hand which she would not eat because she was crying, "Mama, Mama." The women were standing there pitying her, but they did nothing. When I came up to the child, I said, "Hello, come here, little doll." And when I said this, the girl spread her arms out to me. I held her in my arms and still I was thinking what I should do.*

Unable to deal with the child in hand, Leokadia asked about the other one. Mrs. Koklinska explained that since she already had grandchildren of her own to care for, she could not keep the child herself. So she had given her to a certain Mrs. Kossak. Furthermore, admitted Mrs. Koklinska with more than a little guilt, she had gone to the police station where she told the whole story of what had happened that morning. She had made it clear that it was Leokadia who had told her to take the two children home. The captain—a friend of the imprisoned Bolek—had said, "If Mrs. Jaromirska found them, then let her take them to the Jewish community office. Then I want her to come before me and a report will be written up."

I was so mad at that woman! How could she be so stupid as to go to the police on matters which we could arrange differently! I would have worked it out myself that morning if I did not have to get to work. In any case, I now said to them all, "So many widows and women alone manage to raise children that certainly I'll have no trouble getting advice." So I took the child closer to my heart and we went home. A whole procession of women walked after us. They followed right into my apartment and they were looking at me to see what I would do. And all the time the child was crying, "Mama, Mama. . . ."

The only neighbor to offer any help was her friend Mrs. Wakier. Except for her, says Leokadia, "you should have heard the comments! What's happened to Jaromirska, is she crazy? Does she now need a baby? Alone? Doesn't she have enough trouble? Mrs. Sabinska criticized what I had done with an ironical smile and a proverb—'Grandma didn't have any worries so she bought herself a little pig.'"

"In all this time, the child had never stopped calling for her mama. Now I said, 'Come here, I will wash you and be your mama.' Her skin was covered with a rash from lying wet all night. When I washed her, she cried out in pain because the skin was so sensitive. I fed her a whole large roll with milk. She drank a full half-liter. Then, before I put her to sleep, I gave her tea laced with raspberry mash. This is something you make at home by adding sugar to fresh berries, which you cover and leave by the window until it ferments. When you have a cold, it always helps—our Polish home medicine. When I fed this to her, she got a little drunk. She burped and fell asleep. In the evening she awoke. I fed her again and she slept soundly through the night."

Like any working mother, Leokadia had to arrange for day care. That first week, a relative of Mrs. Wakier's took the child. But Leokadia was anxious not to take advantage of anyone's good nature. She quickly found a seventeen-year-old girl named Leodosia, or simply "Dosia," who had fled from forced labor in Germany. As a fugitive, Dosia was grateful for shelter in return for minding the infant. But Leokadia insisted on paying her what she could afford as well. At the same time, she had to solve the problem of clothing the child. *I fixed up a few things out of my own clothes for her, and from friends at work I got underwear and other needs. In two weeks, she already had dresses, a coat, and shoes.* So, each morning now, Dosia would arrive just before six o'clock as Leokadia left while the child still slept. Each evening she was dismissed upon Leokadia's arrival to go to her own mother's house. *It was only on Sundays that the child and I could be together all day long. I would spoil her and we would play very nicely together. I acquired her trust and now when she called out "Mama," she meant me.*

Bialoleka was not, in 1942, an idyllic spot to nurture a child of uncertain bloodline. *In a place like this, everybody knows everybody. Stories passed around about us, and some of them came only partly to my ears. And these rumors raised my ears not for myself but because for these two infants it could have ended tragically. If I didn't know how to get along with people it could have turned out differently. I was lucky that nobody had anything against us in his heart, and that's what saved us.*

The force of rumor was diminished considerably when Leokadia managed to prevail upon the village soltys, or mayor, to register the children to her and to Mrs. Kossak, respectively. Leokadia then had the older child baptized, naming her Bogumila Jadwiga Jaromirska—Bogusia for short. *I named her Bogumila—it means the one whom God loved—because God stood at her side and did not allow her to share the fate of thousands of other children who were murdered in the most cruel way. I lived with her and for her—and as if I grew wings, my indifference and depression disappeared. There was nothing for me to think about except for my Bogusia.*

In another month, Bogusia became round and pink like a doll. She started to walk with more confidence and chat like a bird. When I arrived home from work, even with my coat still on she would hug me and caress me and not let me take off my coat. After supper, I would put her to bed. Then I would wash, iron, and prepare food for the next day. This schedule would have been fine if it were not for the behavior of Dosia. One problem was that the girl was being visited, while Leokadia was at work, by a teenage boy who had also fled from forced labor. Together they brought unnecessary attention to themselves and, inevitably, to the child. But more disturbing was that Dosia was not caring for Bogusia up to Leokadia's standard. Once, in early December, she had come home to find that Dosia had put the child down for her afternoon nap on wet sheets. The girl had airily dismissed Leokadia's concern, muttering under her breath that this was not a child who needed to be treated like a princess. Leokadia did not miss the implication: a Jewish child didn't have to sleep on dry sheets. That was enough for Leokadia. Dosia was dismissed.

For the next week, Leokadia took Bogusia to work with her. She didn't mind carrying her the quarter-mile to and from the train station, but it did upset her to wake the child out of a sound sleep each morning at five o'clock. By the following Monday, she had arranged for Bogusia to be kept by a seventy-five-year-old woman in the building who also cared for her own two slightly older grandchildren. This woman was given a key and instructed to go to Bogusia only when she had awakened. But Leokadia soon heard from neighbors that the two older children were picking on Bogusia. "It was just because of the way children behave at that age," she explains. Just in time, Leokadia now found another seventeen-year-old girl who was hiding from German forced labor. Her name was Irena. Leokadia liked her instantly better than Dosia. *I asked her to stay until the end of the winter. She stayed for three years.*

Her status as an employee of the German warehouses may have provided Leokadia with that all-important ID card, but even by the meager standards of the day the pay wasn't much—50 groszy (½ zloty) per hour, plus a kilo of bread twice a week. In the marketplace, that bread cost 18 zlotys, or the price of 36 hours of work. "When the war with Russia started," says Leokadia, "matters got even worse. A regular-sized roll cost five zlotys—ten hours' work. I know the price because it was a luxury I used to buy for Bogusia."

On her own, she had made do with little. But now with the child and Irena to support as well—she was also sending food packages to Bolek at Auschwitz—50 groszy an hour was not enough. When, as Leokadia measures it, "a whole week went by when I could not buy Bogusia an apple," she knew she would have to moonlight. Having once worked in a sock-knitting factory, she tried first to peddle socks. By her own estimate, she had no talent for it. Then she entered a phase which, a short time earlier, would have seemed as unlikely as instant motherhood. She became a thief. She stole mattresses, blankets, and sheets from the warehouse. The black-market price for a mattress was sixty zlotys. That would give Bogusia an apple day for nearly a full month. *At first I was nervous. At night I didn't sleep thinking about getting caught. But then I came to do it calmly whenever I could. It was not my character to steal. But I did not think it sinful, because all that I was taking they had already stolen from us. Still, I was afraid because for such a crime I could be sent to a concentration camp.*

The Germans were well aware, of course, that thievery would be on the mind of almost every normal Polish subject. So, as each warehouse employee left the premises, they were made to undergo a body search. Booths for men and women were set up for this purpose. Leokadia circumvented the problem by signing up for a few additional hours' work in the evenings as a cleaning woman in the administrative offices. By the time she left at 7:30, the female guards were off duty and only the men were still searched. If she looked a little bulky as she bid the Germans *gute Nacht*, it was because securely wrapped around her basically slender torso were a blanket, a few sheets, or one of the thin mattresses then used. And though at that moment she may have learned to be calm, at night the fear came home to her. "I had terrible dreams that I would be caught," she says. "I dreamed that as I was walking by the guard a piece of sheet would be sticking out from under my coat." Out of those sheets, blankets, and even the mattresses, Leokadia made clothes for herself, Bogusia, and Irena.

Though Leokadia proved to be a perfect thief, she was almost brought down at work one day by a straightforward black-market transaction. In her handbag as she went home was a package of meat which she had bought for cash from the woman who was leaving with her. She hastens to say it was not desirable meat—"just some veal parts which would not normally be eaten, like the ears and so on." Unexpectedly, a German officer asked her to open the bag. It was unexpected because she had been on good enough terms with him to ask if he might in some way intercede on behalf of her husband. "I was petrified," she says, "because under my coat I had a blanket and a sheet. If he searched me, I would be punished. He looked at the meat and said, 'Here I'm trying to get your husband out of Auschwitz and here you are taking meat from us.' I answered that it wasn't meat from the cafeteria but from elsewhere. He put the meat on the floor and called over the police dogs. They ate it greedily, down to the last scrap, while I trembled, wondering what he would then do with us. Luckily, because my reputation on the job was so good, he let us go. That was the end of it. But when the two of us were beyond the gate, we were so upset by the encounter that we cursed and cried. We were too emotional and tense even to board the train. So we walked home in the snow. It wasn't just this one encounter that got to us. It was all the pressures, all the stresses of the war that went on day after day. If you did not live through it, then you cannot imagine what it was like."

By taking in from the edge of the forest a presumably Jewish child to call her own, Leokadia knew very well that she was exposing herself to the gossip of the neighbors and, potentially, to punishment from the Germans. Their policy on this issue was that those who helped the Jews would suffer the same fate as the Jews— either by deportation or, as an example to others, by summary execution. In the western occupied countries, the Germans felt, in general, that they had to be more subtle in this matter. But here in the east, where mobile killing teams had been dispatched to kill thousands in an hour, the Germans would not think twice about putting a Christian Pole up against the wall.

Just the same, Leokadia did not hesitate, early in that winter, to take yet another Jew into her small home. Bogusia's bloodline was at least open to question—especially now that the town records officially recorded the child as Leokadia's own. But with the new arrival, a woman named Sofia, there could be no doubt. Leokadia describes her as a "Jewess, a very cultured person, a former foreign correspondent." With her mother, Sofia had fled to Bialoleka from the big ghetto at Lodz, where her father had owned a factory. Furnished with false papers calling them Aryans, they hoped for a better chance to survive in this village backwater of Warsaw. When Leokadia had fallen sick the previous winter while working in the bottle factory, it had been Sofia who nursed her back to health. Then, in the summer, the Germans began to be suspicious of Sofia and her mother. The two of them decided to take their chances in Warsaw, but there the Gestapo was far more experienced at seeing through false papers. Sofia and her mother were quickly caught and banished into the damned and doomed Warsaw ghetto, where Jews in whom it had been ingrained to sanctify life and help their neighbor now passed the dead and dying on the streets as if they were so much debris.

"Sofia was wonderful and lovely," says Leokadia, "but not nice-looking—quite masculine. But she did have a beautiful sister, very fair, who was married to a high government official. She managed to send oranges and other unheard-of good things to her sister and mother in the ghetto. Then, through her husband's connection to a lawyer named Maslanka—he is very famous now and still alive in Warsaw—she managed to get Sofia out of the ghetto. When I found out that she had no place to stay, I invited her here to stay with me."

Since, after her sojourn of the previous winter, many people in Bialoleka would be sure to recognize Sofia, Leokadia was resolved to keep her hidden. This was quite a trick in an apartment consisting of only two rooms—a kitchen entered directly from the corridor, and a sleeping/living room behind it. The outhouse was in the back yard. Leokadia instructed Bogusia in precautions to protect Sofia. *Though she was very young, I taught her never to make mention of Sofia and that if someone knocked she was to go immediately with me and Irena to the kitchen. Usually it was only neighbors who had come to borrow books, which I had kept in our rear room. Now I transferred them to the kitchen. Though the neighbors were suspicious, they didn't know for sure that someone was staying with us. They gave me a hard time and pressed me, but I smiled and willingly lent them everything.*

Sofia proved not to be the ideal recluse. Leokadia calls her "capricious." Though she knew very well the dangers of being recognized, she railed at staying home. "Once, when she wanted to go out walking," says Leokadia, "at last I spoke my mind. I said, 'I'm grateful to you for caring for me when I was sick, but now I'm responsible for the child and Irena. So if you want fresh air, put on your scarf and coat and sit in front of the open window. But why do you want to risk our safety? You want to live—and so do we.' She knew what punishment would come to us for harboring Jews. She got quiet then. Another time she was sneezing and she wanted the doctor to come. I said, 'Sofia, I'm not sick, Irena's not sick, and Bogusia's not sick. So if the doctor pays us a visit, the neighbors will wonder just who here is sick. I'll give you aspirin, I'll bring you hot tea in bed. But please—no doctor.'"

Despite all these warnings, Sofia went out walking one day while Leokadia was at work. In the intimacy of Bialoleka, the inevitable happened. She was recognized by a certain Mrs. Blinska, wife of a policeman and, as Leokadia puts it, "our enemy." *When I came home, she came over to tell me that she had met Sofia in the street. I, naturally, acted very surprised. Where could she have come from? This Mrs. Blinska gave me a funny look. "She must be staying somewhere around here," she said, looking at me slyly. "But don't worry—I'll find out where." And I said, "What do you have to know that for? Is it your business?" And now the story went around that in addition to a Jewish child, Jaromirska is also keeping Sofia. So then her sister had to come to take her back to Warsaw. It wasn't until years later I found out that three months after the war ended, she committed suicide. Until today I can't understand why she tortured herself for those three years of the war only to do that. I heard only that she said she had nothing to live for.*

With Sofia gone, the books and other borrowables were now moved back to the rear room and the neighbors were again invited to lounge in both rooms of the apartment. But now, too, the neighbors could once again twine their speculations exclusively around the plump figure of Bogusia. And this interest in her origins was not confined to those who knew the family. One morning, a storekeeper five miles away in Legionowo called the child "*bachor*," a nickname reserved for Jewish children. A few days later, Leokadia was ordered to report to the regional commander of the police. "I went with Bogusia in my arms and my heart in my throat," she says. "But first I had dressed her in a maroon tailored coat and matching hat. She looked so pretty. And when I came before the commander, I said, 'Look at this child. How can she be Jewish? It's impossible!'"

Leokadia meant to draw the contrast, no doubt, with those wretched and tattered Jews who, that very April, were rising up against their murderers in the Warsaw ghetto a few miles away, or simply against the equally wretched creatures from right there in Legionowo who were still being routed, occasionally, from hiding places in the forest or holes in the ground. It was indeed hard to connect this healthy, happy, and handsomely dressed child to that miserable tribe. But the commander remained unconvinced.

Scared as she was, Leokadia remained on the offensive. *I asked him, "Does the commander have children of his own?" And he answered that he did. "And if in some way the commander's children were lost by the side of the road, what would he say about people who would just pass by and be indifferent?" I was sure that with all these questions from me he would pounce on me and be angry. But, though the dispute took nearly two hours, I came out as a winner. He promised me that the local Polish police would not get involved with the case. It was the Gestapo that I would have to worry about. He suggested that I should leave the town with the child or at least move to another apartment. But this I could not then do.*

The next evening, feeling more at peace than usual, Leokadia was walking home from work when suddenly she heard shouts that made her blood freeze. The Gestapo had made a raid on her very own Jasna Street. Had the commander allayed her fears only now to betray her? *My God! How I ran home! I stumbled and fell flat in the street and blood from my knee soaked through my stocking. Our street was empty and the building quiet. I banged on our door but nobody answered. I was out of my mind with fear. Mrs. Sabinska heard my sobs and pulled me into her apartment. She told me that Irena had fled out the window with Bogusia and now she was with friends. It was somebody else that the Gestapo had come to get. So I again became calm. But the Gestapo hit somewhere like this each day. And each day I came home from work dreading what I might find.*

In 1943, the nine killing centers in Poland reached the highest output of their existence—nearly 2 million corpses. Three of those centers—Treblinka, Maidanek, and Chelmno—smoked away within a hundred miles of Bialoleka. But for Leokadia, 1943 passed "with no interferences." The big news was the progress of the child. *Bogusia started to talk. There was lots of laughter when she would pronounce words wrong. Each day brought something new in her development. She was so wise and clean. She had a nice coat with a hood. We loved to dress her up. It was not all to the neighbors' taste—they thought we spoiled the child. They never stopped whispering cynical remarks. I don't want to describe these people in dark colors. But it was possible to hate them. Why did they have to give us such a hard time? That we could guess very well. In order to live with them in peace, I had to be a hypocrite. But I would have gladly given them a kick right out of my house.*

The year ended with a proper Christmas for Bogusia. Irena decorated the tree and under it put the presents—a doll, blocks, and a wooden toy dog. Then she lit the candles and called us. What happiness it was! Bogusia couldn't utter a word because she was so excited when she saw her first doll. Together, Irena and I cried out of pleasure that we could cause such happiness for the child.

From the first morning that she awoke as a new and revived foundling in the house of Jaromirska, Bogusia had been a child in exemplary health. Then, one evening in February 1943, it seemed as if Leokadia might abruptly lose her. *I had let Irka* [the diminutive of Irena] *go to visit her family in Warsaw that evening while I stayed home alone with Bogusia. She seemed ready to sleep earlier than usual. I laid her down and she wanted me to sing to her. As I was singing her favorite songs, I looked down and saw that suddenly her eyes were glassy and her mouth was foaming. I began screaming that my child was going to die. The neighbors gathered around, and one—Mrs. Tombilska—called the doctor who lived four kilometers away. He could say nothing except that the child might be having an epileptic seizure.*

For two hours she remained unconscious. Then she was sick with such a wild fever that I didn't dare even to leave her with Irena. I swallowed a few spoonfuls of salt to give myself a fever. That way I was able to go to the doctor and get a special exemption from work for three days. I sat next to her day and night. Everything I fed her she threw up. From watching her small body fight the disease I myself became black with depression.

But at last she fought her way back, and once again we arrived at physical and mental equilibrium. . . .

By the dead of the winter of 1942–43—Bogusia's first with her new mother—the German war machine was stumbling in the snows of Stalingrad. On the western front an Allied invasion was inevitable. For any Nazi who had clear eyes and did not flinch, it became possible to doubt the Führer's prophecy that the Reich would last for a thousand years. Down at her level as the humblest employee of the Reich, Leokadia gauged this new circumstance by the sparser supplies of goods being delivered to her warehouse and an accompanying crackdown on black-market trading.

Being a thief of consummate instincts, Leokadia decided it was no longer safe to barter her blankets, sheets, and mattresses any-where near the premises of her work or even in Bialoleka, where people knew what she was doing. Instead she began to leave from work on Saturday evenings for Krakow, two hundred and fifty miles to the southwest, where she had a brother. *It is hard to describe how people traveled then. As soon as the train pulled up to the platform at the central station, people rushed to the wagons, stormed the doors, even broke the windows. As glass showered down, the German guards hit the people with their batons. Anyone who was lucky enough to get aboard would have to stand toe-to-toe for hundreds of kilometers. It was so dense-ly packed and so dark that if you dropped something or if your shoe was kicked off your foot, it was impossible to bend down to retrieve it. At dawn we would arrive in Krakow. My brother and I then went to the farmers in the area, where we bartered for flour, eggs, pork fat, smoked pork, sausage—whatever we could get. That same Sunday evening, I was back on the train with my bags held close. The trip to Warsaw was all nerves because of the three German checkpoints along the way and Polish police circulating through the wagons checking over people. As they came close, I prayed they wouldn't take my food. If they chose to take it, I could not stop them. Once a German officer gave me a blow on the breast with, his pistol butt, making me spit blood. But in all that time they never took any-thing from me. On Monday morning I went straight from the train to work. In the evening Irena would cook the dinner because I fell asleep like a stone.*

The thirty-six-hour trips to Krakow, debilitating as they were kept Leokadia's household as well fed as any in Bialoleka that winter. She was even able to send a food parcel once a week to Bolek, who, unlike the Jews who arrived at Auschwitz, was considered a slave to be exploited rather than vermin to be exterminated.

Fuel for heating and cooking was another problem. Some firewood was available but coal was as scarce as gold. Thanks to a "nice" locomotive engineer, however, Leokadia was able to steal off into the night after the curfew, once a week, to buy coal directly off the train as it stood at the local semaphore stop. One hundred kilograms of coal cost two hundred zlotys. *We walked home in the snow, not once carrying less than thirty kilograms on our backs. But we were young and we laughed about it. Such a treat awaited us once a week. From work, I also brought home good grey soap for me and the neighbors. I did this rather than take the soap that we were officially rationed, which was made from human fat.*

Bogusia's exact age was still unknown, but in the winter of 1944, she appeared to be three years old. More than thirty years later, Leokadia can still readily pour out all sorts of little stories about her. They are of no special consequence or drama or purpose except to round into life her description *of a child who had a good character, good spirit, and who was worriless.* "Once she was watching a neighbor named Mr. Stanislaw lathering up to shave in the morning. And she asked, 'Are you putting on mascara?' He answered, 'Yes, that's what I'm doing. Would you like to put on some?' The child put her hands or her hips and was very put out with him. 'No, no,' she said. 'I don't use mascara.'"

Then Leokadia, who is a heavy smoker to this day, remembers a time they walked past a man and woman who were sitting on a bench in Bialoleka, kissing. In one hand, the man held a cigarette. "I said to her, 'Don't let men who smoke kiss you.' Quite a few weeks later we bumped into this man, whom I knew. He bent down to kiss the child. But she said, 'No, no, don't kiss me. My mother says not to kiss men who smoke.' And the man answered,

'Yes, but your mother smokes, too.' Right away Bogusia shot back her answer: 'Yes, but she's my mother!'"

Around Bialoleka, the child's penchant for free-spirited engagements with neighbors and friends was more or less harmless. It was less so when she tangled with Germans. Since Leokadia often took her to Warsaw, contacts were inevitable, if less than welcome. "Once we were waiting around a German office for hours to get some minor permit when an officer began to eat a ham-and-cheese sandwich. He offered Bogusia a piece of this delicacy. Here was a child with a ready appetite and, after so long a wait, I knew she was hungry. But she said, 'No, thank you,' and turned her face away. To me, she said, 'I won't eat from the hand of a German.'"

Though her mother cultivated German good will in the interests of family survival, the child remained unbending in her own principle of non-accommodation. On a train once, where seats were reserved for Germans, an officer asked Bogusia to come sit beside him. But she drew away from his extended arms, telling her mother that she would not sit next to a German. "Bogusia said this to me in Polish, of course," says Leokadia. "In translating to the officer, I only said that my child was afraid of his uniform."

With Poles, the child was an altogether changed person. Leokadia remembers the following conversation between Bogusia and the conductor of a tram which they had just boarded in Warsaw.

"I've just come from visiting my aunt for the afternoon with my mother," the child volunteered.

"And what did you have to eat there?" asked the conductor.

"Oh, we ate all sorts of things. And we drank tea."

"Ah, how nice. And did you bring any tea for me to drink?"

"Well, I don't have any with me just now. But please come home to visit with us. My mother is very good and generous and she will offer you some. . . ."

At night, Poles rode the wartime trams and trains in darkness and, for the most part, in silence. But Bogusia was not a child to remain silent, and as often as she conversed with her mother, she bubbled away in monologues of her own invention. "Often," reports Leokadia, "passengers would come up close to peer at us in the darkness. They wanted to see who was this child who spoke so sweetly."

Those peerers would certainly have been startled to learn that this child and this woman, though plainly bonded by fierce love, were in no way related—though not nearly so startled as those German soldiers would have been to discover that the child toward whom they could not resist making friendly gestures was a Jew. Under the astounding and rigid dictates of the Reich, such a soldier would quickly have had to withdraw the offer of a piece of a ham-and-cheese sandwich or a place beside him on the train and send the child off to be stripped of clothing and murdered by gas or bullet. Nobody was more attuned to this consequence than Leokadia. She had sworn to her friends, from very early on, that if the Germans tried to take away the child, they would have to take her too, and if they killed the child, they would also have to kill her.

Wroclaw
February 10, 1966

Dear Yoram,

In this part of the story you will learn of many sad experiences of little Bogusia. At home, her way of life had been fixed. She was pampered to the point that her mother or her aunt (Irena) would run after her in the back yard with a dish of hot porridge. But when she had to leave this sheltered life she was forced to experience many inconveniences as well as hunger and wandering.

When you read about this sadness, don't you be sad, because all that is long since over. You have a beautiful and sweet wife, mother of three fine children, whom you must love and be good to always. You must compensate her for all that she suffered as a child. While you walked happily beside your parents at that age, she was undergoing material privation, danger, and fears of death. You shouldn't wonder, then, at my love for her. It is more than a blood tie. I wouldn't love my own offspring more. She was the only one for me, and my beloved one....

In the summer of 1944, the Russians swept westward across the Polish plain, division upon division, throwing the Germans into retreat before them as implacably as they had themselves been thrown back by the Nazi blitz three summers earlier. This was an eventuality which had been ordained in the winter of 1942–43, when Hitler had allowed a great army to be destroyed at Stalingrad rather than give it permission to retreat from the city. (Stalin had been just as determined to remove the Germans from the city he had named for himself.) Now, drawing endless strength from deep in its heartland—more strength than Hitler ever dreamed was available after their debacle of '41—the Russians arrived in the second week of September at the banks of the Vistula River. On the other bank was Warsaw. It seemed that at any hour the Russian armies would cross the Vistula, restore Warsaw to the Poles, and roll onward toward the Reich itself.

The question of who would liberate Warsaw was not simple. One Polish government-in-exile sat waiting in London, as it had since the war began. It was, of course, Western-oriented and anti-Soviet. Another government-in-exile, created by Stalin for the most part from Poles he had been keeping in gulags and prisons, waited in Russia. The London government-in-exile was well aware that it needed the Russians to liberate Warsaw. But when the Russian tanks crossed the Vistula, it wanted to be the first to have a government in place—a fait accompli that the Russian puppets could not ignore. That is why, on August 1, the Polish underground army got the order from London to rise up against the Germans—not out of hopeless desperation as the Jews of the ghetto had done fifteen months earlier, but to show the world they were in charge. These partisans took it for granted not only that the Russians were coming, but also that their own government in London had arranged for Allied airdrops of weapons, food, and other desperately needed supplies. Nothing of either sort was to occur.

The Russians stood as motionless as a marble army on the far side of the Vistula while the Germans smashed the sixty-three-day-long uprising. Those partisans who were not killed in battle were executed or deported. The remains of the city were destroyed and the population dispersed. While the Germans went about their destruction, moreover, the Russians refused even to allow Allied aircraft to refuel behind their lines after dropping supplies to the partisans. The result was that almost no supplies were dropped. No other conclusion is possible except that the Russians wanted the Nazis to do the work of eliminating an entire class of active, Western-oriented Poles, and thus spare them the job—though it could be argued that nobody did it better than Stalin. It is he, apparently, who had directed ten thousand captive Polish officers to assemble in the wilds of the Katyn forest near Smolensk where, in full uniform, they were shot and buried in trenches for no reason except to rid the Polish nation of men who might later stand up to his dictatorship.

The first blow of the uprising in Leokadia's household fell on Irena. On the last day of July, she had the day off to visit her family in Warsaw. As the uprising began on the following day, the trains stopped running, so Irena tried to make her way back to Bialoleka by tram. For the Germans, the tram was fair game. They attacked it, killing many passengers. Irena, being young and healthy, was spared in favor of the fate she had originally feared—deportation to forced labor in the Reich. For Leokadia, it had been four years since, by another lightning stroke, she had lost Bolek.

By the second week of September, the battle line had advanced so close to Bialoleka that the village buildings shook regularly from artillery and bombs. Once, when a tremor sent things tumbling from a closet, Bogusia asked, "Mommy, are they bombing our closet?" Leokadia decided that the time had come to leave what was, practically speaking, the only home the child had ever known. So, like thousands of other Poles, Leokadia gathered up a few possessions and started walking away from the fighting. Her group of twelve included her neighbors Mr. and Mrs. Wakier, a cousin of Mrs. Wakier named Luda with her fifteen-year-old son Mirek, and several other neighbors, among whom was the wife of an engineer with her son. It was her horse and wagon on which the group's baggage was loaded. *I and the child were last on the parade. It was very hard for me to march in their same rhythm while carrying the child on my back. I walked sweating, my head down, my face red, as if I were following a funeral.*

The march would have gone more easily for Leokadia if only the child could have ridden on the wagon with the luggage. This thought must also have occurred to the engineer's wife. But no such invitation was forthcoming. Leokadia was not in the least surprised. From that first afternoon when the women of Bialoleka had gathered around her to cluck and conspire as she held the strange child, she had been plagued by people like the engineer's wife. Had she been alone, they would have treated her perfectly well, perhaps even with kindness. But these same people, once they knew or suspected she had taken a Jewish child for her own, turned spiteful. In this procession, the engineer's wife played that part. She even invited Mirek, a strapping young man, to ride the wagon. But she pointedly ignored Leokadia's plump burden. Leokadia was irritated. Being more proud than weary, however, she refrained from asking for any favors. But her friend Mrs. Wakier could not restrain herself.

"Madame," she said to the woman, *"why don't you offer to put this little girl on the wagon?"*

Normally, this engineer's wife had a big mouth. But this time she pulled Mrs. Wakier aside and whispered something that I did not hear. Then Mrs. Wakier came back to speak to me, but I turned my head away, letting her know that I wanted no more of this matter. Then the wife of the engineer came back to me herself. "Oh, come on, give me the child and we'll put her on the wagon," she said.

I thanked her politely but said it was no problem for me to go on car-

rying the child. It was only days later, after the engineer's wife had left us, that I learned what she had said to Mrs. Wakier. She said that her horse would not carry a Jewish brat. I kept falling behind and then I would have to run to catch up to the group. As I ran, the child's head swayed from side to side and the sack of valuables that hung from my front kept hitting my stomach and legs.

In this fashion Leokadia walked thirty kilometers northwestward. By the end of the first day, she was left well behind by the pace-setting engineer's wife. But the Wakiers, her cousin Luda, and their two children stuck with her. They settled for the night in a large barn which also served as a makeshift shelter for victims of the shelling. *Our group of six people found a corner to ourselves and lay down. Finding no water, we ate only the dry bread we had brought along. In the darkness, the flashes and roar of artillery fire sent us jumping to our feet. I heard moaning and crying. We remained awake all through the night. I held Bogusia in my lap and whispered stories in her ear. Each time the cannons fired, she would be startled, but she would say she wasn't afraid. Thus we passed our first night away from home. In the morning, I left Bogusia eating another piece of bread in the care of Mrs. Wakier while I went to a farmer's hut with a bottle and a pot. In one I poured a little soup which I bought for the child, in the other some tea. With these cherished possessions I came back and fed her. Then we all lay back and, for an hour, slept.*

At the end of that second day Bogusia had another of her runins with the German soldiers. Having reached a bridge over the Vistula, they had asked a Wehrmacht officer where they might find shelter for the night. As always, Leokadia was careful to put the Germans in the most sympathetic frame of mind by emphasizing that she was fleeing from the hated Russians. *This officer offered Bogusia an English biscuit, saying it had been intercepted from an airdrop meant for the partisans. But even though he offered it nicely, Bogusia would not put out her hand. He offered it a second time, but still she would have nothing to do with it.*

"Why don't you take it?" he asked.

"This gentleman is a German, thank you," she said in Polish.

"What does she say?" asked the officer.

I got worried. Perhaps he understood. I said to him in German, "She's not hungry." So he put the biscuit in my pocket. When we walked away from him, Bogusia said, "Mother, throw that biscuit in the water. The Germans kill people. I don't want their dirty cookies." We were all very surprised that a child could say this. Where did she get such wisdom? But I asked her not to speak to Germans in this way because they would hit us.

In the next several days of wandering, both Leokadia and the child caught colds. Once, as they prepared to settle for the night in a barn along with its normal residents, Bogusia, not normally a complainer, said, "Mother, I want my own bed." *I was very sorry for the child that she had lost her secure conditions of life. Not mine but hers. I kissed her face and caressed her, saying words of consolation without myself being convinced. Myself, I did not know in what fashion we would go on living or even whether we would remain alive. . . .*

Until today I feel the touch of her feet when I took off her shoes before sleep. And even though it is long since over, when I write this, I am crying. I am reliving it all. The child was tired and I was tired. I covered her back with my coat and the rest of her with straw. The cows were chewing their cuds and the pigs in the pen were gurgling and snorting. We lay side by side in the straw like two orphans.

Leokadia's efforts to give the child a decent night's sleep in a succession of barns and sheds were not made easier by her nemesis, the engineer's wife, whom they had rejoined. "Fall was coming, and it was starting to get cold, and one night Bogusia slept badly," she says. "In the morning I got some hot soup from a peasant, and after Bogusia drank it, she fell sound asleep. But the horse cart was loaded up and ready to go. So I said, 'Look how peacefully the child sleeps. Let's wait just a little while for her to awake naturally.' But the engineer's wife said, 'Oh, we can't sit around waiting for that child. Why don't you just leave her?'"

Saying nothing, Leokadia took her bag off the cart. Her faithful friends the Wakiers, Luda, and Mirek did the same. The others went off and the child slept on.

So far, Leokadia had successfully traded off the comforts of home for distance from the fighting. Now, at the end of September, her group trudged into the Kampinoska forest. Today it is a national park. Then it was one of the last strongholds of the partisans, whose uprising against the Germans was, with no help coming from any quarter, deteriorating after two months to its cruel and inevitable end. It was here in the forest, as they stopped one night on the fringes of a settlement called Druzkowice, that the struggle would catch up with Leokadia and her group. *We asked a peasant for a place to sleep for the night. She said, "Go to the hay shed—but I don't know what kind of night you'll have because it has no doors and all our furniture is hidden in the woods." We were tired and hungry and it had been a long time since we had hot food. The Wakiers set up for sleeping, Mirek cut wood for a fire, and I went to buy potatoes and kasha (two kilos of potatoes cost me a spool of thread). Then, as I was cooking, six partisans on horseback rode up. They checked our papers, looked around, and then rode back into the forest.*

I was just bringing a bowl of soup to our hostess when suddenly I heard someone shouting, "Please, gentlemen, don't burn everything down!" Then, at the other side of this cluster of huts, which was arranged in the shape of a horseshoe, I saw German soldiers torching a house. I ran with the soup back to our shed. Bogusia was playing in a field of clover as I helped the others to haul our belongings into the woods. While we were quite frantic with all this, Bogusia ran up to me and said, "Mother, are you taking everything else away but leaving me behind?"

She said this in such a funny way that, in spite of my worries, I kissed her angry mouth and said, "Come to me, my dearest parcel. I am taking you right now." And then I raised my head and saw a terrible sight. This whole settlement of more than thirty huts was burning up. You have never heard such crying and wailing. All this was done, as we learned later, simply because the Germans had spotted those six partisans riding into the woods. They decided on the spot that it would be necessary to burn this place which harbored the so-called "burglars." Bogusia, who was afraid of fire, covered her eyes. Me, practical as usual, I took out spoons so that we could eat the soup which had meanwhile become cold. We ate three from each pot. Only Bogusia, despite my entreaties, was not interested in eating. That's the way she always got when she was worried.

In the morning they awoke in the forest at the edge of the meadow, stiff-jointed and covered with smudges and cinders from the burned-out settlement of Druzkowice that lay before them. While Leokadia stayed behind with the children, the Wakiers and Luda went to scout out a new place to stay—the nearby town of Izabelin. Here they bumped into none other than the engineer's wife. With the source of her dismay nowhere in sight, she could now really unburden herself. "Oh, what a mistake it was to go with Jaromirska!" she wailed. "First, she has this terrible Jewish brat, who was so slow that I had to put her on the wagon. Then she is carrying this pack that is so heavy because she's hiding Jewish gold! Why doesn't she take some of that gold and buy a wagon for herself and that brat? I could have given a German soldier a half-bottle of vodka and we would have been rid of her!"

"When I heard this," says Leokadia, "my God, how worried I was! We cursed this old bitch. What was it with this woman that she wished evil for a helpless child and a woman who is guilty of nothing?" The worst of it was that Leokadia knew that the woman's final threat was true—a half-bottle of vodka would indeed pay for the quick murder of the child.

In Izabelin they bought milk warm from the cow. "Even though Bogusia didn't like milk," she says, "she drank it greedily, because she was hungry and especially thirsty." They stayed only briefly in a store in this village, owned by a woman who had sent her two daughters to a convent because Ukrainian soldiers then in the area were feared as rapists. Then they walked on to a town called Ozorow. Leokadia had hoped to catch a train west from there to a town where she had heard the Germans still operated a logistical center. In the three weeks since she had fled Bialoleka, her only aim was to stay out of range of the fighting. Now, with her little bit of money and few articles for trade running low, she was anxious to find a job at the logistical center. But an endless line of Poles stood at the window of the Ozorow station. Leokadia would still be far back when it closed at three o'clock. After her grim round trips to and from Krakow all the previous winter she was well trained for this moment.

Going directly to a soldier on the platform, she explained how her small group had fled from the Russians. She begged him to let them on the train. He relented, providing that she pay a small fine in lieu of a ticket, and—this was the real catch—that her group ride in the so-called *Totenwagen* ("death wagon"), an empty car pushed ahead of the locomotive which would be sacrificed to any mine planted by partisans on the tracks.

In this time, a train passed through loaded with prisoners from the uprising. Warsaw had surrendered. Seeing those military caps with the Polish eagle, we cried. They threw out messages on scraps of paper in the hope that they might eventually reach their families. These men were being taken to a concentration camp in Germany. As the train pulled slowly through the station, they sang the Polish national anthem.

On Sunday, in the middle of the night, Leokadia's party got off the *Totenwagen*, unscathed, at a stop near the logistical center. On Monday, she applied for a job at a central bakery newly set up to supply the troops in the neighboring village of Niepokalanow. Sticklers for certain procedures right up to the impending end, the Germans put her through a complete physical to determine if she could stand up to the work. On Tuesday, she was accepted. Simultaneously, a refugee committee found her lodging in a private house already occupied by two old women who had been evacuated from Poznan. *After many entreaties, they agreed to give us the kitchen to ourselves. It was filthy, so the first thing I did was to disinfect and paint it. I managed to splash some lime in my eyes. For a few days I looked like a white rabbit, but at least the place was clean.*

I filled empty paper sacks from work with straw and fitted them on the two narrow iron beds for mattresses. Over that went our one blanket and then our coats. These beds were narrow even for little Bogusia alone. So I stayed up until midnight each night to be sure she slept comfortably. Then I'd crawl in and we'd sleep together. At 5:30, I'd get up quietly and go to work. When the child woke up, these two grandmas dressed her and sent her off to the bakery where she shared the ten-o'clock meal with me. Then I would send her back to their care. At the end of the day, she would tell me what she had done, what she ate, what people had said to her. I always brought her cookies sent by the baker—a half moon, a rooster, a dog, and so on.

On October 8, 1944, Leokadia sent a postcard in prescribed format to Bolek, as she had done each week since he was snatched at the Gdansk station. It was nearly a month before it came back stamped in red ink with the words "Wait for New Address." She had no way of knowing that in that very month the Germans had dynamited the human ovens and gas chambers at Auschwitz and forced their surviving slaves to retreat with them westward. So when her card came back, she could only assume the worst. *I cried a lot but I knew that life had to get on. I had to think of those who were left alive.*

Leokadia had never been happy sharing quarters with the two old ladies from Poznan. The problem was not that they were cramped—that was all but inevitable. Since they had been there first, however, she felt like an interloper and, as always, she preferred to be *niezalezna*, or independent. So she was delighted when, on November 1, the manager of her bakery gave her permission to occupy a hut right on the base. In lieu of rent she would have to take a reduction in salary to fifty groszy per hour and, instead of her previous full board, be allowed only one free meal a day. But this was nothing compared to the advantages of being among those few Poles who were entitled to get what the Germans got. *My God, what happiness! It meant I didn't have to steal firewood anymore. At night we had light. Every day a bath and clean underwear. I bought a nightgown. Of course, the hut was small—only two little rooms for the Wakiers, Luda, Mirek, me, and the child. Our one bed served as chest, storage, and table. Everything we owned was either on it or under it. But still this life was paradise.* Relatively speaking, Leokadia had a point. It had been less than six weeks since they had gone for days with no hot food in their stomachs and slept with pigs.

At 5:30 each morning, the soldiers would wake us with shouts of "Aufstehen!" I'd bring us back bread and coffee. At six o'clock, Bogusia would eat breakfast with us. What a good appetite she had! She would eat a huge piece of soldier's bread spread with jam. She became sticky to her ears. She felt good here and everyone adored her. The baker loved to put her on his knee and feed her cookies. At home in Germany, he had five children of his own. Thanks to him, she would walk around with an apron full of cookies. Actually, she didn't even care so much for sweets, so it was I and Mirek who ate them greedily. Her best friend of all was the chef—an Austrian who spoke Czech. She would run into the kitchen saying, "Take down the coffee, take down the soup!" In their broken Czech-Polish, they would carry on and laugh together. She liked to wet his hair and comb it. This cook had a son in the army he always worried about. Bogusia didn't like the German-style noodle soup served here. So once a week I'd make her potato soup, with lots of carrot and cabbage with sugar.

After the ten o'clock meal, I'd bundle her up and she'd go off by herself to the workshop to visit the tailor, the carpenter, and the cobbler, who was a Ukrainian named Miska. This cobbler liked me well enough but he was absolutely crazy for Bogusia. She did what she wanted with him. He never minded. Once I came to the workshop and there was Bogusia poking Miska's rear end with a cobbler's awl. I said, "Bogusia, what are you doing?" She poked him even harder. But he didn't mind. He only said what I said—"What are you doing?" I laugh still, even as I write this. I grabbed the awl from her and told him he was a stupid man to allow her to do it. . . .

These times were good and comfortable. I worked twelve hours a day in the warm bakery. The food was ample and the child was beside me. On nice days she could run around freely outside the big windows where the soldiers came to pick up hot bread from the ovens. She had a ball to play with. If she was hungry, she would run to the window and the baker would give her bread spread with fat or jam or whatever she asked for. She looked beautiful then. She had color in her cheeks and a double chin. Once, however, I discovered lice in her hair. I dipped her scalp in paraffin and oil and tied it up in a scarf overnight. In the morning I washed her hair and the lice disappeared as if they were never there.

Leokadia worked in the bakery with two women named Helena and Ania, both of whom, like her, spoke German as well as Polish. Their papers, perfectly in order, showed them to be Polish Catholics. Leokadia never asked any personal questions, but from her first day on the job, she had felt by the way they talked to each other that they were Jews. Ania, moreover, had a doctor for a fiancé who sometimes came to visit her. Unlike the two women, he did look as if he might be Jewish. Another worker, well aware that Leokadia was friendly with them, commented on that fact. *I said to her, "What do you care? What business is it of yours?" And that ended such speculation—or so I thought. Then one day Ania and Helena called me aside for a conversation between "four eyes"* [i.e., confidential]. *It seemed that Luda, of all people, had been threatening to give them over to the Germans. They still did not come right out and tell me what secret, exactly, Luda threatened to reveal. But I knew.*

Not once but twice before, back in Bialoleka, Leokadia had voluntarily gone to bat for a Jewish woman—the difficult Sofia. She did it then at the risk of nothing but trouble for herself and she did it again now. *I was so mad at that Luda! "What do you want from those girls?" I asked. "What did they ever do to you? Go and tell them also about me and Bogusia, why don't you? Listen, the Germans won't be here forever and when the Russians come, I'll hand you over first! You and Mirek will be the first to go up against the wall!" Luda started apologizing, saying now that she only wanted to scare these two women. But I didn't believe her. It was hard to know what was going on in that idiotic head of hers. From then on, I watched her and I was very careful.*

At the end of the year, after nearly three months on the job, Leokadia passed her third and, from any angle, her oddest Christmas with Bogusia. *We had to celebrate here amidst foreigners and enemies. But the commander of our base understood Poles, and he tried to create a pleasant atmosphere. He succeeded. The baker made all kinds of holiday breads. The carpenter cut down a nice pine tree which we all decorated. We all gathered together for the Christmas dinner, though at separate tables—one for the Poles, one for the Germans, and one for the Ukrainians. The biggest surprises were planned for Bogusia. She got another doll, more blocks, and other little toys. But first one of the German officers stood up and recited a poem he had written for Bogusia. It was about a little girl who watched the stars sparkle in the night. As she was looking up, she saw Saint Nicholas come down from the stars on a sleigh loaded with toys. And then, when the poem was done, Bogusia was given her own gifts. This poem was written nicely and, as this officer read it, I thought to myself, If only he knew this child's origin. . . .*

For four months, the Russian army under General Zhukov had not budged from the eastern banks of the Vistula. They had watched and waited while the Germans first destroyed the uprising of the Polish partisans and then destroyed Warsaw itself. To watch the trashing of the Old City where the uprising had begun, the Russians would not even have needed field glasses. Fall came, winter winds blew in, the Vistula froze over. Still they did not budge. But they did use the time, after the eight-hundred-mile advance from Russia, to replenish and fortify their army. Meanwhile the Germans, battling the Allies on the western front and sustaining tremendous blows from the air to their industrial plants in the heart of the Reich, were only getting weaker. So, when the Russians at last crossed the Vistula early in January, they were ready to do what would have been much harder at the end of the previous summer. They were ready to take Warsaw, then all of Poland, then move on to Germany itself, where, by mid-May, in the center of Berlin, they would arrive at the remains of Hitler's chancellery in the rubble of which—so far as anyone knows—were lost the bones of Hitler himself.

On January 8, the same day that Warsaw was liberated, Leokadia's three-and-a-half-month career as a baker for the Reich was ended abruptly. *I had just gone to the kitchen to get some soup for lunch—Bogusia had already eaten hers—when suddenly I saw out of the window soldiers and also Mirek diving into the crawl space under the storehouse. I ran out to see what was happening when—aye yai!—a bomb fell on the kitchen I had just left. I ran to grab up Bogusia, holding her close and trying to calm her while I brushed dirt from her face.*

Bombs were landing everywhere and I had no idea where to hide. So I just stood there in the doorway holding Bogusia, my blood having left me and my feet like pudding. Bombs hit and bombs missed. I felt as if my end had come. It seemed to last forever, though it was actually no more than ten minutes. Even after the bombs stopped falling, the planes flew over us. To this day I am nervous to hear the drone of an airplane. It was a terror that you will not understand.

The place which had been a source of food, warmth, shelter, and calm for Leokadia was in ruins. Despite many injuries all around them, however, the child was untouched and she herself had escaped with only a few glass splinters from the shattering windows. Still, she had no idea what to do next. Her employers, however, knew their own next move. Fearful of yet another attack, they were already busy loading wagons for a retreat to the west. *We women were so idiotic—instead of just taking off on our own for one of the nearby farms, we stayed rooted there at the bakery with the Germans. We had been so wrapped up in our little world that we had no idea what was happening in the larger world. We couldn't grasp that the Germans were simply taking off!*

The plan was to reestablish the supply center farther to the west in Glowno, within the German stronghold near Lodz. The better Polish women workers, including Leokadia, were to be taken along to resume their work there. So now the Germans, who had set a new and fearsome standard for mechanized advances early in the war, were here reduced to retreating by horse and wagon with the women following on foot. *I wore military boots and a blanket around me. Even though it was very cold, the children had been well bundled up and they were warm.* For Leokadia, at least, this retreat was one step up from the retreat from Bialoleka. Unlike the engineer's wife, the Germans did not hesitate to let Bogusia ride on a wagon.

After dark, tired by now from the slow but uninterrupted march, Leokadia herself was invited to come aboard. But when the German driver tried to make the horse start moving again, it refused. Then, answering the whip, it suddenly jumped forward, sending Leokadia tumbling backward out the rear. *"Oh, mein Gott," said the soldier. He was really genuinely concerned about me. I*

*mention this only to show you that even among the Germans, there were
some who were kind.*

It was just as well that the retreat could not go any faster than
it did, because, as it turned out, nobody knew the way. All night
long they went in circles. Toward morning, Leokadia and her
group decided they had had enough. They decided to bolt the
wagons and take their chances on their own. In truth, the
Germans no longer cared what they did. Without these women
and children, the horses would be able to carry them that much
more swiftly away from the advancing Russians. Each step was
also taking them farther away from Warsaw, which is where
Leokadia and the Wakiers wanted to go now that the city had
been liberated. The only problem was that by jumping off the
wagons in the dark, they lost much of their baggage—including
food. But Leokadia did not lose the sack around her neck which
contained the bit of money she had been able to save from her
job. With this, she was able to rent a room and buy food for them
all in a "nice" village called Chodakow.

"Our mistake," she says, "was to pick a place that was too nice,
because when the Russians came advancing through the next
morning, they immediately commandeered this whole house for a
field headquarters. Then we managed to find a new place. This one
wasn't so nice, but the woman who owned it had an eighteen-
year-old daughter. And while we were there the Russians came
around to 'borrow' her—ostensibly for secretarial work. But probably they just wanted a girl for the night. Her mother complained
that there were other girls to take. Why take her daughter? And
there was so much crying and complaining that these Russians
finally left without taking anyone. We decided not to stay around
Chodakow ourselves. Mrs. Wakier was in a hurry to get back to
Warsaw because she had gold hidden in a basement there. Myself,
I was in less of a hurry because my only precious jewelry—two
wedding bands—was sewn into the collar of Bogusia's coat."

*We started to walk back to Warsaw. I had hung my sack of clothes on
my front, my wallet to the side, and Bogusia on my back—just as it had*

been when I left Bialoleka in September. Only the sack was lighter now and it was snowing. Every few kilometers we found a hut in which to get warm. On the main road, we came upon a German truck upside down, stuffed with files of papers that now were strewn in the snow. Then we came to another destroyed truck which made our hair stand on end. Two German soldiers lay there on the road beside it with their boots and pants removed—I don't know whether by Russians or Poles. I covered Bogusia's eyes and we hurried on. We passed dead Germans like that until I counted seventy. One lay totally naked and somebody had covered the private parts with an old rag. Another had been so run over by tanks that only a uniform lay flat on the road. Thus the child watched all these naked and frozen corpses.

Darkness. We walked from one hut to another looking for a place to stay. The Polish and Russian armies were everywhere and nobody had room for us. Bogusia started crying and I felt helpless. I made her walk a little so that her feet wouldn't freeze. Finally we were directed to a hut where an old couple willingly took us in. It was a cow shed which was now used for living. It had a dirt floor and an iron stove in one corner. We covered ourselves with our coats and the blanket and, with our legs pulled up for warmth, lay down to sleep. But it was cold—as cold inside the hut as outside. So the old lady laid an extra coat on us. In the night, the goat started to pee—it peed right on our heads. Bogusia also wet her underwear, but I didn't dare change it because the temperature was so far below freezing. In the morning, they heated the stove with straw. It became a little warmer and I was able to change Bogusia. I gave the old lady a big slice of our bread because it had been a week since they'd had any. I don't remember the names of these people but their good hearts I'll remember forever. Even the coat she covered us with I'll remember. In the morning I saw that it was so dirty it was glistening. But she offered it to us with the best of intentions.

Leokadia departed from that hovel on the morning of January 19, 1945, determined to reach liberated Warsaw by the end of the day. After some five years of occupation, the city had indeed reverted to the Poles—though, in fact, not a great deal of it was left for their return. The bombing and shelling by the Germans prior to the taking of the city in September 1939, had begun the process. One infinitesimal portion of the wreckage had been Bolek's galvanizing shop. Then, in April 1943, the hundred and forty blocks that had constituted the Jewish ghetto had been eradicated. More was destroyed fifteen months later when the partisan uprising was put down. Then, on personal orders from Hitler, the remaining residents of the city were expelled and, in an orderly fashion, most of the rest of the city was demolished, including even the great Gdansk station where Bolek had been arrested in 1940. The only major buildings left standing were those housing Germans—notably the ornate Hotel Polonia, used for quartering officers, and the handsome building on a downtown park that was Gestapo headquarters, its basement level devoted to the humiliation, torture, and murder of selected members of the citizenry. Exclusive of Jews, the Germans killed about two hundred and fifty thousand people in Warsaw. When Arthur Bliss Lane, the first American postwar ambassador, arrived eight months later in August, he reported that the "smoky smell of long-dead fires hung in the air. The sickening, sweet odor of burned human flesh was a grim warning that we were entering a city of the dead."

The liberators could not even be said to have arrived with anything like impeccable credentials. The Home Army under the command of the government-in-exile in London had been destroyed while the Russians watched. Now Stalin had sent in his own version of a Polish army, nominally under the command of the so-called Government of National Unity he had created in Lublin. Among that army's officers, certainly, there was no trace of the ten thousand Poles whom Stalin had ordered executed in the Katyn forest. Poles though they were, any member of that liberating army was beholden to the Russians.

On foot, and with two lucky rides, first in a farmer's wagon and then in a truck, Leokadia and the child arrived at the western outskirts of Warsaw by midafternoon, only to discover that Polish soldiers were barring entrance to the city until it could be cleared of German mines. "You can imagine how exhausted I was," she says. "So when this soldier told us we had to turn back, I said to him, 'Turn back to where? We have no place else to go. Kill us, shoot us, but we must go forward.' Bogusia was on my back, and as I started walking on, she repeated, 'Kill us, sir, shoot us, because we have no place else to go.' And he did let us go.

"So we walked through the city, keeping to paths that others had already made in the snow, lest we be blown up. All the buildings were skeletons. We walked for two hours in this way to the bank of the Vistula."

Leokadia had wanted to cross over to suburban Praga, which stood relatively unscathed only because, being occupied by the Russians, it could not be demolished by the Germans in retribution for the summer uprising. She had both relatives of her own and of Bolek's in Praga. It was even reasonable to hope they might have a roof over their heads and a spot or a corner where she and the child could stay until she could find out what had happened in Bialoleka. But now, as at the other end of Warsaw, Leokadia was forbidden from going where she wanted to go, this time by Russian soldiers who guarded the temporary bridge over the frozen Vistula.

"I cried and pleaded and finally they let us pass. It was nearly dark and the water rose around my ankles. But I didn't care. When we got to the other side, I sat down in the snow and began to cry again. It wasn't that I had feared death. As long as the child and I were together, I had no such fear. It was the exhaustion and the tension of doing what was forbidden. Bogusia also began to cry. I kept telling her there was no reason to. But as long as I wept, she wept. So we sat there in the snow and wept together."

In Praga now, long after dark, they reached the tiny house belonging to Bolek's sister and her husband. *They stared at us as if we had come back from the world of the dead. Then the brother-in-law began to cry not like a man but like a child. Somebody had indeed told them that we were dead. It was not hard to believe because, as I now learned, Bialoleka had been destroyed to the last stone. Those who had left in time had survived. Those who stayed had died.* Sad as that news was, at least it confirmed that Leokadia had done the right thing.

Though—as she would one day write to Yoram—she and the child had suffered "material privations," wandered, and slept with pigs, they were alive.

Although the fighting had ended, Leokadia quickly discovered that shortages were now worse than under the German occupation. *Ration tickets were given only to workers. Without them, the price of food was terribly high. I exchanged 500 zlotys—all that was left from months of wandering—for the barest existence.* Leokadia hoped to get a leg up on the situation by going to Bialoleka to retrieve her household goods and then, like everyone else, to start trading. But, arriving in her village after a five-month absence, she quickly saw that she would have to revise her high hopes. *All that was left of our building was the chimney. I looked with sorrow on the place where our furniture used to be. Only the springs of the sofa and bed were left.*

I had hidden away our clothing, pillows, bedspreads, blankets, fabric, and my husband's letters. As for jewelry, except for the wedding rings, I had none to leave. Half of it had been stolen—especially little items. What could I do? It had been there and suddenly it wasn't there. My pillows might as well have been stolen—they were rotted from being in the basement. Some of our things had been snitched by a neighbor. But I got back Bolek's suit from her only because he is tall and her husband is short! I also got back six meters of velvet, which I sold for 300 zlotys. With that I went out and bought a huge load of black bread—six kilos—and a challah for Bogusia. The black bread cost 125 zlotys and the challah 25 zlotys, so there went half the price of the velvet already. Though we continued to be short of everything, Bogusia never suffered from hunger. But she did get sick. The doctor said it was bronchitis. In all the time she had suffered cold and inconveniences while we were wandering, she had been healthy. And now this.

In her first weeks in Praga, Leokadia did not lack for places to stay. But she was predictably uncomfortable at living long off the hospitality of others. On top of that, she now felt the brunt of distinctly sour feelings toward the child from her own cousins, just as she had so often felt them from strangers. They did not think it right that she devote herself totally to a Jewish child when they themselves could have used all the help they could get in these hard times. Leokadia ended up, for a while, back at the home of Bolek's sister, where she had arrived on her first night back in Praga. *Then a friend of my sister-in-law's went off to the country and left a small room at her disposal. She gave it to me. Now I was happy. I did housework for my sister-in-law, for which she paid me in bread that came from a bakery where she had connections. I also had to borrow 500 zlotys from her. Then I met the sister of Mrs. Sabinska, who had sometimes taken care of Bogusia back in Bialoleka. From this woman, Jadasia, I heard a sad story. During the bombing, Mrs. Sabinska had gone to take refuge in the cellar with her daughter and aged mother. A direct hit killed Mrs. Sabinska and the child instantly. Her mother survived. But with nobody to care for her, she also died after a few days of being trapped in the cellar.*

I felt sorry for this Jadasia. She had children of six years and nine months. Their wanderings were many times worse than mine. They wore torn clothes and they had nothing. I gave them some underwear and things I had brought back from Bialoleka. Misery went to save misery! Since they had no place to live, I invited them to stay with us. I and Bogusia slept in the bed. Jadasia and the six-year-old, Bogdan, slept on a mattress on the floor. Little Alusia, the baby, slept under the table like a dog. There was no need to lock the door. Anyway, it would have been impossible for anybody else to get in.

Despite the cramped quarters, Leokadia found it easy to live with Jadasia, who willingly took care of the children, cooked, and, most important, was well liked by Bogusia. The problem was money. Leokadia decided to make a trip to the countryside to barter or sell what remained of her household at Bialoleka. By her count, she left with six pillowcases, eight sheets, and assorted other items. Three days later, she returned with butter, oil, flour, dried foods, and a thousand zlotys. *As usual, Bogusia was more than happy to see me, though she said that Jadasia had taken very good care of her. I had promised to bring her a little doggie. Certainly I intended to do so. I had to apologize now, saying that the dog had bitten my hand, and that is why I had to give the dog to an older fellow—a very big fellow—because I was afraid that the dog might bite her and also little Alusia. And thus I managed to convince her.*

This new bounty did not last long, however, especially since it also had to feed Jadasia and her brood. The thousand zlotys went fast, too, since Leokadia insisted on paying back at once the five hundred zlotys she owed to her sister-in-law. *She didn't want to take it. She said she didn't need it and I did. But I insisted, because if I ever needed to borrow again, I wanted to have a reputation for paying back.* The inevitable and nearly immediate result of this policy was, as Leokadia puts it, *poverty again raced down upon us.* She decided that her next career would be as a seller of bread. Making use of her prosperous sister-in-law's connections at the bakery, she was awarded a precious consignment of ten loaves. *I stood in the marketplace for the whole day and managed to sell only two kilos. It wasn't for me, standing like a stick in one place like that without doing anything. I returned the bread to my sister-in-law and never again returned to the bakery.*

Leokadia regretfully came to the conclusion, after her guests had been installed for two months, that it might be better if they left. As decent and as helpful as Jadasia assuredly was, she had even less of a knack for earning money than Leokadia. It had become too exhausting to be responsible for them all. *I couldn't just throw them out on the street. So, in conversation with her, I drew out from Jadasia the fact that she had two cousins who owned a farm. Gently, I persuaded her to take the children there. I sold her the blanket that I had brought from Bialoleka for them to use. Then I bought them train tickets, food for the trip, and I accompanied them to the station. Bogusia and I had the room to ourselves again. How I savored this new relaxation!*

Late in the spring, Leokadia herself got an invitation to go to the country. It came from her friend Mrs. Gienia Pietrokowa, who was going to visit her parents on their farm near Pransk, some several hours north of Warsaw. As usual, Leokadia was not anxious to be somebody else's guest. But she agreed to go along for two reasons. The first was that she and Mrs. Pietrokowa "loved each other like sisters." The other—more important—was that she had known her friend's parents before the war and they were "good people."

It was the Ninth of May, the official end of the war. As was our custom, we decided to take a freight train. At the station, we three—Mrs. Pietrokowa, me, and the child—waited for four hours. It grew dark, and then we saw a beautiful scene. Fireworks spread out over the sky. It was impossible to stop looking. Bogusia was clapping with excitement. Then the train began to move. We spread our blanket on the floor of the wagon and ate our dinner. At eleven that night we arrived at the Nasielsk station where we had to get out and wait for a second train. It was not a comfortable place, but we didn't dare to leave, since we didn't know when the next train would come. It started to rain. We found some shelter and it went on raining. I covered myself and Bogusia and she fell asleep in my arms. She was heavy but warm. Everything was soaked. Thus we waited until morning.

At eight o'clock we heard somebody say that the train was coming. Suddenly, people came pouring out of every little hole. They filled the platform, milling and pushing. Then the train appeared, loaded up with the wreckage and torn metal of destroyed airplanes. The crowd rushed to the train like locusts. I held tight to the child in the crush and cried, "People, help me mount the train." But it was like crying in the desert. How could I climb aboard with the child? There were no steps. Mrs. Pietrokowa was pushed aside. At last somebody yelled down, "Lady, give me the child." I handed up Bogusia but she was crying, "I don't want to go." So they took from me my suitcase instead. Bogusia managed to get up herself and I climbed after her. In the process, I lost my purse. We were wet, sweaty, dirty, and frozen. But we were aboard. I breathed a sigh of relief. I began to ask about the purse. It had gotten somehow to the other end of the wagon and now it was passed back to me. We got settled and ate a breakfast of rolls, sausage, and hard-boiled eggs. I put Bogusia in a spot of her own under the wing of an airplane. I covered her with the wet blanket against the wind and gave her a piece of roll. She nibbled and sat there quietly, sleepy and calmed. At ten o'clock we finally began to move. We got to our destination, Trosk, without any special adventures.

It was only ten more kilometers to the farm. The sun broke through and its beams warmed us. We took off our shoes and we—me with my sweet load on my back—started the hike. Every kilometer we'd take a break.

Halfway along, a farm wagon approached. When the farmer recognized Gienia, he stopped the horses.

"Good morning, Mrs. Pietrokowa. What is the lady doing here? I thought you were a wandering gypsy, and here you've returned. Please sit here on the wagon." We were happy to oblige!

Grandmother and Grandfather were happy to see us. She warmed water and I washed Bogusia, put her in a nightgown, and sent her to bed. We adults also washed and then we sat around talking for hours. Another little girl lived here, Niuzia, and she and Bogusia got friendly. And now, also, she had a grandfather and grandmother who loved her. Soon it was spring and Bogusia was outside, playing all day in the fresh air. Paradise had started.

That life may well have been paradise for Bogusia, but it was something less for Leokadia. She was herself up at dawn and working hard in the fields all day, determined as ever to earn their keep. But while she was certainly earning room and board, she felt the need also to have some spare cash. To this end she decided to embark once again on a career which did not come naturally to her. Just as she had become a thief when she worked in the German warehouse in Warsaw, she now decided to become what can only be described as a pillager. "At the end of the war," she explains, "one of the ways Poles made money was to go to western Poland—the part which the Germans had now vacated—to loot. They [the Germans] had a higher standard of living than we did. They owned more jewelry, more clothing, more everything than we. Much of it they left behind when the Russians kicked them out. We did not feel bad about claiming it. They had stolen from us so we felt we had the right to steal back from them."

So, like a prospector, Leokadia took time off from work on the farm to join the rush to the west, hoping to find treasures that she could sell for hard cash back home. Unfortunately, the trip was less than a big success because the Russian troops who had passed through earlier had already done the job very well. "These Russians looked me over, in fact, as if they wanted to take whatever they could from me. I was young then, and they also looked as if they had rape on their minds as well! I was so scared. So I came home as quickly as I could with nothing to show for the trip except one kitchen pot—and it wasn't a very good one at that!"

One day, late in the summer, Leokadia went to visit a friend in Praga. They were hanging wash on a rooftop line, chatting idly. "Suddenly my sister-in-law came running with but one word on her lips: 'Bolek!' Shoeless, I ran to her apartment. What I saw I couldn't believe. It was a man with no hair, no teeth, and a terrible skin disease. He was swollen up from hunger. I began to cry.

" 'Stop crying,' he said. 'I am here.' "

That day when a shoeless and thunderstruck Leokadia had faced her husband for the first time in five years was a Thursday. She had planned to be in Praga only for washday. But now she and Bolek did not return to the grandparents' farm until Saturday. "As usual," reports Leokadia, "Bogusia was happy to see me and she quickly made friends with Bolek." The one for whom Bolek's return was actually quite disconcerting was Leokadia herself—and not just because he had reappeared from the dead. By great effort, she had established a way of facing up to a hard life on her own. Her sense and style of independence were fully operative. These qualities could not now be automatically diminished or subordinated by his return. And yet enormous changes would be required of her.

The imminent problem was their status on the farm. Given Leokadia's near allergy to living off the good will of others, the situation had been bad enough when it was just the two of them. *Now we were three people living at the grandparents' expense, and I didn't have a penny in my pocket. Bolek ate and ate, and still he was hungry. He had open wounds on his neck, and we had to feed him many eggs. We needed buy certain things, but with what? We could have borrowed from our hosts, but I couldn't bear to ask. They were such nice people. I didn't even know how to thank them for all the things they had already done.*

Leokadia's method of thanking them was to work even harder than before Bolek had come. *At four o'clock I was up to milk the five cows. I fed the pigs, worked in the fields, and also washed the dishes. Bolek began to worry that I was wearing myself out. Sometimes he tried to help me a little bit at hoeing the beets and cabbage. But he really couldn't do anything. I realized that he was sick. While he gathered his strength, he carved a nice pair of wood sandals for Bogusia and also for her friend Niuzia. He also made them toys—wagons and windmills with blades that really turned. The children were always beside him or Grandmother while I worked. Bogusia looked wonderful—her arms sunburned like a gypsy, her cheeks plump and red like apples. Her eyes were bright with happiness.*

Even with the child thriving, Leokadia was now determined that her family give up life on the farm and strike out on their own. The grindingly long days of work were not the problem. It was the lack of time spent with Bogusia. That was bad enough when the child was healthy. It became insupportable when, late in the summer, she came down with chicken pox and had to lie all day in a darkened room while her mother worked. But Leokadia knew they would not be moving anywhere until Bolek got his strength back. That day came some six weeks after his arrival, when he himself announced that he was ready to look for work.

"Take us from here," Leokadia said to him. "I would rather be hungry than to be away from her all day."

Early in August, 1945, according to Leokadia's wish, the three of them left the farm for Praga, where they moved into a single room—the kitchen—at the home of one of Bolek's cousins. While he looked for work, she kept them in food money by selling off the remnants of her household from Bialoleka. The final two items were a blanket and her felt collar. Then Bogusia got sick again with a hacking cough and wheezing. *She would get attacks until her eyes bulged in their sockets and she became blue. It was impossible to take her out in the street, because when she had an attack people would crowd around offering all sorts of advice. The doctor advised a change of climate. But without a zloty, without a grosz, where could I go?*

She went home to Bialoleka, where she and the child stayed with a friend in the ruins of a house. It was, of course, rent-free. The doctor had advised her to walk the child, which she did now on a rigid schedule. *At 4 a.m., before the sun rose, we circled the lake there four times. Later in the morning, when it was warm, I would lay her down in the garden. All day she was out in the good air. The attacks became lighter. They lasted altogether six weeks, of which the middle two were the worst. Once I went to see the battlefields that we had fled from in the previous September. All the beautiful summer houses from the past were ruined and burned. The fields were still full of the bones of the soldiers—a skull here, a hand there, a foot still within a shoe. I was fearful and I thanked God that we weren't there. I could imagine the terror of Mrs. Sabinska with her child and her mother in the midst of this terrible battle.*

By the middle of September, mother and daughter had rejoined Bolek in Praga. They lived in the same cousin's kitchen, in poverty even more abject than before. Bolek was still looking for a job. They picked up meals where they could. Though, as always, Bogusia's good diet was maintained, Leokadia herself ate little more in these times than dry bread. What food she ate in the house was financed by loans from that same sister-in-law from whom she had borrowed before. For reasons of her own, she refused any help from her own relatives. *I wouldn't go to them because they gave me a hard time about Bogusia. Until today, my own brother's wife claims that her son was lost because of me—that because I took strange Jews into my heart there was no room for her son when he needed help. She didn't like Bogusia, and to this day I don't like her. Thus, rather than ask for anything from them, I preferred to walk hungry.*

I remember one evening when I cooked a pot of soup from our last potatoes. Bolek had come in from his sister's, where he had eaten, so he wasn't hungry. I sat thinking in silence. At home, we usually had at least a little bit of something to eat. Now nothing was left at all. The cupboard was bare. There was no place left I felt that I could borrow from. I already owed my sister-in-law one hundred zlotys for the food we'd taken from her to eat. How could I ever find the means to pay her back? I started crying. Bolek sat across the table and looked at me. Nothing. Then, out of the silence, beloved Bogusia said, "Mother, why are you crying?"

"I am crying, my daughter, because we don't have a grosz and what shall we eat tomorrow?"

"Don't worry, Mother. We have a bit of soup still. . . ." And she reached over and caressed my face. You know, I started laughing, and I kissed those eyes and the mouth from which came those words of consolation.

Though she could have no inkling of it, any difficulties which Leokadia felt she was up against at the dinner table that evening would pale to inconsequence in the face of events set in motion on a morning very soon after—on September 27, 1945, to be exact. The signal was an unexpected knock at the door. It was not locked and, without waiting for any greeting or invitation, a man wearing a suit walked in. From photos of the era, he appears to have been strongly built, with a full head of bushy dark hair and heavy brows over dark eyes. His features were firm and he had the air of a man who would not be deterred from getting what he wanted.

I had just come into the front room from doing some laundry in the yard. Bogusia was playing by herself, eating an apple. He looked around the room and then fixed his eyes on her. She was dressed nicely, as always, and she wore a big bow in her hair. He asked for a party I did not know or recognize and I told him that he was in the wrong house. His eyes fixed on the child once more before he walked out. She continued to play without concern while I remained motionless, my heart pounding. But then I expelled all bad thoughts and I didn't let them come back into my head.

From the way this stranger had focused on the child, Leokadia must have known that expelling bad thoughts wouldn't help. He would be back. She had a two-day wait. This time he arrived with a second man, who, to her dismay, addressed her by her proper name without any introduction. While the bushy-haired man stood silently, he introduced himself as an official of the American Joint Distribution Committee, one of the Jewish aid groups at work in the larger Polish cities after the war to salvage what they could of eight centuries of Polish Jewish life.

Some uneasy conversation was in progress when the silent man interrupted: "I am the real father of the child."

While Leokadia stood stunned and silent, he went on to nail down the particulars of his claim. He described exactly where and when he had left the child along the convent wall in Bialoleka. He itemized her clothing—blue dress, blue tights, and black shoes. As Leokadia stared at him, she could not deny the most damning fact of all, even as it went unclaimed—the two of them looked unmistakably like father and daughter.

"If I had known you were alive," she cried out, "I never, never would have picked up the child!"

She meant that she would not have committed the full force of her love to this child—love that was tender, fierce, and boundless—in order now to return her like a lost parcel. But this was indeed the possessor by blood right of the child. His name was Gershon Jonisz, a thirty-five-year-old Jew who, against all odds and in the face of panoramic evil, had survived.

He was born in 1910 in Legionowo, one of tens of dozens of smaller Polish cities with a substantial but, for the most part, separate Jewish life. Jonisz was the unexceptional child of a family of small storekeepers. On May 7, 1938, he married Golda Mischler, who came from the neighboring city of Radzymin, notable, long after its Jewish citizenry was extinguished, as the hometown of the religious scholar Samuel Singer, father of the writers Joseph and Isaac Bashevis Singer. Gershon Jonisz had no such literary ambitions. He moved to the neighborhood where his wife's family lived, opened a store selling knitting goods, and set out to build his family life.

Everything pointed to fulfillment of Jonisz's modest ambitions until, less than two years later, the Germans came, and what he calls the "somber days" began.[*] A daughter was born to the couple on April 22, 1941. They named her Shifra. When, at the end of that

---

[*]Jonisz's memoir is set down in the Memory Book of Radzymin, a big blue tome published in both Yiddish and French some thirty years after the end of Jewish life in that city.

year, the Germans threw up a wall around the most miserable section of the city and herded the local Jews inside, she became one of the youngest inmates of the new ghetto.

The family would have fared no better if they had settled in Legionowo instead of Radzymin. The course and chronology of events were the same there. In each case, the elders of the community were charged with caring for the captives and with carrying out German directives. The captives were subjected first to overcrowding on the order of seven people to a room. Then came starvation, then the inevitable epidemic of typhoid. Finally, in early October, came the order for the citizens of the ghettos of Radzymin and Legionowo to assemble for "resettlement" and "work." In each ghetto about 20 percent of the residents had already died.

Though Jews were normally prohibited from leaving the ghetto, a certain number always slipped out—notably the blond-haired children who were dispatched over the wall to trade with sympathetic shopkeepers on the outside. The local Jewish council had even succeeded, during the worst of the typhoid epidemic, to import a doctor legally from the Warsaw ghetto. The Germans would not normally have agreed to this. It was accomplished by pushing exactly the right buttons in the Gestapo mentality. The council informed the appropriate officer that this particular doctor had been guilty of a theft in Radzymin, and that they wanted him returned for trial and punishment. The Gestapo, ever intent that justice be done, readily agreed. The doctor was duly returned to the community where he spent several weeks among the ill.

The only Jews who were allowed to leave the ghetto regularly belonged to the burial detail which picked up corpses each morning and buried them in trenches beyond the wall. Any Jew found outside the ghetto without permission was shot on the spot. But now that Treblinka was on the following day's travel agenda, what did it matter? On that evening before, according to Jonisz, a number of Jews came to the conclusion that they would be no worse off if, in the "depth of the night," they bolted the ghetto wall and fled into the surrounding forests. Among them were Jonisz himself and his wife Golda, carrying their daughter Shifra.

By prior informal agreement, the fugitives had decided that they stood their best chance to survive in small groups of less than a dozen. Jonisz was glad to participate in the plan. But when, as they huddled in darkness and a driving rain, the turn came for his family to be picked, nobody wanted them. The problem was the infant. These forests, not so far from Warsaw itself, were neither deep nor unpopulated. For the fugitives of the ghetto, silence meant life or, at least, a better chance at living. The piercing cry of a hearty eighteen-month-old infant could only bring on the hunters. Put to a stark choice, there was nobody who volunteered to be in a group with the Joniszes. So, by default, the family constituted a group of their own.

The others had been right. For four days and nights, in the almost continuous cold and rain, the child did cry. In their dash over the ghetto wall, her parents had carried along neither food nor extra clothing. So the three of them stayed hungry and wet. From time to time, in those days and nights, they heard gunshots, signifying that some of the others had been hunted down. Yet they, with the crying child, remained alive. It was nothing they could celebrate. By luck, the inevitable seemed only to have been postponed. Jonisz and his wife knew full well that their chances of escaping the Germans were practically nil. "We decided to do something, at least, to save the life of the child we adored," says Jonisz. "Coming to this decision wasn't easy, but the only thing we could see to do was to abandon our child at the edge of the forest in the hope that some merciful soul—one of the local people—would discover her and be willing to give her shelter. Thus we approached the village of Bialoleka and left our little Shifra on the wet earth.★

★Though he does not touch on the point, it would seem that Jonisz and his wife made contact in the forest with another fugitive couple with an infant and that the abandonment decision was taken jointly—hence, the two children discovered by Leokadia. The disposition of that second child is unknown to the author.

"Heartbroken now as well as exhausted, we staggered off once more into the forest. Each step which took us farther from our daughter seemed like an eternity and her bewildered cries remained loud in our ears: 'Mama, Mama . . .' To this day, I don't know how we managed to resist that desperate call." It was the dawn of October 6, 1942.

Bereft or not, the couple now had a freedom of movement which gave them, as well as Shifra, some hope of surviving. That morning, in a place called Pelcowizna, they peeked out from the underbrush along a rail line and saw a group of Jewish workers bent over the roadbed. This was one of the details sent out each morning from the Warsaw ghetto to do hard labor for the Reich. If the lives of these men and women were unremittingly hard and poor, at least they were officially authorized. Jonisz and his wife, bedraggled as they were, found it easy to slip in among them. When, at dusk, the workers were loaded into trucks for the trip back to the ghetto, there were two extra passengers aboard.

The trickiest moment came at the ghetto gates. Here the Germans made a careful head count to be sure that the same number who had gone out in the morning had returned— minus, of course, any who fell and were shot. Luckily, the counters were more vigilant in their search for escapees than for new volunteers. With the help of others in the group, it was not hard for the Joniszes to fudge the count. Had they arrived in the ghetto six months earlier, they would have found it as woefully overcrowded as their own Legionowo had once been. But now that the population had been diminished by deportation, as well as by deaths from disease, hunger, and suicide, the couple had no trouble finding accommodations. It is a measure of the astonishing times that to them the Warsaw ghetto was what could only be called a haven.

Each morning now, the Joniszes were loaded on a truck to be taken out to Pelcowizna to work on the railroad. In Gershon Jonisz's succinct analysis, "This was a routine which kept us from getting shot." But it was also a routine which taunted the father and the mother. "We were so close to the spot where we had left our baby," Jonisz says. "Endlessly, we asked ourselves the same question: Had some decent soul actually gathered up our baby, and was she saved? . . ."

By the end of 1942, the hundred and forty square blocks of the Warsaw ghetto were, of course, nearing the end of a three-year agony unique in history. Deportation and deaths from within the ghetto had reduced its population from about 360,000 to about seventy thousand. Those who remained were, for the most part, no longer normal human beings. A secret emissary of the Home Government exiled in London, Jan Karski, slipped into the ghetto for a look at life there in October 1942—the same month that Gershon and Golda Jonisz arrived.

> To pass that wall was to enter a new world unlike any-
> thing I had ever imagined. A cemetery? No, for these bodies
> were still moving . . . still living people, if you could call
> them such. For, apart from their skin, eyes, and voice, there
> was nothing human left in these palpitating figures.
> Everywhere there was hunger, the atrocious stench of
> decomposing bodies, the pitiful moans of dying children. . . .
> Frequently we passed corpses lying naked in the streets.
>
> "What does it mean?" I asked my guide. "Why are they
> lying naked?"
>
> "When a Jew dies," he answered, "his family removes his
> clothing and throws his body in the street. If not, they have
> to pay the Germans to have the body buried. They have
> instituted a burial tax here which practically nobody can
> afford. Besides, this saves clothing. Here, every rag counts."

With all this, Jonisz and his wife continued to hold tight to life into the new year. But by this time, he reports, "the turn had come even for those Jews who were doing forced labor. On January 18, 1943, I was arrested by the SS and taken with other workers to the *Umschlagsplatz*—gathering place. During this same *Aktion*, my wife managed to hide from the Germans in a bunker at 10 Zamenhof Street. As for me, I was put on the train for Treblinka."

This memoir of Jonisz is not so detailed as Jaromirska's. But others have written a great deal about the events of January 18 and about the *Umschlagsplatz*. On that date, for the first time, the Germans encountered Jewish gunfire. For months the clandestine Jewish Fighting Organization had been dealing with Polish smugglers to acquire arms. By January they had, by one count, 143 revolvers, one machine gun, and seven rounds of ammunition per gun. They had also built a series of tunnels and bunkers. In answer to the deportation order, the ghetto fighters put out their own mimeographed directive: "Jews! The enemy has moved to the second phase of your extermination! Do not resign yourselves to death! Defend yourselves! Grab an ax, an iron bar, a knife! Let them take you this way, if they can!" Then, at 58 Zamenhof Street, 44 Muranowska Street, and other locations, the fighters opened fire. How many casualties the Germans suffered remains unclear. In terms of changing the outcome, it did not matter whether it was one or a thousand. But the event was auspicious, first, because it was the precursor of the full-scale uprising to come in April and May and, second, because these Jews had decided not to be martyrs to the glory of God—*kiddush hashem*—but to fight back.

As for the *Umschlagsplatz*, it was an ample, high-walled courtyard at the north end of the ghetto. On one side was a former hospital which had been converted to a holding barracks. Like a lobster trap, the *Umschlagsplatz* had only one barbed-wire entrance, with no exit except to a rail siding. Here the Jews were dispatched.

When it had become clear to all but the most obtuse, in the summer of 1942, that death was only hours away from the *Umschlagsplatz*, the Germans found it so difficult to get volunteers for "resettlement" that they made the Jews an offer which many could not refuse. Those who agreed to report voluntarily would receive three loaves of bread and one kilogram of jam. Offered for only three days at the end of July, the premium was so successful that it was extended several times. About thirty thousand starving Jews accepted. Postcards sent back from "work camps" were another potent form of bait. Usually the writers were kept alive only long enough to sign the card. To further the resettlement illusion, the Germans authorized a small Jewish hospital to operate at the *Umschlagsplatz*. They even supplied it with certain medical items. Would the Germans bother with such a sham, asked the wishful thinkers, if the deportees were scheduled to be killed?

So they went. As a young woman named Feigele Wladka observed, "They are loaded with sacks, baskets, suitcases in which they drag the last remnants of their poor belongings—all marching toward the *Umschlagsplatz*. . . . From the hiding places and the shops people look at them with sorrow and admiration. . . .'They have found the strength to take a decision.' . . . Crushed under the burden of ghetto life, shriveled or swollen from starvation, haunted by the constant fear of being seized, these Jews could no longer go on with their fight. . . . How enticing were those three brown loaves!"

By the time Jonisz was arrested by the SS, bait like bread and jam had long since ceased. So had most illusions about what the end of the train ride was to be. Jonisz, of course, had already forgone such illusions when the Radzymin ghetto had been called to its own small version of the *Umschlagsplatz*. During the overnight train ride to Treblinka, he and five other young men managed to jump off the train and dash into the night. The SS guards on board, well attuned to this sort of thing, picked off two of the escapees with rifle fire. Jonisz and the other three were able to escape.

Then, at dawn, came a repeat of his first attempt at survival. At a place called Zielonka, the escapees found and joined one of the few remaining Jewish labor gangs working on the railbed. As long as there was unrest back in the ghetto, the laborers were not returned there each night, but were quartered at Zielonka instead. But then, after several days, word came that the ghetto was calmed.★ Once more, Jonisz was back within its walls. "It was the night of January 25, 1943," he says. "I raced directly to the bunker where my wife had last been. She was still there. When she saw me, she could not believe her eyes. She had assumed that by now I had already died in the gas chambers of Treblinka. . . ."

When the final revolt of the ghetto fighters broke out in April 1943, Jonisz and Golda were among their pathetic numbers. As the Germans set fire to their buildings, they burrowed like rats into the subcellars until they were driven out by heat and smoke. As a record of their own prowess, the Germans, under orders from General Stroop, took care to make photographs of these ghetto fighters emerging. Though their hands are up, they look uncowed, even defiant, and for the most part incredibly young. The soldiers aiming their rifles at them are puffed up and swaggering.

"We were lucky," says Jonisz. "Instead of being shot on the spot, we were both deported to the extermination center at Maidanek, near the city of Lublin. Here a new hell commenced. I would be simply incapable of describing all that our eyes saw and all that we ourselves suffered. At the end of June 1943, there was a large-scale 'selection' at Maidanek. On this day five thousand women were sent to the ovens. My wife, Golda, was among them. I was now alone."

By anyone's measure, Gershon Jonisz should have been dead himself several times over by now—if not with his townspeople of Legionowo and Radzymin in the ovens of Treblinka, then in the forest where he, Golda, and their infant had dashed about for four days and nights. And if not there, then in the deportation from Warsaw on January 18, 1943, or else in the uprising of the

★Surprised by the Jewish attacks of January 18, the Germans had indeed backed off from intensive deportations. The Warsaw army command appeared at first to fear that the Jewish fighters might be stronger than they actually were, and that any uprising might spread to the Polish populace at large. So for three months— until the ultimate uprising of April and May—the Germans resorted to soft-selling what they still insisted was a "resettlement" to the clean country air of work camps in the east.

ghetto fighters which began that spring. Or if not before, then surely at Maidenek, a killing center as foolproof as any the Germans created. His was a curriculum vitae in reverse. Then, soon after the gassing of his wife, Jonisz got the ultimate promotion. He was sent to Auschwitz.

There he lost his name in favor of the number 126415 tattooed on his left forearm. He became a slave. "I arrived at Auschwitz on July 2, 1943," he writes. "From that moment I saw the smoke of the crematorium ovens. I smelled the smell of burning flesh. I heard the moans and screams of Jewish women and children. I still hear them, thirty-two years later. . . ."

For eighteen months, Jonisz's skills as a mechanic kept him alive at Auschwitz. When, on January 18, 1945, the Germans scrapped the institution and retreated westward in the face of the Russian advance, he was among the slaves taken with them. This was the notorious midwinter death march which finished off so many men who had survived all that had gone before. To stumble was to be shot. When Jonisz's group finally arrived at the Czech frontier, less than half of those who had begun the march were left. This remnant was now stuffed into windowless freight cars for a trip to the slave camps at Mathausen, deep within the tottering Reich. Day upon day went by. Without food, water, latrines, or light many who did not die went mad. A twenty-one-year-old voyager in another train named Jorn Gastfreund tells that when the first death occurred in his overstuffed car, the others were at a loss to know what to do with the body. "And then a way out occurred to us. We had a blanket with us, so we wrapped the first dead man in the blanket, and tied him to the iron bars above us . . . like in a hammock. But soon we discovered this would not work because we had more and more dead owing to the heat in the car. And the bodies began to smell. And that his how we were traveling."

For all his suffering, Jonisz mentions only one time that he felt his end had come. It was at Mathausen and it was, seemingly, the direct result of his own sojourn in a sealed railcar. "My will to live was simply slipping away," he says. "I knew that in a few hours I would no longer be one of the thousands of living skeletons all around me. . . ." But as he lay down to die, Jonisz had a vision.

"I saw the image of my baby. I saw her precise face, her adorable smile which had given us joy. But why was our Shifra crying? I remembered. I was seeing her now lying on the soaked earth at the edge of the forest, crying out for her mother. . . ."

On the day of that vision, perhaps the last he would ever have, Americans entered the camp. It was May 6, 1945. Jonisz's prodigious will to live had outlasted the unspeakable. But only just barely. When he tried to rise to meet the Americans, he found that for the first time in his life he did not have the strength to stand.

As soon as he did feel the strength, Jonisz went back to Poland. "I found myself in an immense cemetery," he says. His parents, Yaacov-Shlomo and Yetta, his brothers and sisters, his friends and enemies, were all gone. He went to Bialoleka. As Leokadia herself had found, whatever had been there before the Russians came through was now in ruins. "When I recognized the spot where I had laid our child," he says, "I began to weep. I called out aloud, 'Shifra, my baby, where are you? . . .' "

Jonisz's shout could just as well have been for his whole community. It was snuffed out fifteen hours after he and his family had bolted the ghetto wall. No formal account of the end of the Jews of Legionowo is available. But the end of his hometown of Radzymin, whose Jewish citizens were combined with those of Legionowo, Wolomin, and several smaller towns for deportation, has been chronicled in the Memory Book of Radzymin by a survivor named Michael Kossover. The timetable selected by the Germans begins on the eve of the normally joyous harvest holiday of Simchat Torah.

> . . . All traces of the festival disappeared. Simchat Torah, Festival of the Law, took on the atmosphere of Tishah Be'av, commemorating the destruction of the Temple. People wandered about, speculating on their fate. Some had already

begun to envy their kinfolk who had already died "naturally" in the ghetto. They, at least, died "deluxe" in the sense that they were buried according to the laws of Moses. . . .

In the midnight hour before the first Jews were to jump the ghetto wall, Kossover recalls the farewell of their rabbi, Yehudah-Arieh Wisokinski:

> . . . "Unforgettable are the years, the days, and the nights in which we have shared the persecutions heaped upon our community. Together we have carried the weight of eight thousand souls born in Radzymin as well as refugees from Wyszkow, Serock, Pultusk, and other communities to be destroyed.
>
> "Now is the hour of our separation. You leave—you *must* leave—to fight for life. We send with you our warmest wishes and prayers. Take with you as well our last wish. In the name of our sainted martyrs and in the name of those who have fallen on the 'Aryan side,' whose remains even now are blowing in the wind, we ask you to bury their remains as quickly as possible according to the laws of Israel. And in the name of thousands of Jews who in a few hours may no longer be among the living, we beg you to avenge us against these bloodthirsty enemies for the spilling of all this innocent blood."

All the following morning, Jews who had been herded on foot from the other towns arrived at the square in front of the Radzymin railway station—fifteen thousand men, women, and children.

> The pious Jews, with Rabbis Eliezer Hendel, Schlomo Kapelusznik, and Leibich Nadel of Wyszkow at their head, had wrapped themselves in their prayer shawls and were holding their Torah scrolls up high. For a moment, the

Germans and their colleagues in "navy blue" [Polish police] were taken aback. They did not expect Jews to go to their deaths in this fashion. They didn't know what to do. But Landskommissar Mons gave the order not to interfere and to let the Jews carry their Torahs.

In these hours, a few Jews still thought they were leaving for work camps. But most—especially the women—cried bitter tears. They could be heard from afar. . . . The Polish villagers just stood around watching this bewildering spectacle. Very few among them—women in particular—seemed moved.

About four o'clock in the afternoon, the trains came into the station. German and Polish police, joined now by the cruel Ukrainians, began beating the Jews. . . . To anyone who might somehow escape, the president of the Wolomin Jewish Council made a pathetic plea: "My son is at the work camp at Izabelin. Tell him to say *Kaddish* for his father!"

And then he prayed the words of the final prayer: "*Ashamnu, Bagadnu . . .*" ["We have sinned, we have been false . . ."]. Then he recited the prayer for the dead: "*Shema Kolenu . . .*" ["Hear our voice . . ."]. Thus fifteen thousand persons being hauled off to death prayed out their last cry of distress. And there was also heard another cry never to be forgotten by the Jews who survived Hitler's beasts, and the entire world: "Never forgive our assassins! Avenge us!"

Following this description in the Memory Book of Radzymin is a page filled with photos of children on that train—a knock-kneed and fat-faced bunch like most any other—under the admonition "Even Satan has not invented punishment strong enough to pay for the murder of a little child." There is also a photo, further on, of a plain-featured and expressionless woman named Malka Wagman. "She was," says the caption, "the last Jewish soul left alive in Radzymin at the liberation of the city. After several years, she emigrated to Australia, where she was killed in an auto accident."

• • •

So it was that Jonisz cried out to the forest and nobody answered. "From the forest I went from village to village," he continues, "asking the local people if anyone had heard of an abandoned child. Nobody knew anything. As fate would have it, I had not asked anyone in Bialoleka the question, for the simple reason that it was in ruin and nobody had yet returned. Resigned and sorrowful, I returned to Warsaw and, several days later, I took the long road to Italy from where I had decided to go illegally to Palestine."

On a hot day in July, Jonisz was waiting for his boat in the Cinecitta refugee camp near Rome when he had a curious, not to say revelatory, experience which would change more lives than his own. He and a pal named Bielowicz were taking a stroll when they came upon a knot of people gathered around a gypsy telling fortunes. She had plenty of takers, since, as Jonisz explains, "Everyone wanted to know what awaited them after years of suffering." Jonisz himself could not resist holding out his hand to the gypsy.

"'What language do you speak?' she asked me in German, looking at me with black eyes.

" 'Polish,' I answered.

"Her voice was raspy but to me it seemed the voice of an oracle. 'Far from here your child remains alive. She waits for you. She waits for you to find her. . . .'

"I stood as if nailed to the spot and my legs began to tremble. Once more I saw in a flash the forest of Legionowo and the bit of earth where my child lay crying, 'Mama' . . .

" 'Gershon,' said my friend Bielowicz, 'you have no choice except to go back.'

"That same day, I was back on the road from Italy to Poland, the idea of leaving for Palestine on ice. Nothing stopped me—not the borders which I had to slip across illegally and not the lack of money."

Many more former residents—Christians, at any rate—had returned to the environs of Bialoleka when Jonisz reappeared. And this time he began to make headway. With the help of the local soltys, he found in the communal register an entry for a child who had been found in the forest in October 1942. She had been adopted by one Leokadia Jaromirska. The child had been named Bogumila. Nobody knew where Jaromirska had now gone, but a man who against all odds had denied death was not about to be denied by life. Clue by clue, he tracked Leokadia Jaromirska to the tiny house at 10 Mala Street in Praga.

He stood at the door in fear. As Leokadia would remember, he recalls knocking and then entering at once. "Seated next to a table was a young Polish woman and beside her on the floor was a girl, pretty and blonde. When my eyes fell on her face, my heart began to pound. . . ." Jonisz had no idea what to do next. He only knew for sure that he could not face this woman with the truth just yet. In the truth there was danger. Suppose Leokadia were to flee with the child and hide? This was not an idle thought. An acquaintance of Leokadia had told him that she had sworn that if anyone—even Bogusia's real parents—tried to take the child away, she would not give her up at any price.

So Jonisz stood in a strange house trying not to stare too hard at his child. Suddenly, finding her seemed like the easy part. Now came a more demanding and delicate task—"How to get back my child, how to return her to her people." His mind blank on that issue, he could do no better than to make his excuses and back out the front door.

Jonisz walked away the rest of the day on the ruined streets of Warsaw, alone in his enveloping quandary. That night, "building plans in my head and knocking them down as unworkable," he did not sleep. The next morning, he was walking again when he met an old friend named Abraham Binduski, the son of a tailor from Radzymin. Being that rarity, a Jewish officer in the Polish army, when the war broke out, he had survived on false papers. Now he worked for the J.D.C. Jonisz explained his situation and Binduski agreed to go with him and lend moral support when he returned the next morning to 10 Mala Street.

As it turned out, Binduski did more than lend moral support. He began to carry the conversation with Leokadia. But Jonisz could stand it no longer. "I broke in and announced, 'I am the real father of the child. She belongs to me and I want to take her with me.'

"Leokadia went pale and for a moment she was silent. Then she began to weep and lament: 'Why did I ever have to pass that spot beside the forest? What tragedy has hit me? . . .'

"Then she looked at me with a steady gaze. 'I am not giving up the child,' she said quietly. 'I am not giving up my Bogusia to anyone. God sent me this child and He means for me to have her.'

"She picked up the child then and held her close to her heart. 'This stranger says he is your father,' she said. 'Do you want to go with him?'

"The child looked at me with fear and dislike. 'He is a stranger and I will never go with him,' she said like an adult. She held close to Leokadia and said, 'You are my mother. I love only you and we will always be together. Please don't be worried.'"

So ended Gershon Jonisz's recollection of the second meeting and first real confrontation between a natural father who was a stranger and an adoptive mother who would yield to nobody in matters of maternal instinct. Each of them now had to think about how to proceed in a situation for which there was neither precedent nor, certainly, any clear course.

Leokadia knew quite well what she would have done had her way been clear. *If Bolek had not come back from the war, I would have taken the child and run far from here. Nobody would have found me. But what could I do? He had kept alive for five years with the hope of return-ing to me. If I left now, it would have been a blow straight to his heart. Besides, we three were penniless and I had nothing left even to sell. I felt helpless like a child.*

Despite these limitations, Leokadia might well have fled with the child if Jonisz had threatened, or seemed to have threatened, to take Bogusia away from her. But he had not. He wisely assured her, in fact, that he was planning no such action. There were, in addition, two other factors which may well have weighed heavily in her decision not to fight him. One was that in her heart of hearts she knew the child was as much his daughter as hers. The other was that if this man had had the will and fortitude not only to survive against stupendously cruel odds but also to find his child, then most likely he would not fail to rediscover her again if Leokadia disappeared now. And so she made a pragmatic decision. As long as Jonisz remained friendly and unthreatening to the child and to her, she would not be unfriendly to him.

The burden of action fell on Gershon Jonisz. Cautious and thoughtful by nature, he spent the following days seeking advice from the few surviving friends and rabbis who had returned to Warsaw, from lawyers and staff members of J.D.C. All agreed that the child could not be wrested from Leokadia by force or stealth. With the bones of the natural mother lying at Maidanek, she *was* the child's mother. She had been correct, moreover, in telling the child that Jonisz was not a father but a stranger. And the child had spoken the unassailable truth—she loved her mother. As for a father, she had one. When Bolek had returned, just a few months earlier, Leokadia told her this was the father who had been taken away by war. That left Jonisz with a miracle shrouded in bitterness. Against all odds, his daughter had survived, and yet she was not his.

Jonisz settled now on a course of gradualism. The first step would be for the child to get to know him. This could best be accomplished if he was not a visitor to the household, however frequent, but a member of it. He would give Leokadia and Bolek good reason to invite him in. Baldly put, the incentive would be monetary. By borrowing cash from the J.D.C., as well as through his own abilities as a businessman, Jonisz would not only carry his own weight, but would try to provide the needs of life for a family now destitute. Then, with time, when the child had come to know him as her true father and even to love him, he would be able to take over her upbringing and protection. She would be returned not only to him but to the nearly vanished bloodline of Polish Jewry.

Jonisz did not make his proposal at once. For a time he contented himself with frequent visits to the family, during which, by Leokadia's estimate, "he tried to behave in the best way." After that traumatic second visit, he borrowed money from the J.D.C. and returned the next day with what, by the standards of the time, was bounty overflowing. In line with her decision not to reject him as long as he did not threaten, Leokadia allowed him in. *He brought a doll that could close its eyes for Bogusia, as well as things to wear. He'd heard we were hungry, so he brought us food—a loaf of bread, butter, sausages, and even little cakes for dessert. We made a supper like before the war. The next day we had goose for lunch. We couldn't satisfy ourselves— the stomach was full but the mouth wanted more. For this meal, we even invited the cousins.*

As long as Bolek, his wife, and the child lived in the cramped kitchen of his cousin's apartment, Jonisz's proposal that they join together would have to wait. Bolek was stuck here until he could find a job and, so far, he was having no luck in the environs of Warsaw. Late that fall, he began to consider moving to the city of Jelenia Gora, where the prospects were much better. This region in the southwest, long ago annexed by Germany, had now been returned to Poland by common consent of the Allies. Anxious to repopulate the area with Poles, the new government had invited skilled workers like Bolek to go to Jelenia Gora.

But Jonisz had another suggestion. Why not go, all together, to Wroclaw, formerly Breslau, in the same region. Jonisz had made several forays to Wroclaw where the black market was especially active and profitable. Next to this big, wide-open city, Jelenia Gora was small potatoes. And since the Germans had for the most part fled to the west, housing was more easily found in Wroclaw. Jonisz promised to find an apartment big enough for all of them. Bolek was willing but Leokadia was wary. Then Jonisz sealed the deal with one more promise—if she agreed to establish the new household in Wroclaw, he would give his word not to try to spirit away the child.

I left Bogusia in the care of Bolek's cousin and the three of us went down to Wroclaw by train to see how we could arrange for this new life. I myself planned to stay for two weeks so that I also could look for a job. But after one week I missed Bogusia so much that I went back to Praga. It was two o'clock in the morning when I arrived, and I began to talk to the cousin in whispers. But Bogusia, sensing that I was back, woke up anyway. I kissed her and she said to me, "My treasure . . . my millions . . . my sun . . . my sweet fish"—the same names that I called her when I came back from a trip she now called me.

Two days later, I took her with me on the train back to Wroclaw. It was a twenty-four-hour trip but with her it seemed like forty-five minutes. She was shy about going to the bathroom on the train—there were no bathrooms, in fact. So I had to tell the other passengers to look away and pretend they weren't there. And then I would take out the pan and she would use it.

Now life in Wroclaw began.

February 2, 1966

Dear Yoram,

The third chapter of our story now comes. For me it is the most tragic. I am looking out the window now where my child ran and played twenty years ago. When we were in hunger and wandering homeless, I was a lot happier than I would turn out to be in Wroclaw.

It never entered my mind that one of the child's parents would come back from the dead. I assumed that I would raise her and educate her and that after the war I would go back to my job at the sock factory. Our life would become routine. But we have a saying in Polish that "man makes his plans but God paints them." So it was that my dreams melted and I lost my peace of mind forever. . . .

As far as comforts went, Wroclaw proved to be all that Gershon Jonisz had promised. The three-room apartment they found in the center of the city was ample—Gershon had his own bedroom and the child had a bed of her own in the Jaromirski bedroom. The one minor problem was that the roof of this otherwise sound structure had been jarred loose by bombs, and Leokadia had to be constantly on the lookout for "stones falling down." There could be no complaints, either, about money. Gershon was earning enough at black-market trading to make life easy. Just two months after she had sunk to her lowest ebb of penury back in Praga, Leokadia was able to hire a thirty-year-old German woman to be the family maid.

Clashes were all but inevitable in such a unique household. They began with its two masters and the fact that only one was earning a living. While Jonisz dealt handily in the black market, Bolek was at first reduced to spending his day rummaging for stray pieces of coal in wrecked buildings. "He came home sometimes with nothing," says Leokadia. "And all the while people in this part of Poland were making fortunes. Fortunes!" Leokadia had done no better herself, of course, in her own scavenging foray in the west during the previous summer. Her one triumph, apart from bringing home a single pot, was that she had avoided being raped. By the end of 1945, however, Bolek had managed to establish a machinery repair shop in their building. But he would never replace Jonisz as the prime earner.

Leokadia did not much care who earned the money. She only hated their bickering. "I knew they both suffered the disease of those who have spent years in the concentration camps," she explains. "They were sick in the head as well as the body. I had to make allowances for that. But I couldn't stand the constant arguing between them. Once I got so mad that I threw a plate at them—and I didn't care which one it hit. Better to hit both!"

Thanks to a somewhat macabre irony, these two men had not met at the house on Mala Street back in Praga as total strangers. In the vast slave-labor operations at Auschwitz, Bolek had served for a time in the eating hall. One of the slaves to whom he ladled out a ration of soup each day, beginning in the late summer of 1943, was Gershon Jonisz. "When I met him as a free man," says Jonisz, "he said to me, 'If I'd known it was you, I would have given you soup from the bottom of the pot.' Instead, because I was just another Jew,

I got from the top of the pot, where the soup was like the coffee—just dirty water." After more than thirty years, this is what Jonisz remembers as if it were yesterday, and it appears that by the time they were again eating together in Wroclaw, their mutual enslavement at Auschwitz had become less a bond than an irritant.

So the two of them couldn't agree on anything, and I was the victim. But Bogusia spent her days with no worries. Around here were many children for her to play with. Though she didn't have a bicycle of her own yet, she was able to borrow one from her friends. She was herself unselfish and her heart was sensitive to the troubles of others. She was always inviting children home—both German and Polish—for dinner. The one she liked best was a boy named Piotr. He was strong and big but not the quick-witted type. He protected her and whatever she asked him to do, he did. They would play below this window where I am writing. And she would call up from the yard, "Bread, please!"

I had already prepared two sandwiches. Now I threw one down to her and waited.

"And what about a sandwich for Piotr?" she would ask, shining her eyes up at me.

"With what am I supposed to feed your friend?"

"But, Mother, I have already given him his sandwich. Shall I not have one?"

What could I do? I threw down the other sandwich and she would say, "Ah, my fish, I knew you would give us one more." And all the time she was looking up with her cute, sweet smile.

In this household with two fathers, the role of disciplinarian to the child was never in question. That was Leokadia's job. *Never did I lie to her and always I fulfilled what I promised her. Therefore, she knew only one authority—mine. If she "did something," she would go with me to the bedroom for her punishment. Then, after the spanking, she would ask me to pardon her. I would give her many kisses, and though I had to be serious, I tried to make her less sorry for what happened. It was hard for me to punish her, but I had to teach her to discern between good and bad.*

If Leokadia found it difficult to discipline the child herself, she drew the line absolutely when it came to the others. *I knew her character, having molded it myself. She couldn't stand to take orders. My own requests of her were always made in a polite way. When Jonisz or Bolek ordered her to do something in a peremptory tone, she would refuse. Because of that, many times we ended up in quarrels. But not once did anyone hit her. I didn't allow it. Nobody but me had the right to touch her. Jonisz claimed he had the right to discipline her because he was the real father.*

"You have a father's right to provide for her," I answered, "but as far as punishment goes, only I am allowed to do it. Because I am the one who raised her. If she isn't behaving right, you must tell me. But to raise a hand to her—that I won't allow to anybody. She will listen to me. If you don't know how to talk to her politely, she is right to refuse. She is used to a different style."

So she continued to develop very nicely, with many kisses and caresses. We would tell each other all kinds of stories and also our dreams. (My dreams were always made up!) Together we were happy. Then, in the spring, Irena came back. After returning from forced labor during the war, she had not been able to find a job in Warsaw. Until this time, I had been afraid to leave the child alone with either Bolek or Jonisz. Now, with our Irka back, I could relax. We talked about the old days in Bialoleka. We decided that it was much better then than now. Even Bogusia said to me once, "What do we need these men for? Let's go to Bialoleka. Gershon could give us money, and we'll build ourselves a house. But only Auntie, Mother, and me. . . ."

Nothing of the sort was going to happen, of course. Jonisz was then thinking hard, in fact, about just how to undo the bond between mother and child and how to dissolve this artificially constituted household. This was not a new or a vindictive intention. It had been part of his plan from the beginning to give his daughter time and a way to get to know him and even to begin to love him. Now a fall, winter, and spring had passed. He was ready to leave Poland—now nothing more than a graveyard for his family, his people, his culture. He saw several options. One was to send his daughter to a distant cousin who lived in Detroit. But the immigration regulations would not allow him to follow immediately, and he did not want to separate again from the child. He could also try to find a new home somewhere in Western Europe where they could stay together. There was one more option. Along with the majority of the surviving European Jews, he could take her to Palestine, soon to become Israel. While he could not be sure yet where the future lay, Jonisz had decided one thing immutably. He wanted to take his daughter elsewhere. One warm evening in the early summer of 1946, after the child had been put to sleep, he told his decision to Leokadia.

Until this hour, Leokadia had done her best not to think about the future—just as she had tried, that previous summer, not to think about the stranger who had entered her home in Praga. *Now the future had arrived. This blow just shocked me. I couldn't imagine my life without her. Whom should I live for? If she would not be with me, who would care for her? At last I started thinking. If her mother were alive, I'm sure that we could agree between us on a solution. We would live together or I would give her the child—her child—without any restraints and with peace of mind. It would have been enough for me to visit with them and them with me. We would educate her together. But to give her to a man whom she hardly knew—even if he was her father? Who would understand her? Who would have the same patience and loyalty? Who would wipe away her tears when she was sad or hurt? Men are not attuned to this. They think more about their own convenience. Even in the best of fathers, there is no motherly feeling. . . .*

Jonisz, backing away from this emotional fire storm, decided now to see if he had any sort of legal redress. Surely this child, his own flesh, belonged to him by law. But in the office of the prosecutor of Wroclaw, Jonisz got a different opinion. The child was indeed his flesh and blood. On the other hand, he had abandoned her, albeit unknowingly, to a stranger who had cared for her unstintingly in the midst of war. What meager money Leokadia could earn she had spent on the child. She would have given her very life for the child. In the absence of the natural mother, consequently, she was the de facto mother. She had as much right to the child as the father. The only way the law might be on his side, suggested the prosecutor, was to prove that Leokadia took the child against his will. In a word, kidnapping.

"*Mein Gott!*" says Jonisz, remembering that conversation. "I didn't want that. In my heart I could never do it. She was a lovely woman and I wanted to thank her very much. But I was the father of my daughter and I wanted her back. That's all. I didn't want to send anyone to prison. So I gave up trying to do anything legally after this. I decided not to do anything at all for a while longer and see what time would bring."

The atmosphere was subdued but guarded as Leokadia and Jonisz circled each other like a pair of cats. "She was watching me to be sure I didn't steal away with the child," explains Jonisz. "I was watching her to be sure she didn't commit some folly." Though Bolek had stayed out of this affair from the beginning, he and Jonisz continued to bicker and to agree on nothing. "Even the child felt something," says Leokadia. "Again she asked, 'Can't we go to Bialoleka or Warsaw, but without them?'" After that first meeting on Mala Street the summer before, the child had not been told again that Jonisz was her father or that she had been born Jewish. But in the street the word was out. *Once I heard her coming up the stairs crying. I jumped out the door. "What happened, my love?"*

"*Renia* [a playmate] *told me I'm Jewish and that Gershon is my father," she said.*

What was I to tell this child? She was only five years old. I explained to her, "Your mother is a Catholic and you go to church to pray with me. So how can you now be Jewish? When you are older, you will understand many things better. Now take a kiss from me and go play." She believed me, as always.

Now that I could no longer ignore his intentions, I became a bundle of nerves. I went to a lawyer, but he was no help. He claimed the law was on the father's side. But where was my right? I was the most miserable person in the world. I would go alone to church and pray before the Holy Mother and I would ask for an outlet from this closed circle of suffering. There, with no witnesses, my tears could run without restraint. Jonisz saw my sorrow. He asked me to go with him to Palestine, not as his wife, but as the child's mother. When he remarried, I would be a part of the family. If not for Bolek, I would have given it a lot of thought. But how could I leave such a man? His belief in me had kept him alive for five years when he should otherwise have died. Now he was helpless with the disease of those who come out of the concentration camps. He was without steady work and without ability to think. If I had left him, he would have gone on vegetating.

In a last-ditch effort at getting authoritative backing on her side, Leokadia wrote a letter to Pius XII asking for his wisdom on the subject of Bogusia. In less than a month came an answer that struck down all hope. She was instructed by the Pope to return the child to its father. If she were to keep the child by force or stealth, in the end she would regret it, since, at school or elsewhere, the child would eventually learn the truth. It was her duty as a Catholic not only to give back the child, but to do it with good will and in friendship.

A sticky point in the struggle for the child was money. Curiously, the principals differ as to who brought up the subject, which for Leokadia remains not only odious but the source of searing guilt. Jonisz claims that he offered Leokadia a sum of money as a sign of gratitude and also to neutralize the opinion he had received from the prosecutor of Wroclaw that all she had spent gave her standing as the child's mother. But Leokadia claims that she herself demanded a large sum of money from Jonisz on the theory that he would not have it or else would refuse to give it and that this would "drag out the whole thing, maybe for as long as a year."

As it happened, the J.D.C. in Lodz had a special budget for the express purpose of paying bounties for Jewish children who had survived the war in Polish families while their own families were being wiped out. Without such a bounty, many Jewish children would be lost to their people forever, even as they lived on contentedly as Polish Christians and, almost inevitably, took into their blood the prevailing anti-Semitism of the land.

So it was that Jonisz soon arrived with a woman official from the Lodz office of the J.D.C. who handed over to Leokadia the sum of seventy-five thousand zlotys. *I was stunned. If the money had come from his hand, I would never have accepted it. But she was gracious. I felt that I could not retreat. If we were to be poor again, with Jonisz gone and Bolek still not working, how else would we get by? Even then, it would only last for a month or two at best. I took the money. The bills burned my hands like the silver shekels of Judas Iscariot, who betrayed Jesus. For myself, I bought nothing. Even so, I was glad when it was gone.*

The day of our separation came. Jonisz asked if I would be the one to explain to her about the trip and, sick in my heart, I agreed. On that morning, when she awoke, I explained I was sick—a form of heart disease—and that while it wasn't serious, I probably would soon have to go into the hospital. That is why it was better for her to go with Gershon to another place, where she would attend a very nice kindergarten. She didn't want to hear about it at first. But then she wanted to know why she couldn't stay here with Irena while I was in the hospital. I explained that Irena would also have to be away, helping her family in Warsaw. She would be left alone. "Who will cook your lunch for you?" I asked. "Who will mend your dresses? It will be better for you to be with all the nice children in the kindergarten."

I was calm when I told her this. But later she saw my tears. "Why are you crying?" she asked. I told her it was because I had just heard from the doctor that he had arranged a bed for me at the hospital, and I had to go that very day.

"Mother, you'll see—everything will be fine," she said. "Soon you'll be healthy again. I'll come back and we'll have fun spoiling each other again. I'll come to you in the morning first thing, before you're up, and you'll say, 'Who is this little dog who comes to my bed?' And I will say, 'It's your little daughter Bogusia! Don't you recognize her anymore?'"

She knew how to ease my tension. But as she made up this little dialogue, speaking in two voices, my throat filled to choking, because I knew that these were only dreams and that I had to separate from this child forever. One last time, that morning, I spoke to Jonisz.

"You can have other children," I pleaded. "And I'll never deny your

fatherhood of this child. . . ." But he didn't want to listen. He only wanted to go. I prepared her things and cooked her lunch for the last time. When they went out the door, I stretched out only one hand, because with the other I covered my mouth so that she wouldn't hear me cry.

Jonisz may have been certain that his daughter could never truly be restored to him until he left Leokadia's household and just as certain that, under no circumstances, did he want to remain any longer in Poland. But the truth is that, beyond those certainties, once he walked out of that house with the child, he had no clear idea of where to go or what to do. Did he want to find a new home in Western Europe? Did he want to go to America? Or should he try to get to Palestine? Then there were questions requiring more immediate answers—namely, how does one fix lunch and mend the dresses of a spirited five-year-old accustomed to the very best attentions? How could he carry on his peripatetic trading business with a child in tow?

These last questions were temporarily answered that same day when Jonisz and his daughter arrived in the southwestern Silesian town of Pietrolesie, some sixty miles from Wroclaw. Here, as in Lodz, the J.D.C. had established a front-line orphanage, meant to salvage Jewish children from the Polish countryside and then prepare them for emigration to Palestine. For the time being, while he pondered his future and went about making a living, Jonisz deposited his daughter at the orphanage. This was hardly the way to hasten the closer relationship with her that he longed for. But he was comforted to know, at least, that for the first time she would be among Jewish children—albeit children who were as handy as she was at making the sign of the cross or reciting the rosary.

Leokadia, in the meantime, was finding no solution at all to dealing with the sudden hollow at the center of her life. Bolek, on the other hand, now emerged at last from his emotional as well as physical lethargy in order to support his stricken wife. He made arrangements for Irena or a neighbor always to be with her. He called a doctor, who gave her a tranquilizer. He made her swear to him that she would not harm herself. "I cried in the daytime," she says, "but it was the nights I could not bear. In the dark, I saw the face of my child, not smiling but crying. And from her bed, I heard her crying, 'Mother, Mother. . . .' It was her own voice, so clear and piercing in the dark that I would run to see if somehow she had gotten away from her father and come home, or if perhaps it was all a dream. In the dark I would touch the bed but it was empty."

It did not help that in the process of his trading forays Jonisz now returned frequently to Wroclaw—staying, no less, in his old room in the Jaromirska apartment. He was solicitous and he even brought gifts. He assured Leokadia that, for the time being, the child was in the good hands of a Jewish orphanage. But he was careful not to say where. Just the same, in an uncharacteristic moment of stealth, Leokadia was able to sneak a glance at Jonisz's rail ticket to a destination in western Silesia. Nearly a month after the child's departure, with her cries still ringing unabated in the night, Leokadia knew what she had to do. With a suitcase filled with Bogusia's clothing and toys, the last of the money from the J.D.C., and faithful Irena for support, Leokadia set off to find her child.

They got off the train near the German border and began to ask for places were Jewish orphans were being kept. Going from one institution to the next, Leokadia asked for her daughter—to no avail. Her charm being as real as her determination, however, she was invited to sleep overnight at two such orphanages. On the third day, by a process of trial and error very much like the one Jonisz had used to find the child in the previous summer, Leokadia now arrived at the door of the orphanage in Pietrolesie—though, unlike him, she had no way of knowing she was at the right place. She asked for the director. In a few moments, from upstairs, a slender young woman appeared. Her name was Helena Goldberg and she was one of that strain of Polish Jews who appear more "Aryan" than many Christians.

Again, Leokadia asked for her daughter. The answer was as always. Helena Goldberg claimed she had no such child at the orphanage. Until now, Leokadia had accepted this answer and trudged on. "This time," she says, "I saw something in the face of that woman that made me go on the offensive."

"'What do you mean she's not here?' I shot back at her. 'I was told that she is here. I am her mother and in this suitcase are clothes that she will need. Don't tell me she's not here, because I know that she is. And don't tell me that her father told you not to allow me to see her. Because I am the only one who loves her. I am her mother. . . .'"

Helena Goldberg had not lied . . . quite. But neither had she told the truth. The child had been admitted, a few days earlier, to a nearby children's hospital with a case of scarlet fever. Until then, however, she had been at the orphanage, and upon her recovery she would return. And so the directress was now in a quandary. Gershon Jonisz had alerted her to the possibility that somehow Leokadia might find this place. He had instructed her that under no circumstances was she to reveal the whereabouts of his child. Helena Goldberg had been prepared to follow such instructions— until this moment. Just as Leokadia had seen something in her face, she now saw the face of a woman—the dusty, anxious face of a mother—who could not be denied.

Helena listened to Leokadia's tirade in silence. When it was over, she said, "Please come in. I can take you to the child you seek."

Over tea, Helena delivered some news that all but floored Leokadia and also confirmed her opinion that it had been wrong to let Jonisz take his child from her. Bogusia, that paragon of social virtues, had turned into a misfit. She started fights with the other children. She hit them. She would obey nobody. "But this Hela," says Leokadia, calling Helena by her nickname, "was both good and wise. She understood that this was no ordinary bad child. So she took Bogusia to stay with her in her own room, apart from the other children. This is how my daughter, who would be friends with anybody, had changed in a month!"

They walked together to the hospital. Helena had called ahead to say they were coming, and Leokadia was startled to see Bogusia was already hanging out of a second-story window awaiting them. Just as the child had so often looked up at her mother from the courtyard of their building in Wroclaw, Leokadia now looked up at the child. Since Bogusia was in quarantine, that was as close as she would get. *So I stood at the gate and, putting on my glasses to see her better and to hide my tears, I showed her what I had brought to her in the suitcase. She was not very interested. I could see that she was not herself. And so we talked.*

"Bogusia, my sweet, how are you?"

"Good. Why did it take you so long to come? There was a place in the hospital for you right here. I asked the nurse if you could have it because you were sick with heart disease. But then another lady came and took the bed. So I made the nurse promise to give you the next bed."

"Why are you scratching your head, my angel?"

"Because I have lice. The nurse put powder on my hair. Now the lice are all dead and lying on my pillow."

"Ask the nurse to cut your hair shorter and to put on more powder."

"Okay, Rybciu [little fish]."

At first they didn't want to let me stay there to take care of her. But I insisted. So I sent Irena home and, as I had done before, I nursed her back to health. I carried her in my arms again and told her the stories she had loved. But she accepted this attention absentmindedly—even with indifference. Constantly she repeated the same words: "Mother, don't go. Don't leave me again. . . ." Perhaps she was thinking did I really love her? I tried to make her understand a hundred times that no matter how much I loved her, now she must go with her father. But what could she understand, this little one? "Finally, when she saw it would not change, she said to me, 'I will kill that Gershon with an ax!'

"That was the only way she could translate her grief. But I was firm with her and told her she must never say that or even think that. She nodded but I saw that her mind was running.

"'Then I will commit suicide,' she said.

"'And how will you do that, my child?'

"She held up the locket around her neck which I had given to her. In it was a tiny photo of the two of us. It was not made of silver, but a false silver. I had always warned her not to put it in her mouth because this kind of metal was poison. Now she said, 'I will put this locket in my mouth, Mother, and I will hold it there until I am poisoned to death.' She saw the way I looked at her. 'If that doesn't work,' she added, 'then I will jump out the top window of the hospital.' This too I told her she must never think or say. But I recognized that, as well as being still sick from the fever, she was as sick at heart as I.''

Arriving back in Wroclaw, Irena had found Jonisz carrying on business locally and living in the house with Bolek. Realizing that Leokadia had found the child, Jonisz hurried back to Pietrolesie. This time he asked Bolek to come with him in the hope that he could comfort his wife, now that the knot would have to be broken once more. "At the orphanage she held out money to me," says Jonisz.

" 'Here, take this money back,' she pleaded. 'I will make up the rest. I can't live without her.'

" 'You're worth not just this money but fortunes,' I answered. 'Thanks be to God and you, my daughter is alive. We will be like relatives—close and loving relatives—and I promise to write you all the news and send photos. But what you want can't be.' "

In truth, Leokadia knew by now that indeed it could not be. But she could take a certain bitter comfort in knowing that for Jonisz the victory was hollow. He had won the child, but the child's love remained with her. Bogusia hated her father. "We were sitting once in the cafeteria at the orphanage," says Leokadia. "Bogusia was drinking an orange soda and she offered me a drink. Then he said, 'Don't you also offer a drink to your father?'

" 'I don't want my glass to touch his pig's snout,' she answered, looking away from him. This is how she felt. Yet this was the man with whom I had to leave her forever. The other women who worked at the orphanage were all on my side. Bolek also shared in my sorrow. He was sorry also for Bogusia. Once she fell asleep on his knees. He didn't move so she wouldn't wake up. Before, he would not have done that."

Now the time came for our departure. I said goodbye to her. I went with

Bolek without seeing the road. Before, Bogusia had been calm. Now I heard her crying after me in a voice of despair. Even from the distance I still heard her. With each step my heart tore in shreds. I hear her cry until now. I returned to Wroclaw not the same person. When Irena saw me, she made the sign of the Cross. My hair had turned white.

Bolek tried to take my thoughts away from her. He was very good and caring. He asked me to go to the movies. This movie that we saw described a girl Bogusia's age—an orphan—who was wandering in a forest in a storm. I started to cry with convulsions, and Bolek had to take me out of there. I didn't go to the movies anymore. Irena bought me a puppy dog to cheer me up. I cried and this made the dog lift its head and start howling. Everything made me nervous. I walked around the apartment like a shadow. Every detail reminded me of the child. Every toy, every rag that belonged to her, I flooded with tears.

By summer's end, 1946, the Pietrolesie orphanage had been disbanded and the children moved across the German border to another displaced-persons camp. Jonisz got a job there distributing clothing from the J.D.C. to Jewish refugees. True to the promise he had made, he wrote often and sent photos of the child back to Wroclaw. Two years passed, and still he had not decided, as a member of a community which no longer existed, where to put down new roots. Then, with the establishment of the Jewish state, the decision was made. In November 1948, Jonisz married a woman who, like him, had lost a mate in a killing center and whose child had survived. She would be—at least he meant her to be—the new mother that the child needed. The next month, they sailed from France for the fledgling State of Israel.

In that same year, Leokadia had adopted another infant girl. She named her Elzbieta and called her "Ela." If those close to her had thought that this new child might fill the void, it was hope in vain. Leokadia was hardly more consoled by the child than by the puppy that howled with her. The momentous arrival, in fact, she dispatches with these terse words: *Ela came. I didn't feel anything toward her. As I cared for her I thought of a different girl. I looked at other young girls who were the age she would be. "What is she doing just now?" I'd ask myself. "How is she feeling? What is she thinking about?" Jonisz wrote to me from Germany that she was losing her baby teeth. Then from Israel that she was in school. Though he never mentioned it to me, he wrote to other friends that she cried whenever Wroclaw was mentioned and that she said she would walk there by foot. Again, I began to torture myself. Once, he sent a parcel of dresses that had belonged to her for Ela to wear. I held them to my cheek and cried. As I went to work each day, she was always in my thoughts. Where was my sweet child? At night I would think—if only she would dream about me. Thus twelve years passed. . . .*

As a condition of sending Leokadia regular progress reports, Jonisz did not want her to be in direct contact with the child. From his point of view, this was not meanness. He simply felt that if Shifra—formerly Bogusia—was to be properly settled in the nest of her new family in a new land, then it was not fair for her to feel tuggings from the life left behind in Poland. She could have only one mother at a time. In return for her silence, Jonisz had kept up the reports as promised. Then, in the spring of 1958, on the eve of entering the hospital for surgery, Leokadia violated this informal agreement with Gershon Jonisz and wrote a letter to her daughter. Despite the assurances of the doctor, Leokadia was not convinced that she absolutely would survive the operation.

She sent the letter in care of Jonisz in Tel Aviv. *I thought that perhaps somebody will translate it for her, and it will cause her to think about me and perhaps even to write to me—something in her own language. . . .*

On June 26th or 27th, I got a letter—the unforgettable first letter from my beloved child.

> Dear Mother,
>
> This is my first letter to you and I ask you to forgive me this. I often wanted to write to you but there was nobody to translate from the Hebrew and I was afraid to ask my father. I have so much to tell you and you must have much to tell me after our separation of twelve years. I have changed a lot because so much has happened to me since then.

I'd like to describe for you a bit of my life right now. I'm in the army. Here girls also have to serve automatically. Now that I've finished basic training, it's not so difficult as before. It's even interesting to meet different kinds of people.

I don't live with my father. They live in the city and I live on the kibbutz. It's like a big family—a collective— and we work together and share the profits together. I've been on this kibbutz for three years now in the care of my mother's brother.* This life has been a big influence on my well-being. I visit my parents from time to time. But after my service I would like to come back to live here at the kibbutz.

You might wonder why I've selected this life. The first reason is that I never could get used to the noise of the city. I wanted the peaceful life. And after the working day I want to find myself close to my friends.

The second reason has to do with the attitude of [step]mother to daughter, which upset me. My father wanted to help smooth things over but it was too complicated. Now her attitude toward me has gotten much better. It also helps that we see each other rarely.

Dear Mother—I think about you often. Suddenly I see you bend over and kiss me with a mother's tender care. Nothing could make me ever forget you. I would like you to write me often. I would like to see you with my own eyes. I send you a daughter's kisses.

Your loving daughter,
Bogusia/Shifra

With that first letter came a photo of the writer outfitted in khaki fatigues, smiling delightedly and also a little sheepishly, as would any teenage girl who is posing with a machine gun held at

---

*Having left Radzymin as a youth to go to Palestine as a *halutz* (pioneer), this uncle helped found kibbutz Sha'ar Hagolan in 1933.

the ready. *I reacted to the shock* [of that letter] *by being sick for four days. I cried out of gladness until my eyes became swollen. I couldn't write an answer because my hand shook. Slowly I calmed down and I started to look differently on the world. Since then, her letters to me have been balm to the heart. I know that she is well, that she has a loving husband and three charming sons, that her material conditions are good. So when I think about her now, I'm not sad anymore. I have so many photographs. I look at them and it seems we are together. When I have worries of my own, I spread them in my thoughts before my child and she is my consolation. She is my good and beloved child. Surely she feels and understands my love, as she did long ago.*

In the same clear and generous scrawl with which she began, Leokadia now comes to the end of her chronicle. The first of the letters to Yoram had been dated January 18, 1966. She had hoped to be finished by the end of her ten days' sick leave from work in the factory. But the last letter was not written until February 22. It is addressed first to Yoram and then to his wife.

My dear Yoram,

I've finished my story. It's not my fault that there isn't a lot of joy in it. As much as possible I tried not to touch on matters which would scratch old wounds. But you asked for it and I have tried to fulfill your request.

I know that my story will interfere with your quiet for a long time. For me also it won't pass easily. But now, at least, you won't be angry with me anymore for being surprised that Bogusia is working in the kitchen.* I felt it from your first letter.

In my eyes, she deserved the crown of a queen. But love is more important. You love each other, you have your own treasures, and this is worth more—because the hands of a

---

*A true "Jewish mother" forever, Leokadia had questioned whether her daughter should ever have to see the inside of a kitchen. Yoram, a true kibbutznik, reminded her that in a collective all chores are shared and all forms of labor are honored. If anything, those which are more onerous are more honored.

child on a mother's neck are the most beautiful necklace and nothing can replace them. Excuse me if some parts of this story were not likable in your eyes.

Kisses from Mother

My dear daughter,

After reading this story, tell me frankly what thoughts you had toward me first as a child and then as a young woman. In what light did your father explain these events to you? Did you bear any grudge in your heart because I gave you away? You probably felt my attitude toward your father. Now you will judge whether it has any basis. If I wrote to you in my letters about loving you and missing you, the words sprang from the depths of my heart.

Yes, my daughter, now you'll believe that I lost twenty years of my life. It's not your fault and it's not mine. It's the fault of fate which caused us to meet and the cruel war. Were it not for the war, you would have your true mother. You would have been a happy child raised in the home of your parents instead of living a young life of sorrow and misery. My life, too, would have been settled differently. But fate wished otherwise. And it didn't spare us any mental and physical hurts. You are young, so that with you it passed quickly. But with me it will stay until the end of my life. Now, though, I am much relieved. I have spilled all the sorrow and all of my missing you in forty pages.

The thought that you have judged me guilty, that I gave you away to your father for material profit, has always tortured me. I don't know what fairy tales were fed to you, but the fact is that I had to do it because the law was on his side and I had no other way out. I couldn't leave there because I felt an allegiance to Bolek. He loved me very much, he married me when I was poor and hungry, and he created good conditions of life for me. For the five years [before the war] I didn't know what it was to need money. Could I then leave him when he was poor and sick? I fought a lot with myself over whether to leave him. But I could not be so bad. You had a father, at least, but for Bolek I was the only one who remained. And he wasn't in a normal state, either. If I had left him, he would have vegetated and that would have lain on my conscience.

When I wrote to you that I was the victim of fate, I wasn't kidding. But now it's all the same to me. I am fifty-eight years old and those struggles are all in the past. We are together here, living as a family. Many people are around. But I am lonely.

My beloved daughter—I promise that this is my last sad letter. Now you know everything about yourself. A burden has been lifted from us. I will only add that while you were sick, you weren't a good girl! You tired out your mother! You had all sorts of caprices and whims! Yet I fulfilled them even though it made Irena angry at us.

I forgot one last cute story about you from the days in Wroclaw. You were lying in bed one evening, supposedly asleep, when on the radio they broadcast a jingle:

> "Our link sausages are best quality—
> On this you can depend . . ."

And you piped up, in rhyme:

> "Yes—if only we had the money to spend!"

We all burst out laughing.

And now to the point—for this story of your childhood, for the uncooked dinners (and those that got burned), for the work I postponed, write me a long letter. The older boys should draw a picture for me and Omer [Yoram and Shifra's youngest son] can put down his fingerprint.

For what they will draw for me, I'm kissing them warmly

now on the forehead, eyes, nose, and palms. The adults I bless and kiss, wishing everybody good health, good moods, good weather, and good crops. Bolek asks for you warmly.

Your loving mother,
Leokadia

Sha'ar Hagolan
April 25, 1966

Dear Mother,

After weeks of anxious waiting, we were moved by feelings that are difficult to put into words when we read your beautiful letters. We were overwhelmed by this story of our common fate in the war. . . .

Dear Mother—when I write these words, my heart contracts with pain. I am trying to picture myself in your place as a mother—and yet you were far more than a normal mother. When I think of what you went through in those years—all the suffering and worry—only your good heart points the way. Your letters are full of love and so many tears. For me, in my memory, you will always remain my loving mother. And yes, as you sense, I am happy now. Yoram is a wonderful man and the children are a joy.

I remember very well that time when Daddy took me away from you. I used to call him Genek.★ I did not want to call him Father. For a long time I was angry with him and I did not love him—although he was good to me and tried to make me as happy as he could. I used to ask him why other children had a mother as well as a father but I didn't. I did this so that he would find me another mother. He soon found her. At first I was happy but as time went by my disillusionment grew. She was not even able to provide a

---

★The Polish nickname for Gershon.

small part of what you gave me. Even today I remember how much I cried. It is true, of course, that she was a clean and industrious woman who had gone through a lot in Germany.

We arrived in Israel at the end of the War of Independence. Right away I fell ill with typhoid fever. I didn't yet know Hebrew and all day long in this hospital, which was run by a Catholic order, I would cry in Polish, "Sister . . . Sister . . ." Then my mother also fell ill, and had to be operated on. The surgery wasn't successful and she had to stay in the hospital for six months. Daddy had to work, and I, a nine-year-old, had to cook, clean house, and also care for her six-year-old son.

Our neighbors took pity on me and offered help. They knew this woman was not my real mother. When she came back from the hospital, she was not pleased with me, her "substitute." And she reminded me of this at every possible occasion. I told Daddy I would run away from home. He loved me and tried very hard to help me, but a father cannot replace a mother. I remembered how I longed for a good-night kiss, for caresses, and for a kind word that came from the heart—or even just a smile from someone who loved me. I was looking for love, but in my own house I always felt like a boarder.

Whenever I tried to discuss things with my stepmother, she complained to my father. Coming home late from work, tired, he would try to settle these conflicts. Often, rather than be in the house, I would wait outside for him on the stairs. Sometimes quarrels would break out between them because of me, and I felt that perhaps without me around the atmosphere would have been better.

Sometimes Daddy would sit with me and talk about the war. He explained that the whole family was sent to the camps, and if he had taken me with him, I would have met a bad fate. Daddy told me about his sufferings—hunger, beatings, and how he escaped the gas chamber by jumping from the death train. My mother was gassed by the Germans and Daddy knew about it. He was completely depressed—in fact, he did not know what he was struggling for. He did not know if the war would ever end. When that day did come, Daddy simply couldn't believe it. After he was free, he came across a group of people gathered around a fortune-teller. He gave her his hand and she said someone was waiting for him. At that moment, a spark of hope was awakened in him. He started to look for me.

I didn't like to hear Daddy's stories about the war. He told me all about you—how you didn't want to give me back, and how he gave you money and a sewing machine, which you did not want to accept. He said he had no choice and no other way out. He always spoke of you in the best possible way. How could he, in truth, do otherwise?

Dear Mommy—I remember many details from your letters. I remember the baker who gave me fresh rolls. I remember my doll Loda. It seems to me that Bolek made her a little bed. I remember that story about drinking milk, which I hated. There remains in my memory a church, and a cross at my neck. I remember how I ate with a knife and fork and how you told everybody about it with such pride. Once, Bolek gave me a puff on his cigarette and I coughed a lot. I used to be very scared of drunkards. But much of my memory of the last period is as if hidden behind mist.

What I remember best is our parting—you are standing at the window of our building and Daddy is leading me by the hand and both of us are crying. When Daddy read me your letters, I always cried. I was ashamed that Daddy saw me crying, and I asked him not to read them to me anymore.

As I grew up, I thought a lot about you. I wanted to see you. I did see you in my dreams. I wanted to write to you but I had nobody to turn to. I didn't want Daddy to read about my feelings. But finally I did let him translate the first letters.

When I was thirteen, an uncle from Mommy's side invited me to the kibbutz. His family received me warmly and persuaded me to come live on the kibbutz. I was accepted for work with others my own age. I went with the group that summer to camp and I no longer wanted to return home. I found in the kibbutz all that I sought—peace, work, a home. My uncle and his wife were good to me. I studied five hours in the morning and then worked two hours in the fields. I liked the work very much. In the evening, we had discussions, games, and socials. I had an excellent teacher—like a mother. Daddy wanted to take me out of the kibbutz. He tried many ways. He wanted me to get a better education. He promised to send me to school abroad. However, I did not give in to him. Thus three-and-a-half years passed in a good and homelike atmosphere.

Then I was drafted into the army. I did my service at Yad Mordechai. That was when we wrote each other regularly. As I was then far from home, a friend, Mrs. Reginka, translated for me. I missed my family and the kibbutz. But in those days your letters helped me to overcome all obstacles.

By the end of 1966, Yoram, who had set this chronicle in motion with his own first letter to Leokadia at the start of the year, decided that nothing else would do except for Leokadia to visit her daughter at home, here on Sha'ar Hagolan. The cost of the trip was to be shared equally by the kibbutz and Gershon Jonisz. These arrangements were made final against the rising cacophony of broadcasts from Arab nations calling for a jihad—holy war—that would push the Jews, once and for all, into the sea. But in a letter to Leokadia dated May 28, 1967, Yoram allows no shadows to fall on his enthusiastic planning for her trip:

Dear Leokadia,

. . . We got your letter of April 28th. We are glad to hear that your health and your mood are both better. Gershon has agreed to our request to send you his share of the money for your trip this coming fall. We insisted on it. Shifra gave up the trip she had planned to take to America and everything is agreed upon. In his letter he proposed that you and he both come in October—that's good because of the weather and we hope you will be able to prepare for the trip by then. Write to me as quickly as possible about what papers you will need from us so that there will be no delays. In the meantime, we will try to find out what can be done at this end ourselves. The only obstacle that remains is bureaucracy. I hope that we shall overcome even this.

Nothing can prevent us now from fulfilling your dream and our dream. You will be able to stay with us for as long as you wish. I am sure you will be satisfied here. We shall have a bit of trouble with language but I hope Shifra will be able to express a few words in Polish. Perhaps she will study it this summer before you come. We also have many members who speak Polish—including my mother, Shifra's father, and Tula [translator of the letters]. . . .

Your letters about Shifra's story got quite a bit of publicity here. . . . There is much sensitivity to this topic among us. I hope you are not angry about it [allowing others to read the letters]. We could not resist the pressure.

And now a little about us. Today is Independence Day. Israel is already nineteen years old. When the State was born, I was eleven. That day, war started here and, four days later, Arabs managed to occupy Sha'ar Hagolan. But the adults had already taken us children to underground shelters. It took three days for us to win the kibbutz back. Despite their counterattacks, we held on. Three of our members were killed in the war. The settlement was totally burned down and nothing from those days now remains.

The children especially enjoy the holiday. We adults fixed up all sorts of games for them and also a puppet show. Omer saw it and he understood it quite well. We adults, naturally, got tired out by the whole process. I will close now. Best regards.

See you,
Yoram

Eight days after he wrote this letter, Yoram was at war with his tank unit first in the Sinai Desert and then, closer to home, on the Golan Heights. Despite the high casualties—particularly among kibbutzniks—suffered in the armored charges up those slopes, he survived unhurt. But then on December 27, six months later, during a stint of reserve duty on the border with Jordan, he was killed in an exchange of tank fire.

Yoram was carried the next day on the shoulders of eight soldiers who were his friends to the burial grove of Sha'ar Hagolan, where he had been born thirty years earlier and where his own three sons were born and would continue to grow up. In a photo of the cortege, you can see that the winter wheat is white, that the slender pines remain green, and that the hills are bleached to paleness. Slumped with her head down, Shifra follows the coffin. The children—aged two, four, and six—were judged too young to join the mourners.

• • •

Wroclaw
January 16, 1968

My dear and beloved child,

The message about the disaster struck like thunder. Only two days ago, I got such a relaxed letter from you in which you told how Yoram took a walk with Omer and in which there was also a nice drawing by Yuval. I didn't have a chance yet to answer you and then on Sunday two letters arrived together— one from you and one from Mrs. Reginka [the translator]. This occurrence surprised me to anxiety. Did anything happen? When I saw the words, "Yoram fell . . ." I wasn't able to read any more.

My dear child—what a disaster has come down on us! In

June, I was worried about him. But now that the formal war was over, why did he have to be killed, bringing disaster to our homes and making our most beloved creatures into orphans?

I know there is nothing I can do to soften your suffering. Nobody is able to do that except your children. My beloved daughter—my tears have also run dry. I am as full of agony now for my dear Yoram, my good child, as I was in those days when you were taken from me. In twenty-one years I haven't shed so many tears.

Yoram's picture is engraved in my heart beside you and your children. It will be engraved there forever, that figure of the noble man, son, husband, good father. My heart aches that I will never be lucky enough to see him, and to thank him for all that he did for you, and for his good attitude toward me—a foreign woman to him—for whom he kept a special corner in his noble heart.

Why did he leave us, our good son, in such a terrible sorrow? He lies now in peace and feels nothing, but we are left with our pain and agony for many years. What a cruel fate— to take a life of such a happy and young person when many miserable old people remain alive. I can't accept it, my daughter, my dear little Bogusia. Our Yoram will always remain alive in our hearts.

My daughter, many friends are left to you: Yoram's parents, your children, and me, your mother. You know what a treasure you are to me. In my life I haven't loved anyone the way I loved you. Since we've been corresponding, you have been my spiritual support. Your letters have added to my will to live. If it weren't for you, I would be miserable—if only I could suffer now instead of you.

Don't break, my child. Yoram has attained complete peace. He won't come back but the children are left. You must save them from any vision of tears. They don't yet grasp the scope of the disaster. Don't take away from them the joy of life. If they see your tears, they too will be sad. When they are older, they will remember their good father who fell as a hero. It's not only your loss—he gave his life for the country in which he was born. You are not alone. Think of all the others who were killed and who will be killed, because the road to peace is long. . . .

My child, you have to be brave. You have to think about your living treasures . . . they will be like sunbeams. Seeing them, you will be forced to smile, even though out of pain . . . time does its work. Life will force you to return to balance. You will be healthy together with the beloved children. I kiss your grey-green eyes, the sad and tearful eyes.

Kisses to the cute children.

And to our beloved—put a flower on his grave and give him regards from the loving mother and grandmother.

Leokadia

Simultaneous with the Israeli victory, Poland joined all Soviet-dominated nations except Rumania in breaking off diplomatic relations with Israel. Polish citizens were forbidden thereafter to visit Israel, making it seem that Leokadia's long planned trip would be just one more casualty of the war. Her October visit was indeed canceled. But she wrote a letter to the visa authorities in Wroclaw explaining her circumstances. That letter was persuasive enough to make her, apparently, the only Polish Christian to travel to Israel in the following year, 1969.

One morning in May, seven months after her original trip had been scheduled, she boarded the overnight train to Venice and from there sailed for Haifa. Well before the ship had docked, mother and daughter had spotted each other. They embraced for the first time in twenty-three years. Leokadia held tightly not to a child, of course, but to a twenty-eight-year-old mother, freshly widowed. Shifra, just the same, was smiling. That same extended family of the kibbutz, which, as she had once written her mother, she preferred to Tel Aviv society, had gathered around her to make the healing easier. Even Yoram's parents put their own grief in a position subordinate to Shifra's. "At least we have the two other boys [Yoram's grown brothers]. But she has no men left to comfort her. . . ." But, quick and unstinting as it was in its support, the kibbutz family did not put up with a great deal of emotional dawdling. Work had to go on. Seven hundred eaters needed Shifra back in the kitchen.

Leokadia's seventy-five days on the kibbutz spanned the Jordan Valley's gentlest season—after the wet, cool winter and before the baking summer. She communicated with her daughter and grandchildren in a mixture of German, Polish, and sign language. She was made to feel at home by all, even though this was a kibbutz founded by Jews from Poland who felt they had no future in that country and, in many cases, had never known a Polish Christian whom they could call a friend.

On May 8, she and Shifra were driven south through the valley, turning right at the Dead Sea for the long climb on a winding road that brings you up to the Judean hills and the clear air of Jerusalem. Taking a spade that day, while her daughter stood beside her, Leokadia planted a tree on the Avenue of the Righteous.

It is a one-mile walk from the highway that runs south from the Sea of Galilee to the kibbutz called Sha'ar Hagolan. If the breezes are up here in the valley, you will hear nothing on this side road except the rattle of the big, floppy fronds of the banana trees that fill the acreage all around. Sha'ar Hagolan is the largest producer of bananas in Israel—a curious distinction, considering that the founding group, heavily weighted toward East Europeans, had probably rarely in their own birthland seen a banana.

I had only to ask for Shifra by her first name to be led to the last of a group of attached houses at the north end of the kibbutz. Like most such quarters, it is very plain stucco, laced and garlanded all around with brilliant flowers. The woman who came to the door had a handsome wide-cheeked face and calm, green-grey eyes. Anyone who had seen a snapshot of her as a three-year-old would have had no trouble recognizing her—even, as she was now, nearing the full term of a pregnancy. Along with the three boys from her marriage to Yoram, she now had a fourth son, five years old, from her marriage to Adam Ivri, director of the kibbutz repair shop and also a lifetime friend of the late Yoram.

Owing to the vagaries of getting any kibbutznik on the telephone, I had arrived at her doorstep unknown and unannounced, giving Shifra every right to be startled at this confrontation with a strange American inquiring into the story of her and her Polish mother. But she was as matter-of-fact as if I had come to read the gas meter. If anything, she seemed most pleased that after two years of evening classes in English, she now had somebody on whom to practice what she had learned.

Her twelve-year-old, Ronen, had been peering at me quietly since my arrival. Now he jumped on a bike and, with a few shy words in English and many vigorous gestures, offered me a larger bike for a tour of the kibbutz—the children's dormitories, the dining hall, the factory for plastic pipe (much of it shipped to West Germany), the smelly pens where cattle, having no natural grazing lands here, spend their whole lives, the stables, the endless banana and cotton fields, the Olympic-size swimming pool. Thanks to chance discoveries during the excavation for this pool, the kibbutz now has a small museum displaying the tools and pottery of settlers who had preceded them at this site by some thirty thousand years. Throughout this tour, Ronen kept peering back, still shyly, to see if I was following. Just as his mother is easily recognizable from snapshots of her infancy, Ronen's dark, oval face marks him, to anyone who has seen an old snapshot, as the son of Yoram.

Near each of the children's dormitories, we had passed odd mounds of grassed-over earth that looked like the burial places of American Indians. But they were only fortified shelters for the children to use during air raids or shelling alerts. Later that night, I pulled open the door to one of these shelters, found a light switch, and descended a narrow stairway. The place was filled with small cots, storybooks, first-aid boxes, and the dampness that comes from being underground and from disuse. These shelters were, however, used actively during Leokadia's visit. All the kibbutz children, in fact, slept here every night for two years—regularly waking to the whistling of Katusha rockets fired into the valley by Palestinians from the nearby hills of Jordan.

"I remember something she said during one of those alerts," said Shula, the mother of Shifra's second husband, Adam. "It was during the festival of Purim. The children had been in the shelters all day. But this is a happy holiday, celebrating the triumph of Queen Esther over the wicked Haman, adviser to King Ahasuerus. So a decision was made to bring the children up into the night. They sang and marched with sparklers. Then they went back down into the shelters to sleep. And Leokadia said to me, 'When I was a young woman, I lived in a neighborhood where there were many Jews. And I would hear young Zionist groups sing songs about how the Jewish people will always live. I used to wonder about it. What did they mean? Now I see how you love and protect your children and yet, on this holiday, you are not afraid to bring them up in the night to sing and even to light sparklers. And I understand now that those young Zionists whom I heard singing were not wrong. The Jewish people shall live.'"

Before I left the kibbutz, three days later, I went to say goodbye to Shifra in the kitchen where, despite the misgivings of her Polish mother, she still worked even now in her ninth month. It was three o'clock and she was sitting at a stainless-steel table while two Dutch volunteers peeled vegetables for the evening meal. She wore a sundress in which she appeared tanned, soft, and relaxed. As women sometimes do at the full term of pregnancy, she had the look of someone who, despite her burden, is floating. After having three boys by Yoram and one by Adam—who himself had a son by a previous marriage—she was resigned to another boy.

Several days later, I knocked on the door of Gershon Jonisz's second-floor apartment at 136 Dizengoff—the busiest avenue in Tel Aviv. In his photos from just after the war, he had looked astonishingly strong in the light of what he had undergone. Now, at age sixty-six, it seemed as if the suffering of those days had caught up with him. His bushy hair was gone, his face looked almost as if any previous softness had been chipped away, and he walked stiffly. But he was smiling broadly.

"Shifra just called," he said. "She had a girl."

The building where Bolek and Leokadia Jaromirska have lived for thirty-two years stands beside the trolley tracks at a busy corner of Ruska Street in the center of town. Wroclaw may be a Polish city now, but buildings like this one which have survived the war still belong to Teutonic Breslau. It is a solidly lugubrious, four-story pile, fronted by a pair of giant black gates, their ironwork coiled into beasts and gargoyles with nasty tongues. Inside, the double-staired, unlighted lobby was—despite a fine morning sun—shrouded in darkness.

A wrinkled face, set with a pair of restless, wide-spaced eyes and framed by a head of uncombed white hair, appeared at the crack in the door when I knocked at a few minutes before nine o'clock. At my side was a young woman named Elzbieta Otawska, who would interpret for us. It was clear from Leokadia's startled look that the letters telling of our visit had not yet come. But, drawing her house robe closer around her, she did not hesitate to invite us in. She led us down a dark hall to the living room, where she now resumed dressing eight-year-old Michael—son of her adopted daughter Ela—for school. Though it was not cold out, she carefully buttoned up his pale blue jacket. Both jacket and pants, she explained, had been sent to him by Shifra, making him perhaps the only schoolboy in Wroclaw to be wearing Israeli clothing.

At the door, with a last check to be sure his shoelaces would not trip him and that his book bag was strapped properly on his back, she leaned down and he stretched up to give her a kiss. Then he was out the door. Leokadia went to the front window, dragging one leg. Not long after her visit to the kibbutz in 1969, she explained, she had suffered a stroke which left her with a useless arm and leg. Because of the steep stairs and lack of an elevator, she had been confined to the apartment ever since. Peering down now at the busy street, she said, "I always watch him until he crosses over. It's a dangerous place. . . ."

We watched for several minutes. Trams went by, the traffic light changed several times, people crossed. But Michael had eluded the gaze of us all. Finally, Leokadia turned away from the window and shrugged. "Well, the grandmother has done her duty," she said. And only now did she turn her less than happy eyes full on us.

Against the walls at the two front corners of this long living room were the narrow cots in which Bolek and Leokadia slept. His was neatly made and on hers the covers were thrown carelessly. On the wall above her bed was a small head of Christ in ikon style, with a spray of fresh purple violets floating in a water glass beneath it. There was one bookcase, well stuffed, and other books lay everywhere. Leokadia cast an appraising eye around the room—especially at her own bed—and rattled off what seemed to be a dry comment.

"Her husband is at a two-day meeting of concentration-camp survivors," translated Elzbieta. "She says he will be sad not to have met you. But the *worst* will be that the house isn't clean and in order. He is very strict about things looking just right."

We sat at the dining-room table at the other end of the living room, where the two women began an animated exchange— Elzbieta talking in rapid bursts, wide-eyed, Leokadia holding her own in the dry voice of a lifelong smoker. It was a long time before Elzbieta turned to me.

"She says she will ask her husband to bring back a book from the camp at Maidanek. In it is a picture of a barren hill built up from the bones of people who were burned there. It is the place where Bogusia's mother was killed. Most probably, her bones are part of that hill. She says you must look carefully and you can even see pieces of bones. Leokadia has visited Maidanek and Auschwitz several times. She has visited Treblinka also. She says you don't know over there [in America] what we had over here. . . ."

"You know that my child's name means 'loved by God,'" said Leokadia. "God loved her because he allowed her to be saved by such a wonderful miracle. If you knew how Jewish children were hidden in wooden boxes under beds, in holes in the ground, and how they were pulled out and shot. . . ."

Leokadia began to cry. It was not a choking cry, not a sob, but a steady wail, as if the years had evened it out to this monotone of grief.

"What was Bogusia like?" Elzbieta asked in her soft voice.

"*Slodka*—she was so sweet," answered Leokadia. "And as I never lied to her, she was very trusting. She loved me a lot. . . ."

On my last morning in Poland, a Sunday, Elzbieta and I walked up five flights of filthy stairs, in a building amid an endless grid of such buildings in a huge housing development north of Warsaw, to the immaculate studio apartment belonging to Irena Akaska. As a teenager, her first job had been as nurse to Bogusia. Now she works for a state pharmaceutical exporting company. She is a handsome and well-turned-out woman, never married, who is a bit tanned now after a week's vacation in Bulgaria. In honor of our visit she has baked an apple cake, which we eat with tea on a lace tablecloth. Irena is a personable, polite, but reserved woman. It is easy to see how, as Leokadia wrote, she would have been altogether trustworthy without going nearly so far as the mother in satisfying the caprices of Bogusia.

Irena appears to be happy with her work and with her life. Her only complaint is with the management which has neglected this ten-year-old building to the point where it is all but run into the ground. Her own apartment is a bastion against the neglect all around. It contains fresh flowers, curios from trips abroad, a few books. Like Leokadia, Irena keeps a box of photos from the war days. One photo shows her sitting in the back yard of the house in Bialoleka with smiling Bogusia in her arms. Any stranger who rummaged through this box might even gather that in Irena's past there was a love child.

Helena Ackerman (née Goldberg) lives today in Montreal with her husband, Ignac, a fur cutter. Her fine-boned good looks could not have changed much from the day she stood at the door of her orphanage in Pietrolesie, staring at the dirty, weary, and desperate figure of Leokadia in search of her daughter. When the orphans had gone to Israel in 1948, they were escorted by others, including Gershon Jonisz. Helena and Ignac went to Canada to be near her brother, who lives in New York. " 'You and I are the only two left out of a family of sixty,' my brother said to me," explains Helena. " 'If you go to Israel, I will never see you.' "

She tells a story from the days in Bialoleka, told also by Irena and even by Jonisz, which Leokadia herself brushes aside—possibly because it is so traumatic. "Soon after Leokadia found Bogusia, somebody had tipped off the Germans that this woman was harboring a Jewish child. It wasn't long before two soldiers arrived and confronted her. They ordered her to hand over the child, and said they would spare her.

" 'Take the child and you take me,' answered Leokadia. 'And if you kill the child, then kill me.'

"So they took her at her word. They marched her, with the child in her arms, to a back yard where there was a low stone wall. And they put her up against this wall and raised their rifles. But Leokadia said, 'Please, sirs, grant me one last wish. Shoot me first so that I don't have to see the blood of my child.'

"The two soldiers looked at each other. Always before, Poles had been only too glad to give up such a child to save their own lives. And the senior of the two soldiers said, *Das muss die richtige Mutter sein!*—'This must be the real mother!' And they went away."

When I search for an image on which to rest this whole chronicle, my mind flashes a series of quick images—Leokadia awakened in the hay by an ailing goat's warm pee; Bogusia cheerily inviting a tram conductor home for tea; a German officer standing up to recite for the child a poem about Saint Nicholas coming down from a cold blue, starry sky. Those images came by way of Leokadia. Others I saw with my own eyes—a seventy-year-old shut-in, grey and unhappy, dragging her bad leg behind her in Wroclaw; tattooed numbers still bright blue on the aging arms of Gershon and Bolek; Shifra sitting at a kitchen table in the kibbutz, carrying her daughter at the full term of pregnancy and yet seeming to float.

But the image that comes last is not alone. It keeps company with another and earlier image which has remained with me like a glowing ember since an evening in May 1976, when I had just touched down in Israel. Fresh off the plane, I jumped on a bus for Jerusalem. It was crowded and I stood in the aisle next to two children seated beside their mother. Plump-cheeked and blond, they had the look of seraphs. Then, perhaps because I was tired and disoriented—I'd had my morning coffee in the Italian hill town of Orvieto—I saw something strange. As these two children opened their mouths to speak, a full circle of flame appeared around their heads. It danced pale orange and white hot. And I wondered, Is this how they looked when they burned, all those children of the Holocaust? Could this have been their final expression—not pain, fear, or horror but this wide-eyed, open-mouthed freshness as they left the body behind and saw eternity?

In the next instant, tugging at their mother's dress, the children spoke. The language startled me. It was Hebrew—not as I was used to hearing it in synagogue prayers, but in the piping voices of children. That sound banished the flames. But when, at odd moments since, I have thought of what Hitler did—and failed to do—I again saw those faces licked by a rim of flame. I never willed it or wanted it. But, on my bike in front of Saks Fifth Avenue, eating in a French restaurant, looking at nectarines in the market, it just pops into my mind, like a snatch of irresistible melody.

Now that I have investigated Leokadia's story, that image fades seamlessly into another. This other one comes from a Sabbath morning in the Jordan Valley. Ronen has invited me to come waterskiing from the kibbutz's new speedboat on the Sea of Galilee. We bike the back roads through the fields of banana, cotton, and avocado, flushing out doves and a quail or two from the bushes along the way. Barefoot, we scramble down the bank of sharp stones to the cool water. On the boat, piloted by his stepfather, Adam, Ronen insists on giving me a turn on the skis first. Then he adjusts the size of the ski shoes for his own turn.

Ronen is not so sure of himself or so bold as many other twelve-year-old males. But when Adam guns the powerful motors of the boat, he pops up in perfect form on the skis. Then, at full speed, Adam puts the boat into a turn. Ronen is swung across our wake, his speed accelerating as he bounces. He is worried that he will fall. But he hangs on and, suddenly, at the far swing of his arc, he is back on smooth water. Ronen's dark, oval face breaks out into a shy, relieved, and enveloping smile that seems to fall directly on me.

That is the image into which, at the same odd moments, the other now fades. It is also a place where this story can end. Leokadia and the men, Gershon and Bolek, all suffered. Their suffering, unlike hers, was beastly. But it is Leokadia's suffering which for this story is indispensable. Without it, there would be no boy smiling—only a flat patch of blue water with a Sabbath sun shining down and, at best, a fish or two beneath. Ronen knows this as well as anyone. After he read Leokadia's letters to Yoram, he wrote her a letter in return:

Dear Grandma,

I have read your story, and I must say that I admire your courage. And also, I want to thank you, because without what you did for my mother, I wouldn't be here.

Love,
Ronen

EPILOGUE, 1999

Leokadia died in Wroclaw in 1987, pining to the end for her Bogusia. Irena, who had cared for the child while Leokadia worked, still lives in Warsaw. Shifra keeps up a warm contact with her. Zuvit, the youngest of Shifra's children, traveled with her senior high school class to Poland a few years ago. Her parents also made the trip. They visited places where Polish Jewish life had flourished as nowhere else in Europe—and where it had been extinguished.

For the teenager, this journey reached its emotional climax on a grassy field at the edge of a convent wall in Bialoleka: the spot where Leokadia had found Zuvit's mother weeping, cold, and rash-covered. In a brief ceremony, as nuns from the convent looked on, Irena was honored by the Israeli group for her part in saving Shifra. Zuvit threw one arm around Irena, the other around her mother, and began to weep.

"Be happy," said Shifra to her daughter, "because in this place, positive things happened for you." Her words were another way of expressing what Zuvit's brother, Ronen, had written in his childhood letter to Leokadia: Without their safta *Polonia—or Polish grandmother as the children had called Leokadia—Zuvit would not be there today.*

Monsignor Schivo

Ursula Korn Selig—born in Germany, raised and rescued in
Italy, tossed somewhat unwillingly onto American shores at
age twenty-four—remembers precisely what sparked her into
belatedly seeking recognition for her rescuer. Uschi, as she has
been called since childhood, had been watching the evening news
in her modest apartment in Marble Hill, an out-of-the-way community in the northwest corner of Manhattan. It was May, 1985.
What Uschi saw made her livid: President Ronald Reagan flying
off to Germany to lay a wreath of flowers at the German military
cemetery at Bitburg. Buried there, along with Wehrmacht soldiers,
were also 419 SS members. Unlike the soldiers, the SS men had
voluntarily sworn a blood oath to Hitler. They were self-chosen
executors of savage Nazi crimes.

It's not always easy for a survivor, no matter how grateful, to sit
down and write the all-important letter to Yad Vashem asking that
a rescuer be honored as one of the Righteous Among Nations.
Even with a life saved at the end of the story and the buffer of

decades, the rush of piercing memories can be too difficult to face. And so the years pass with the survivor unable to take action.

So what makes people who were saved finally "come out of the closet," as Mordechai Paldiel, the director of the Department of the Righteous, puts it? He answers: "A woman's husband is killed in an auto accident, and she decides to square her own accounts before it is too late. She sits down and writes us a letter. Or a man complains to his doctor of pain in the left side of his body. The doctor finds nothing physically wrong and asks if the patient is under any kind of pressure. He has been pressured—by that need to close a circle."

A small, spunky, restless woman, Uschi had lived alone in Marble Hill since 1977. That was the year her husband, Stanley, collapsed from a heart attack outside their building as they were heading off to play tennis. He died two weeks later. The next month, Uschi's mother died. Her father had died five years earlier. An only child and childless herself after three miscarriages, Uschi was suddenly the last of her family. But, back in a graceful old walled city in Italy, there remained the one person who came close to being her real family: a tall, white-haired priest as coolly reserved as Uschi is ebullient—"the only one in the world," she says, "who knows what I'm thinking, who really, truly loves me."

As Uschi watched President Reagan at Bitburg on TV that evening, she says "it made me so goddam mad! I decided that if he could throw flowers on SS graves, then I had to do something to honor the opposite kind of people."

And so she sat down the next day and typed a letter to Yad Vashem, asking that the priest, Monsignor Beniamino Schivo, be honored among the Righteous. "I know I should not have waited forty years to do this, but now I must," Uschi wrote. "Every gentile who risked his life to save a Jew should be honored for posterity so that the world will not forget the many true and noble heroes. Please help me make this possible for my friend and savior. Here is my story. . . ."

So many Holocaust survivors remember their childhood as warm, loving, and happy even if they were poor—until that world was blasted apart. Uschi is too clear-eyed for that. She was born in 1925 in Breslau, then a German city which was ceded to Poland in 1945 (and is now called Wroclaw). Her parents, Paul and Joanna Korn, were both from wealthy, worldly families. "Back then, " she says, "rich never married poor." Each morning, before Paul Korn went off to manage his family's department store, he went horseback riding. Joanna Korn, according to Uschi, was a handsome, headstrong woman who "bought her dresses in Paris, wore them once, and threw them on the floor." The family kept a cook, a butler, and a nanny for Uschi. "My parents didn't have time for me," she says. "We didn't even eat dinner together. I always ate with my nanny." Occasionally, Uschi was known to bite people.

Taking a break from her troubled marriage, Joanna Korn took Uschi to Berlin in 1932 to be near Uschi's maternal grandparents and aunt. Paul stayed behind to continue running the family business. But time was closing in on the German Jews in the Third Reich, and the Berlin sojourn was short. In 1934, Uschi's grandparents moved with her aunt's family to Alassio, a serene, fashionable resort town on the Italian Riviera, where they bought a beachfront hotel called the Imperiale. Thanks to an influential Italian friend, the family arrived with a personal letter from the dictator Mussolini authorizing them to stay in Italy indefinitely and to own property. Uschi and her mother followed in 1935. They seemed safe from the evil rising against the Jews back home. Uschi's father, who remained in Breslau, thought that he was protected. Having served as a German army officer in World War I, he couldn't imagine that he would become Germany's enemy. Even a beating he suffered one night at the hands of Hitler's brownshirts did not change his mind.

An incident occurred on the night train taking Uschi and her mother from Berlin to Milan, never to return, that was in keeping with the dark mood of the times. As the train was about to cross the German border into Switzerland at Basel, German police checking papers found something amiss on Uschi's passport, which by Hitler's law was marked with a "J." She and her mother, along with other passengers, were ordered off the train. "I started to scream bloody murder," remembers Uschi, "and I didn't stop. I was afraid my mother was going to leave me behind." Another passenger suggested to Joanna that she quiet the child and then take her back aboard and hide her behind the window curtains in their first-class compartment. The man thought that the police would forget about the child. And so they did.

Those screams turned to smiles in Italy. "I never, ever encountered anything but kindness from the Italians," says Uschi. The snapshots from those first days show a slender, feline adolescent, promenading on the elegant, palm-studded beach with new friends—mainly boys with dark slicked-back hair. After six months of being privately tutored in Italian, she was enrolled in a public high school. The only downside was having to leave her classroom during Catholic instruction. "Why am I different?" she asked. In Germany, where stones smacked the windows of her Jewish school in her final days there, she knew well why she was different.

By 1939, even Paul Korn was driven from Germany. He showed up in Alassio. His timing was awful. After refusing for years to emulate Germany's racial laws, Italy suddenly enacted its own in November, 1938. Jews were banned from key professions, and schools, and from owning property. Uschi's maternal grandparents were forced to sell the apartment they kept in Milan. She remembers the embarrassment of the purchaser, an Italian air force officer, at getting the place at a bargain price—including "the beautiful furniture, the carpets, and the crystal that my grandparents had managed to bring from Berlin." In Alassio, the Imperiale was also forcibly sold. The family, bereft of possessions, moved into a rented villa opposite the hotel. A few days later, Paul Korn was arrested. "Then he was gone and the police didn't say where," says Uschi.

The turn of the women came two days later. Uschi, her mother, aunt, and cousin were handcuffed by the carabinieri. "All I took with me was a tiny suitcase, my teddy bear, and a photo album," says Uschi. They were taken by train to Perugia, the Umbrian hill city whose 2,500-year-old Etruscan walls still hold firm. Nuns operated a women's prison there. Uschi remembers that the nun who opened the door looked dourly at these well-dressed women and asked, "What did they do?"

"Nothing," answered one of the carabinieri, who was unhappy with this duty. "*Sono ebrei*" ("They are Jews").

Joanna Korn and her sister were to be separated from their daughters. But she insisted that they stay together. "So they put us all in a large cell for delinquent girls who were pregnant," says Uschi. The food was bad. "My mother had some money hidden in her underwear," she says. "She used it to get us better food." Meals was served by another inmate, "a nice woman" who wore prisoner's stripes.

"What did you do?" asked Uschi.

"Killed my boyfriend," she answered.

The Catholic prisoners attended daily Bible study sessions conducted by the nuns. Curiously, the Jews were assigned to read *Uncle Tom's Cabin*. Uschi's family was among thousands of foreign-born Jews arrested "in solidarity" with Hitler after Mussolini declared war on the Allies in June 8 1940. But the Italians went about it in their own way. Their inclination was to minimize the victims' pain. Rather than keep Jews under arrest, the government leaned toward releasing them into "open internment." That is, Jews were placed in apartments, houses, and vacant hotel rooms throughout the country. Their rent was paid and they were given a stipend for meals. Those Jews who had their own funds were allowed to upgrade their conditions. But all had to report to the local police morning, noon, and night. Native-born Jews were not arrested in the first phase of anti-Jewish restrictions. But they were stripped of their jobs, their property, and most other basic civil rights.

After a week in prison, Uschi and her mother were transferred to a small town called Collazzone. Here, she got a taste of the inimitable Italian way of making war on the Jews. Uschi developed a bad toothache. After the local police chief cabled Rome for instructions, an appointment was made for her at a dentist in Perugia (there was none in Collazzone.). "I traveled by bus to Perugia," remembers Uschi, "guarded by two carabinieri wearing white gloves." Several trips that week followed—at one of which the dentist, who Uschi says was an antifascist, asked the guards if they weren't ashamed to be guarding such a "criminal." Apparently, they were. For her future appointments, Uschi was permitted to travel to Perugia on her honor.

It could have been infinitely worse. If Uschi were unlucky enough to be in neighboring France, for example, she'd have suffered her toothache behind the barbed wire of a network of internment camps such as Gurs, Rivesaltes, and Compiegne. They were filthy, miserable places which were a first step on the way to Auschwitz. Thousands of interned foreign Jews died of disease and malnutrition in these camps operated by Frenchmen, not Germans. The Italians, to their eternal credit, had neither the stomach nor the heart for treating anyone that way. What the authorities did do, along with stripping Jews of jobs and property, was to shower them with endless small humiliations. In Collazzone, for example, the Korns had to sign in at the police station four times per day, yet the chief still checked to see if they were home after the 8:00 P.M. curfew. He also monitored Uschi's friendship with several teenage boys in the town; socializing with non-Jews was forbidden. "So we met outside the village," Uschi says. "Sometimes the police chief would approach on his bike and we'd hide in the bushes."

The village priest, unlike the police chief, was kind to the Jewish strangers in town. He often talked to Uschi, which was against the rules. When the Korns were about to be transferred to a new internship in Città di Castello, the priest told her to look up a former classmate of his from theology school who'd become rector of the bishop's seminary. "His name is Don Beniamino Schivo. Go see him and give him my regards," advised the priest. "He is a person you can count on."

This offhand suggestion, coming from a priest whose name Uschi no longer remembers, would mean the difference between life and almost certain death by gassing for the Korns.

. . .

A medieval wall still encloses Città di Castello, today a city of thirty-eight thousand. The upper Tiber River flows lazily by the west side of the city, whose Latin name was Tiphernum, after the river. This region is called Alta Valle Del Tevere—Upper Valley of the Tiber. To the east rise the Marches, their peaks normally snow-capped before Christmas. The train doesn't stop anymore in Città di Castello, isolating it from the main tourist route. Visitors to nearby Assisi and Perugia rarely make it here. The city's winding streets go from narrow to narrower, with graceful overhead arches supporting passages between ancient buildings. Everywhere are churches and the high walls of convents. Even in daylight, most residents keep their fir-green shutters closed. As cool autumn evenings come, the stone walls seem to give off the fragrance of wood fires within. While most of the world seems to be shod in athletic shoes, in Città di Castello even the teenagers who hang out on the Piazza Gabriotti still favor finely crafted soft leather shoes not so different from those Romeo and Juliet would have worn.

Città di Castello is named for the several sixteenth-century palaces of the Vitelli family. At the main palace, now the municipal art museum, there is a small window above an arch over the street. Allesandro Vitelli's mistress, Laura, so goes the story, would watch for pleasing young men to pass by. Choosing one, she'd drop her handkerchief to him. After a few hours of bliss with Laura, he would be directed to a door. It was, in fact, an airdrop to the street. If the young man survived the fall, Laura's henchmen pounced on him and made sure he'd never tell the tale.

Uschi was fifteen when she arrived with her mother in Città di Castello in early 1941. There, they were reunited with Paul Korn, who had been released from an interment camp near Salerno. The family was assigned to a single small room in a building near the duomo. The rent was paid by the government. Like everyone else, the Korns were issued food ration coupons. In keeping with the racial laws, Uschi was permitted to go only to a Jewish school. But there was none in Città di Castello. The handful of Jews in town were, like the Korns, internees from somewhere else. The adults could not work. Reporting to the police station four times daily was their main activity.

With nothing to lose, Uschi walked one morning to the bishop's seminary, a stern-looking building just within the city's northwestern quarter. She knocked on the big dark door. An unsmiling nun appeared.

"I've come to see the rector," said Uschi.

The nun was hesitant. What business did a teenaged girl have with the rector of a boys' seminary? But Uschi would not be turned away. She was led to a large reception room. The rector entered through a side door from his private office. "He was tall and blond," remembers Uschi. He wore a round hat and a long black skirt. "From the first moment, I felt he was the kindest person I'd ever met."

Schivo also remembers that first visit: "She seemed like a well-bred girl. We chatted, but she asked me for nothing—even though, in her situation, she had nothing." Schivo was then thirty-one years old. Remarkably, Uschi was the first Jew he had ever met.

As a boy, Schivo had been a refugee himself. He'd been born to a farming family in Gallio, a town in the rugged Veneto region in northeastern Italy. Schivo's father died earlier than he can remember and his mother remarried. Unable to eke out a living at home, the family tried to find a better life in Bosnia—only to be interned in a refugee camp soon after the outbreak of the First World War. (Italy entered the war on the side of the Allies against the Austro-Hungrian Empire, part of which was Bosnia.) "Many Italian farmers were interned in Bosnia," Schivo says. "We were treated badly." After a year, the family was released. At age six, Schivo went to school, learning in the Serbo-Croatian language. At home, he spoke both Italian and a Venetian dialect. "My upbringing was very multiethnic," says Schivo. "Lots of Turks and Moslems. Catholics were in the minority. We didn't even have a church."

At the end of the war, Schivo's family returned to the Veneto. He almost got left behind. "There was chaos in the train station," he remembers. "I thought I was holding my mother's hand. But when I looked up, I saw it was a stranger's. A train was starting to pull out of the station. I decided to jump aboard rather than do nothing. There, I found my parents." The incident shows that decisiveness had already formed in Schivo's character. Most any other child his age, upon discovering his mother gone, would have stood there and cried. Schivo took action.

Only upon his return to Italy did Schivo attend his first Catholic mass. "My strongest emotion was curiosity," he says. "What was this all about?" The switch to Italian in the classroom slowed him down and he was tutored by the parish priest. In 1923, he was impressed by the preaching of a local priest who had been transferred to Città di Castello. The priest asked if any boy in the audience was interested in attending the seminary school. "I was the only one," Schivo says. He began his studies in Assisi at age fourteen. A strong student, he stayed on an academic track rather than become a parish priest. Only twenty-five years old when he was named rector of the bishop's seminary in Città di Castello, Schivo found himself in charge of fifty boys.

Life in Città di Castello was calm yet precarious for its handful of Jewish internees. Paul and Joanna Korn, in their enforced idleness, passed their days bickering and worrying. Uschi, too, was idle—and that did not escape Schivo's notice. He could not free her from internship. But he did ask Uschi, who visited him weekly, if she wanted to go to high school—even though, according to Italian racial laws, she was forbidden to do so. Uschi jumped at the offer. Schivo arranged an appointment for her with the bishop, Filippo Maria Cipriani.

Uschi was enrolled in a boarding school operated by Benedictine nuns. She was the only day student. Being the only Jewish girl in a Catholic school might have been a daunting experience. But Uschi, lively and affable, was accepted by the other girls and clucked over by the nuns—especially Donna Anselma, who taught Spanish, French, and Latin. Sophisticated, secular, and well-off, this nun had not answered the religious calling until age thirty. "She loved me," says Uschi.

Each morning at eight o'clock, Uschi walked five blocks to the convent doors and rang the bell. "I couldn't wait to get to school," she says. Unlike the other girls, Uschi left school at one o'clock. The bishop had arranged for her to be excused from reporting daily to the police station at noon. She continued to report in the morning, afternoon, and evening. It wasn't all schoolwork. Uschi hung out with a group of students at Paci, an antifascist bookshop on the Piazza Matteotti, one of whom was a gentle and darkly handsome chemistry student named Giovanni Bianchini. He became Uschi's boyfriend. Joanna Korn opposed the budding romance.

"She liked Giovanni very much," says Uschi. "But we weren't supposed to have contact with non-Jews. She worried I'd get the family in trouble. I asked the advice of Monsignor Schivo. He didn't tell me to stop seeing Giovanni. He just told me to be careful."

By enacting harsh racial laws in 1938, Italy became the first Western European country to join Hitler's war on the Jews. Yet Italy spent the next five years fighting off German urgings to squeeze the noose tighter. That refusal extended beyond Italy to places it occupied, including Greece and Yugoslavia. By the summer of 1943, more than one hundred thousand Jews had been hunted down and deported from France, Belgium, and Holland. None had been deported from Italian-controlled territories. Thousands of Jews, for example, found haven in the seven departments of south-eastern France under Italian control—especially Nice. Despite German cajoling, the Italians kept finding excuses not to arrest them. Meanwhile, Vichy police in the rest of the France were busily delivering Jews to the Germans for the trip to Auschwitz.

Toward summer's end of 1943, the rules of the game changed for the worse for Jews in Italy. On September 3, Allied forces invaded the southern tip of the Italian boot and started to head northward. The forty-five day old government of marshall Pietro Badoglio, which had replaced the increasingly unpopular Mussolini in July, had no taste for waging war at home after ghastly losses fighting with the Germans in Russia. The new government announced an armistice with the Allies on September 8. Hitler responded by reinstalling Mussolini as a puppet dictator. And he poured fresh troops into Italy and into the former Italian zone of France. With the troops came less SS deportation specialists. They moved fast. On October 16, a sabbath, 1,259 Jews were arrested by a large SS force that struck Rome's Jewish community. Eight hundred and ninety-six of those were women and children. Some of the victims believed their forebearers were "deported" to Rome from Jerusalem in 70 AD after the Roman general Titus sacked the holy city and destroyed the second temple. Now these members of the old Jewish community in Europe were deported to Auschwitz. They arrived one week after the round-up. One hundred and forty-nine were spared for slave labor. The rest were gassed.

The deadly new situation was felt by the Korns in still-peaceful Umbria one evening that same October. A policeman did them the favor of visiting them at home to warn them that at six o'clock the next morning, they would be arrested and delivered to a prison in Perugia newly under control of the SS. "Take care of yourselves," said the policeman. And he left.

When the foreign Jews were first being interned, Joanna Korn had seriously considered trying to escape across the Alps into neutral Switzerland. Her husband didn't agree. This time, the family didn't even think of running. "We had no documents and no money," explains Uschi. Under curfew, she didn't dare to venture out to seek counsel from Schivo.

They were led off in handcuffs, as had happened in Alassio three years earlier. Uschi remembers that the carabinieri were apologetic at having to slip on the handcuffs. Sixty-eight hundred Jews would be deported from Italy. The Korns seemed fated to be among them. But, a miracle occurred in Perugia. The SS prison was full to bursting due to the inflow of Jews from many cities and towns. The Korns were sent back to Città di Castello until further notice. They had no way of knowing what they had been spared.

Beniamino Schivo had not been a rescuer until now because until the previous evening, the Korns had not needed rescuing.

For Uschi, it was enough that he'd arranged with the bishop to get her into school and that he'd been the one person to whom she could "pour out my heart." She wasted no time in knocking on the door of the seminary upon her return from Perugia.

"Now is the time we must prepare," Schivo told her. That same day he approached Bishop Cipriani, who agreed that the family had to be hidden. He left it to Schivo to make a plan and carry it out. "I had a problem," says Schivo simply. "I tried to figure out the best way to solve it."

The most obvious solution would have been to find a hiding place in the city's labyrinth of church property. But Schivo felt that the family would be safer beyond the city walls. And he had a place in mind. High in the hills to the east was a remote summer retreat owned by the Salesian Sisters, whose convent adjoined the seminary. Called Pozio, the retreat was already closed for the season. "I felt this place would be safest," says Schivo, "because there was no road to it. Only a path. The older nuns made the trip to Pozio by oxcart. The younger nuns had to walk. That took seven hours. I didn't think the Germans would be likely to go up there."

The Mother Superior hesitated. But, under Schivo's gentle prodding, she gave him the key to the mountain retreat. He and a young *seminarista* escorted the Korns. With them came Uschi's boyfriend, Giovanni. A few months earlier, he'd been drafted into the army and, because he was a university student, made an officer. "When he heard about the armistice," says Uschi, "he told his platoon to take off their uniforms and go home. He did the same." As a deserter, Giovanni could have been shot. Numerous fascist thugs were ready to do just that.

The Korns and Giovanni, escorted by Schivo and his assistant, lugged along a bare few belongings on the arduous hike into the hills. It was especially hard on Paul Korn. "He just sat down and didn't want to continue," remembers Uschi. If her father knew the hardships that awaited the family at Pozio, he'd never had been persuaded to keep going. For two years, the Korns had been unhappily squeezed into a single room. Now, exhausted after the long hike, they found themselves the sole denizens of an entire convent. Under other circumstances, it would have been an idyllic vacation spot, with its sweeping views of the wooded Marches. But a chill autumn wind pentetrated the unwinterized place. The electricity had been turned off. Beds and most other furniture had been removed for the winter. Shutters had to be kept closed. After the departure of the priests, the Korns and Giovanni lay down in the dark and shivered.

A trustworthy caretaker named Lazzaro lived with his family in a stone cottage adjacent to the convent. Schivo had arranged with him to deliver a basic meal to the family each midnight. "He didn't trust his wife or children to know that we were there," says Uschi. "So he waited until they were asleep, and then he brought us soup and bread, maybe some pasta, but never very much, because he didn't want her to notice the food was missing." The signal of Lazzaro's arrival was three knocks on the door. "We weren't starving, but we always hungry," says Uschi. Foraging in the cellar, she found a cache of potatoes that must have been forgotten by the departing nuns. "We ate them raw," says Uschi. "Like animals." Giovanni made several trips back to town, returning each time with extra food, sanitary supplies, and—luxury of luxuries—bedsheets! If only they had beds.

While the retreat stood in isolated splendor on its promontory, farmers who eked a living out of the hills did pass by on the ox-path. They would have been instantly curious to see any signs of life at the closed-up convent. Still, Uschi and Giovanni traded the risk for private sojourns together to a walled garden at the rear of the convent.

Christmas Eve 1943, was just another frigid and lonely night. Giovanni had gone to his father's house for the holiday. At midnight, the Korns heard three thumps on the door. They assumed it was Lazzaro with soup and bread. But when they opened the door, it was Beniamino Schivo standing there. On this holiday, when he'd normally be in church, he'd hiked up to Pozzio, waiting until after dark, to bring the Korns a sack of holiday food. Schivo wore farmer's clothing—the first time Uschi had seen him not in clerical garb. With him was the same young *seminarista* who had accompanied them to Pozio in autumn.

"I've come to spend Christmas Eve with you," said Schivo.

He stayed with the family until five o'clock that morning. Almost as eagerly as they ate the cold food, the Korns took in the news of the slow Allied advance up the length of the Italian boot. Fifty-five years later, in testimony recorded by Steven Spielberg's "Survivors of the Shoah" project, Schivo spoke of that night. The conditions in which the family was living, he called *deplorevole*—lamentable: "Given the family's social background and wealth in Germany and in Italy before the war, it was particularly hard for them to be so deprived. When I think of how they were living, even now it makes me sad. But at that point, the most important thing was for them to stay alive and await the arrival of the Allies."

Schivo wanted to be far from Pozio once dawn came and he could be seen. As it was, he and the *seminarista* chose to trek through the woods rather than on the trail because, explains Schivo, "If we'd been on the ox-path, the farmers along the way would have noticed us. As it was, every time we passed a farm house, a dog started barking." By the time they returned to the seminary late on Christmas morning, they had hiked a total of fifteen hours.

Early in 1944, the Salesian Mother Superior approached Schivo. She was worried. If the Korns were discovered at Pozio, it could mean trouble for her nuns from either the Fascists or the Germans, who were approaching Città di Castello. No longer willing to bear that responsibility, she asked for the key back. "I understood her concern for the safety of the nuns," says Schivo. Preserving the safety of the Korns, however, was top priority. The priest arranged to return the key to the Mother Superior. But not before he made a duplicate for the Korns. As a precaution, Schivo also decided that the family should vacate the convent and hide in an adjacent building, small and windowless, which contained an oven in which the sisters baked their bread. If anyone entered the convent, they'd find it empty. "We sat there on the floor in the dark," says Uschi, "staring at each other and wondering what the next day would bring. My parents were fighting and yelling. It was beyond getting on each other's nerves; we were slowly going mad."

The decision to move the family to the oven building was prescient. One night the Korns heard shouts in German outside. Soldiers were checking out the convent as a potential field head-quarters for Field Marshall Kesselring, whose forces were, at that very moment, stubbornly resisting the Allied advance up the Italian boot.

The Germans banged on Lazzaro's door and demanded the key to the convent. Lazarro had been cautious. Now he was shrewd. They were welcome to the key, said Lazzaro, but he didn't have it. They'd have to go to Città di Castello the next morning and retrieve it from the Mother Superior. And then he offered the soldiers wine from the hillside vineyard that he tended. They drank and went away merry. Then he knocked three times on the oven door to bring the news.

The Korns cleared out in the morning. Giovanni was with them. It was late afternoon as they reached the outskirts of Città di Castello. Seeing a German patrol on the road, they scrambled into a high-walled cemetery. They came out after dark. A single German soldier crossed from the opposite side of the street and approached them. "I thought this was the end of the line for us," says Uschi. "A Jewish family and an Italian deserter. But the German only asked, '*Fiammifero*?' He just wanted his cigarette lit." Giovanni went home, the Korns to the seminary. Schivo himself opened the door at the first knock—"just enough for us to slip in," says Uschi. Joanna Korn, a normally strong woman, collapsed on the stone floor—apparently from tension as much as fatigue.

Schivo had a plan ready—"new holes to hide them in," as he puts it. He'd dispatched his trusted *seminarista* to a farmer in the hills north of the city to ask if Paul Korn could be hidden there. Meanwhile, he'd hide him in a room on the top floor of a little-used building across from the seminary. And he'd arranged for

Uschi and her mother to hide in the adjoining Convent of the Sacred Heart. Uschi remembers being guided down long halls to an isolated and empty wing of the convent. The two women were locked into a second-floor room, but not before they were each outfitted in the black-and-white habits of the order. They were not to leave the room. A single nun, Sister Lucina, would bring them their meals twice a day. Nobody else could see them.

The change was enormous. For the first time in months, the Korns were no longer cold. And no longer starving. Uschi explains that the nuns, with their familial connections to farmers in the countryside, did not lack for food. She especially savored the hot pasta that Lucina delivered each noon. And now that they were dressed as nuns, the Korns permitted themselves the luxury of opening their shutters to the daylight and a pleasant courtyard view. One of the sisters became intrigued with the two strange "nuns" in the isolated wing of the convent who never dined with the others. One evening, she came with a ladder and climbed up to the window.

"Who are you?" she asked.

"Sisters from Milan," answered Uschi in her flawless Italian. "Our convent was bombed out." Seemingly satisfied, the nun retreated down the ladder.

One Sunday in June 1944, Uschi said to her mother, "*Mutti*, I hear airplanes. Maybe they're going to bomb Florence." A moment later, she knew the truth: "They were bombing us!" The two of them crawled under the bed as the bombers pummelled the city, in wave after wave. "My main fear was not for us," says Uschi. "It was for Don Schivo. If something happened to him, we were surely lost."

At day's end, when the bombers had gone, there was a knock on the door. The women assumed it was Sister Lucina. But it was Schivo. He wanted to be sure they were safe. And to let them know their father was unhurt.

"Have you seen Giovannino?" asked Uschi (using the affectionate diminutive).

Schivo shook his head. But hours later, he returned with the boyfriend. "He'd told the nuns that Giovannino was an electrician," says Uschi. "Otherwise a young guy would never have been permitted in the convent."

The bombings became a regular event that June. Schivo sent his students home and converted the first floor of the seminary into a hospital after Città di Castello 's own hospital was requisitioned by the Germans. "They emptied all the sick people into the street," says Schivo. "I took them back with me." His makeshift hospital was attended by two Italian doctors, deserters from the army, to whom he'd offered refuge. After each bombing, Schivo scouted the streets for victims and carried them back to the seminary, where beds awaited them in the long central hall shielded by thick stone walls.

For the Korns, locked in their convent room, the deadliest threat did not come from the sky. Late one June night, they heard drunken shouts from the courtyard. Then blows against the door. Uschi peeked out and saw a group of staggering German soldiers. Joanna wanted to stay put. "*Mutti*, even if they don't kill us, they'll rape us," said Uschi. And she convinced her mother to climb down into the vegetable garden. On the far side was the main wing of the convent. "We were crawling on our stomachs in the dark," says Uschi, "but in our billowy habits, we were easy to see." Shots were fired at them as they scampered to the main entrance of the convent. The nuns, fearful of the Germans, at first didn't want to open the door. But, hearing Uschi's voice, they relented. At dawn, the two women, still in their habits, slipped across the street to the seminary.

"Now it's time to stay here with me," said Schivo.

At night, they slept in a locked room in the rear of the seminary. Then the Germans, preparing to hold the city against the approaching British land forces, ordered all civilians, except those maintaining essential services, to leave. By this time, Schivo had sent Paul Korn to the farm in the north. Uschi and her mother departed with the Sacred Heart nuns, along with a group of orphans in their care. They were walking to the convent's summer residence, a stout, square building on a hillside not far from the city. The two women looked like the other nuns. Still, as they walked along the road crowded with refugees, a woman suddenly said loudly, "Oh, look—those are the Jews who were interned. I thought they'd been sent to Germany."

They could not hesitate, lest they be delivered to the Germans. Joanna Korn took her daughter's arm and wheeled around. They retraced their steps and fell in with other nuns who were escorting children to a Franciscan Brothers abbey in the valley. Called I Zoccolanti (the word means "wooden shoes," or "clogs"), it seemed to be safe because it sat on a gentle rise in full view. Neither aircraft nor artillery spotters could mistake it for a military target. But, as the refugees huddled in the courtyard of I Zoccolanti, it took a direct hit. Two nuns and several children were killed. The survivors fled the smoking abbey. Spending the night in the woods, they were told by partisans that the Germans were preparing to retreat from Città di Castello. And so they returned—the nuns and orphans to the Convent of the Sacred Heart, Uschi and her mother to the bishop's seminary.

With electrical power knocked out in the city, the Germans demanded candles. The bishop had selected Schivo to offer the commandant hundreds of prayer candles from local churches. Giving them up voluntarily was preferable to the Germans searching the churches for them. As it was, the Germans and their fascist henchmen were combing church property for army deserters, partisans, and Jews. A few days earlier, Germans had entered the seminary and scouted the chapel. "Look in the confessional, behind the altar . . . anywhere you want," Schivo had told them. He acted as if he had nothing to hide—a steely response, considering that a pair of Jewish women were locked away upstairs.

For two more days, the city shook from battle. Uschi worried when Schivo went out to collect the wounded. If he were killed, who would protect her and her mother? The bombing and shelling became so savage one night, the two women huddled under a stairwell stout enough to withstand a direct hit. The next evening, an eerie silence came. What did it mean? In the morning,

Schivo came and found Uschi. Taking her by the hand, he led her out to the street, bright with sunlight. "I saw British soldiers," Uschi says, "wearing khaki shorts and knee socks." It was July 14, 1944. Uschi was nineteen years old—and still in love.

Uschi dashed to Giovanni's house on a narrow, ancient street just behind the police station where she had endlessly reported like a parolee. Now nothing could stop them from being together.

"We are free," she said as she hugged him. But Giovanni did not share her joy.

"You're free," he said. "But for us Italians, we are rid of one occupier. Now that the British are here, we have another."

That wasn't the response that Uschi had expected—not from the man she hoped to marry. Still, Giovanni was a rock in her life. All her clothes had been stolen, but he'd brought her a large, fine linen curtain he'd torn down from a window in a school that had been attended by children from wealthy fascist families. A seamstress made it into a stylish summer dress for Uschi. In the first days of their freedom, Uschi and her mother had continued to live at the seminary. Then the British town commander installed them in a handsome apartment that had belonged to a Fascist who had fled to the north with the Germans.

What had happened to her father, Uschi tried not to think about. Just to the north, where he gone, the Germans had dug in against the Allied advance. Then, after three months, a friend of Uschi's named Riccardo—he was one of the group that hung out at Paci's bookshop—rushed up to her. "I saw a man dressed in rags standing on the piazza in front of the duomo," said Riccardo. "He looks like your father."

Paul Korn had safely passed the summer at the farm. But even though the Germans still held on to the area, Korn couldn't bear to hide any longer. Come what may, he had hiked back to Città di Castello. Now displaced persons, the family had no other place to call home. Joanna Korn, who a decade earlier had thrown her French dresses on the floor after one wearing, now peddled army blankets and secondhand clothing in a flea market. Paul Korn went with her a few times, but he couldn't bear the smell of the goods his wife was hawking. "My father was a gentleman," says Uschi, "but my mother was a survivor."

Uschi had loved living in Italy before the war. She loved it just as much after. But her parents never did put down roots in the country. In 1949, they received visas to emigrate to America. Uschi's hope was to be wedded to Giovanni, but he still backed away. "He wanted to be a doctor, and he said he had too much education ahead of him and not enough money to support me," says Uschi. In her mind, the war had changed him—in particular, a ghastly incident that occurred while Uschi had watched in horror as nuns and children were blown up in the courtyard of I Zoccolanti.

Giovanni had taken refuge in a farmhouse with several of his school friends. A young woman, apparently thinking there was a lull in the fighting, ventured outside. A shell exploded, ripping her body apart. What happened next was a scene out of a Boschian hell: the same shell that killed Giovanni's friend had also blasted open the gates of the hog pen. The animals, suddenly roaming free, gathered around the torn body and dined on it. "When I first met Giovannino, he was totally together," says Uschi. "But after that incident, he was never the same."

The Korns arrived in New York in 1950. They were put up in the Marseilles, a faded immigrant hotel on the Upper West Side. Answering classified ads in the *Aufbau*, the German Jewish newspaper, both women quickly got factory jobs. Paul Korn had a harder time. Eventually, he found work as a night watchman at an old-age home. Joanna, once a spoiled woman of leisure, loved America and its "get-ahead" work ethic. Her husband felt beaten down. Yet, from his meager earnings, he sent monthly donations to the bishop's seminary in Città di Castello. "First he sent five dollars," says Uschi, "then, when he could afford it, ten dollars."

Uschi was lonely in America. Why not go to the Central Park tennis courts, suggested her mother. Uschi loved tennis and she was bound to meet someone interesting. That someone turned out to be Stanley Selig. Tall and handsome, as was Giovanni, he'd been born in Frankfurt and raised in France. Arriving in New York in 1939, he went directly into the army. Now he worked for a wool importer. Uschi and Stanley were married by a judge in the Bronx courthouse five months after they met. He doted on his bride, picking her up in the evenings when she attended night school. But he sensed that she still pined for what was left behind in Italy. In 1955, the fifth year of their marriage, Stanley suggested that his wife go back for a visit—and even to stay with Giovanni, if that was what her heart dictated.

Joanna Korn was not about to let Uschi make the trip alone. The two of them arrived in Città di Castello that fall. Giovanni was working for a chemical company in Perugia, an hour away by bus. Propriety demanded, Joanna insisted, that she accompany her daughter, a married woman, to Perugia for her first meeting with Giovanni in six years. Uschi resisted, but her mother was not one to back down. Uschi turned to the one person who had never failed to help her in an hour of need. Having been called on to save her life, Beniamino Schivo now interceded in a different mode: "He convinced my mother to stay with him in Città di Castello."

Perugia, with its wide and lively central promenade, dotted with the coffee and chocolate shops for which it is famous, had all the right atmosphere for the reunion. But it had not changed Giovanni. He still pleaded poverty and unfinished studies. Uschi had taken a room overnight at the Brufani, Perugia's most beautiful hotel—not that they would have been allowed to go up to the room together. So they sat in the small park in front of the hotel until late in the evening, their conversation going nowhere. At the other side of the park was the entrance to an ancient stone fortification. It had been the prison where the Korns had been taken in 1943—and miraculously escaped deportation. In the morning, Uschi returned to Città di Castello. The torch that she'd carried for Giovanni was dimmed, maybe extinguished.

Returning to New York, Uschi took a job as a fur model in the ultrachic, East Fifty-seventh Street showroom owned by Ben Thylan. To better enjoy their trips to Italy, Stanley learned Italian. He and

Schivo grew fond of each other. After hearing the Mother Superior of the Benedictine nuns speak of her wish for a vacuum cleaner, Stanley sent one from America. Uschi's sadness was that, with all her love of children, she could not carry through any of her pregnancies. She believes that, somehow, the ordeal of her teenaged years in hiding was to blame. The couple shopped on the Italian Riviera for a retirement apartment. They were on the verge of making a deal in 1977 when Stanley had his heart attack. He died two weeks later. The next month, Joanna Korn also died.

Uschi kept working. She liked her job in the showroom—up to a point. There was the time her boss asked her on short notice to deliver a mink-lined raincoat to Ingrid Bergman in London. Her instructions were to fly over on a Friday night and return in time for work on Monday.

"I said I'd go," says Uschi, "but I'd like to stay in London for an extra day or two, and take advantage of the theater. Ben said no. So I told him to find somebody else to deliver the damn coat. Anyway, I wasn't hired to be a delivery girl." Not long after her refusal, she was fired. Free to do as she wished, Uschi went off to Italy for three months. Much of the time, she stayed in Naples with her "adopted family"—the several sisters and brothers of Sister Anselma, her "special" nun at the Sacred Heart convent. "If anything happened to my parents in the war," says Uschi, "Sister Anselma had told her family to always take care of me."

When the Bitburg affair erupted, Uschi was working part-time for an import firm and a bit at loose ends. She did not get an encouraging response when she first called the New York City office of Yad Vashem to ask how to nominate Beniamino Schivo as one of the Righteous. "Boy, were they unfriendly," she says. "They said the process would take two years, and with my parents dead, I wouldn't be able to get their affidavits about what the priest did for us." Uschi kept the pressure on. Once the dossier reached the Committee on the Righteous, she was regularly on the phone to Jerusalem, where the time was seven hours later, to check on the progress of the case. "I was getting very anxious," she says. In the spring of 1986, Paldiel called her and said, "You won."

On the morning of the tree-planting ceremony that September, Uschi and Schivo knocked on Paldiel's door in the Yad Vashem administration building. She introduced herself and Schivo—a pair whom time had not withered. The staff, she remembers, appeared disconcerted. "They expected a bent-over wrinkled woman wearing a kerchief and a fat old country priest," says Uschi.

In the dim grey light of the Hall of Remembrance, Schivo and Uschi descended to the stone floor engraved with the names of the killing camps. He lit a flame over the ashes representing all the Six Million. After a cantor intoned kaddish (the Jewish prayer for the dead), Schivo recited a memorial prayer in Latin. Uschi doesn't easily lose her composure, but she admits that the ceremony "got to me." Schivo reached for her hand and steadied her.

Uschi laughs, recalling how Schivo came down to the Hotel Laromme's breakfast room each morning of their stay in Jerusalem, nattily dressed in civvies, carrying the Jerusalem *Post* under his arm. "Never mind that he can't read English," she says. Uschi caught the glances of the desk clerks. She understood their meaning: This must be a dalliance between a lively woman from New York and the handsome Italian gentleman.

Uschi marched up to the reception desk. "You should understand," she instructed them, "that this gentleman is not my boyfriend. He is a priest who saved my life. And also my parents' lives. He is here to be honored as one of the Righteous of Nations." That evening, Schivo found a bouquet of flowers in his room from the hotel staff.

Schivo was interviewed by Steven Spielberg's Shoah Foundation in June 1998, in Città di Castello. Tight-lipped and poker-faced as the tape begins, Schivo evidently doesn't relish this attention. Remarkably, he tells the interviewer, a young Milanese journalist, that he had never met a Jew until that day in 1941 that *la signorina* Korn knocked on the door of his seminary—though, he hastens to say, he knew the Jews through the Old Testament and took pleasure in teaching his students its most beautiful parts.

Diverse in other ways, rescuers are mostly the same in their distaste for broadcasting stories of their heroism. But Schivo takes that inclination to its extreme, telling the interviewer that he never revealed to anybody—not even the bishop—the details of his rescue of the Korns.

"Not even members of your family?" he is asked.

"Nobody," repeats the priest. Not even when badgered, he might have added. When Uschi and her family suddenly vanished from Città di Castello in the autumn of 1943, her beloved Sister Anselma was worried to distraction. She pleaded with Schivo to tell her where the Korns had gone. He was silent. "For the rest of her life, even when she was very old and sick," says Uschi, "Sister Anselma always said that she loved Monsignor Schivo—but she'd never forgive him for not sharing the secret of our being hidden."

Did Schivo receive any guidelines from the Vatican on the rescue of Jews? None at all, he insists. "We were isolated in Città di Castello. We didn't hear from Rome. We didn't even know what was going on in Assisi"—a church stronghold only twenty-five miles from Città di Castello, where the local bishop presided over an extensive church rescue effort. Convents which had been sealed off to outsiders for centuries were opened up to hunted Jews. Only the Vatican could have allowed such a breach of hallowed tradition, Schivo insists. "In Rome, Jews were packed into Catholic institutions. I'm convinced that the church did all that it could to help the Jews."

Asked at the end of the video interview if he has anything else to say, Schivo answers quietly: "As a Catholic, I believe in Jesus Christ and the light that comes from the Gospel. If people understood the message of the Gospel, none of this could have ever happened."

Marble Hill, where Uschi has lived since she was a bride, is one of Manhattan's oddest neighborhoods. Eccentric Victorian-era homes, turreted and topped with their original weathervanes, nestle in the shadow of the sterile facades of oversized modern residential towers commanding views of the mighty Hudson River and the soaring New Jersey Palisades on the far shore. Smaller art deco-period apartment houses like Uschi's are also scattered about Marble Hill. Once an Irish bastion, the neighborhood is now multiethnic. On my first visit, Uschi was waiting outside with her cream-colored poodle, Oggi ("Today" in Italian). But I passed right by her. She seemed too youthful to have Holocaust roots more than a half-century old.

We stepped into the elevator to go up to Uschi's fifth-floor apartment. But the ceiling light was out and Uschi, agile as a sandpiper, backed out in a flash. "Ever since I was hidden," she explained, "I never go into dark places. I don't even sleep in the dark." I tried to keep up as she and Oggi sprinted up the five flights. In her modest, cheerful apartment, Uschi told me that she planned to go to Italy in May, when the days would be warm. This was December. Expressing my own wish to meet Monsignor Schivo with her, I asked if she'd be willing to go to Città di Castello sooner.

"How soon?" she asked.

"At your earliest convenience."

Without another word, Uschi went to the telephone and dialed. "*Buona sera*, Monsignor Schivo, it's Uschi. *Come sta?*" When Schivo said he was available for a visit the following week, Uschi lit up into a high-wattage smile that would have floodlit the dark elevator.

The train from Rome to Arezzo, the closest rail point to Città di Castello, was almost two hours late. It wasn't hard to pick out Beniamino Schivo amidst the crowd on the platform: a tall man, standing straight, dressed all in black except for his white clerical collar. His blue eyes were worried until he spotted Uschi—and cautious as she introduced us. Uschi had confided to me that Schivo had telephoned her in New York to express his reservations at being written about. He'd read a book about the rescue of Jews in Assisi which struck him as romanticized, even inaccurate. Schivo himself had edited, while in his seventies, a scholarly history of the Nazi occupation in Città di Castello.

In the week of our visit, Schivo would prove to be a nimble and decisive driver as he deftly negotiated the serpentine streets of Città di Castello. But for the thirty-five-minute trip from Arezzo to Città di Castello, he left the driving of his Alfa Romeo sedan to Irene Baldicchi, who with her sister, Antonietta, has provided a home for Schivo since his retirement after thirty-five years as rector of the bishop's seminary. That was almost thirty years ago. He attributes his extraordinary youthfulness at age eighty-eight to their devoted care.

The road to Città di Castello twists through rugged hills leading into the valley of the Tiber. A clunky steel bridge over the lazy river leads to the walls of the medieval city. It replaced an old span with graceful stone arches—blown up by the retreating Germans in 1944.

Schivo and the sisters Baldicchi live in a roomy apartment in square red-brick building just outside the city walls. A print of the Madonna and child by Raphael hangs over the priest's headboard in his small, immaculately neat bedroom. Books are everywhere, including a multi-volume history of the Bible. Opposite the dining room, where Schivo recites grace before each meal, is his spacious study. Over the desk is an antique map of Città di Castello, a portrait of the Taj Mahal, and a certificate of honorary Israeli citizenship. Most mornings, Schivo goes to the diocesan library at the former seminary. He is its director, sole employee, and most devoted user.

Memories stay fresh in the Catholic institutions of Città di Castello, as Uschi found out when she visited the Sacred Heart Convent on the morning after our arrival. Wandering the unheated halls as she looked for the room where she and her mother were hidden, she passed a nun, Sister Graziella, who peered closely at this stranger. As a teenager, Uschi didn't have blond hair or a black mink coat, but that didn't throw off Sister Graziella.

"You're Uschi!" she exclaimed. "Do you remember how that nun was so curious about who was in that second-floor room? And she climbed up a ladder to the window?" Sister Graziela embraced Uschi. The warmth of the nuns had not gone cold after fifty-five years.

Memory was also quick at the former bishop's seminary. We entered via the same imposing doors at which Uschi had stood and asked for *il rettore*. Now the building is a research center. The director, Monsignor Luigi Guerri, recounted how the porter, Giuseppi Bucci, delivered food twice a day to Paul Korn, hidden in a garret across the street from the seminary. Bucci was wary of prying eyes: How to make the deliveries without causing suspicion? "Bucci arranged the food in a pail," explained Guerri. "On top, he sprinkled seeds. Anyone could see that he was going to feed the chickens."

Schivo listened admiringly. "I only told Bucci to feed *signore* Korn," he said, "but not how. I didn't realize he was so clever."

Città di Castello, under Vatican rule until 1860, would seem to be a redoubt of pure Catholicism until the wartime internment of the Korns and a smattering of other Jews. But in the 1980s, stucco was removed from the facade of an old building on the Via del Vingone. The structure had long been relegated to use as a church warehouse. Underneath the stucco, elaborately carved in sandstone, was a Star of David. Research by Ariel Toaff, a professor of medieval Jewish history at Bar Ilan University in Ramat Gan, Israel, revealed that Jews had been invited to Città di Castello in the fourteenth century with a mandate to help cure a municipal budget that was in the red. The building on Via del Vingone had been their synagogue.

Poking in the municipal archive, Toaff discovered a trove of Hebrew texts on parchment, including talmudic texts copied as early as the twelfth century. Toaff has a personal connection to Città di Castello. His father, Elio Toaff, current grand rabbi of Rome, had been briefly hidden in the city during the war. In the fall of 1998, Mayor Adolfo Orsini hosted an international conference on the revelation of the city's Jewish heritage. Schivo spoke on "Jews in Città di Castello in WWII." Mentor of the event was Marisa Borchiellini, a historian who grew up steps away from the yet undiscovered synagogue. When Borchiellini showed the site to Uschi, she was startled. Walking to school each morning, she'd passed by the hidden Star of David.

It would seem to be an impossible contradiction: A woman has only fond memories of a place where she was in double peril, endangered by both the "regular" war and by the particular war against the Jews. Yet she did love those times in Città di Castello—being doted on by the nuns, hanging out at Paci's bookshop, romancing Giovanni, pouring out her heart to Don Schivo.

Uschi's one relentlessly dark memory is of serene and beautiful Pozio. We went there on the last day of our visit. The ox-cart path has been improved. It is open to cars now, but just barely. Wending into the hills, the paving soon turns to rutted dirt. Farmers' dogs still bark furiously at passersby. You catch sight of Pozio, nestled amid cyprus trees on a high ridge, well before arriving there. Then the road turns sharply and the view is lost until just before reaching the retreat. A trio of Salesian nuns had driven up from town to open the place for us. In Città di Castello, the weather had been mild. Here, the wind was a knife. Just as Uschi remembered, it cut through the walls of the retreat house, which is now used as a summer camp for city kids in need. Just as in the war, a few raw potatoes had been left in the basement. The oven building, where the Korns had huddled for months in darkness, was locked. Uschi eyed the place as warily as if snakes were coiled within.

Before we left, the nuns brought out a bottle of brandy and some glasses. They bowed their heads as Schivo, a silk scarf at his neck, closed his eyes while intoning a benediction. It included thanks to God for having permitted this place to be used for the rescue of human lives. It was a solemn moment. But when Schivo opened his blue eyes, they were dancing as he looked over at Uschi.

"Now don't you go getting in any more trouble," he said.

EPILOGUE, 2004

Monsignor Schivo continues to work two days a week in the archives of Città di Castello. At age 94, he still does not need eyeglasses. In August, as is his custom, he drives to a vacation spot in the mountains of northeast Italy, where he was born. Each week, he and Uschi Selig speak by phone and most years she visits him.

A few years ago, an Italian journalist approached Uschi with the idea of writing her biography. Related to Pope John XXIII, the journalist had good entrée to Catholic archives concerning Uschi's schooling in Città di Castello and Monsignor Schivo. At first, Uschi and her rescuer talked with the journalist. But when they started to sense that he was trying to "create" a romance between them, they cut him off.

On Holocaust Remembrance Day in January 2004, a popular Italian daytime TV show flew Uschi from New York to Rome to film a segment on the story of her rescue with Monsieur Schivo. As Uschi's passport was checked at the Rome airport, the officer looked up at her and said, "Ah, yes, I recognized you. You're going to be on TV tomorrow with the priest who saved you!"

Pieter Henry and Family and Henriette Regina Chaumat

Brussels, **September 24**, 1976, 7:36 P.M.: Yet another cloudless and dulcet evening to lengthen an almost unnaturally perfect strand of such evenings here in a city which, under the spell of the North Sea, is normally forced into a sort of rueful pride at its seasonal excess of drizzle, fog, and rain. But this particular evening and this moment are special only to the Jews of the city for still another reason. They mark the beginning of Rosh Hashanah, the New Year 5737 according to the lunar calendar that commenced with the Day of Creation. It is also some thirty-three years since the peak here in Belgium—as well as in France and Holland—of deportations to the killing centers of the east. But despite the best efforts of the neighboring Germans, the Reich is gone and, at this hour, the great nineteenth-century synagogue on the rue de la Régence is full.

Among those praying in one pew toward the front is sixty-four-year-old Abram Lipski, a big but oddly delicate man, topped off with a thatch of energetic white hair, who seems even taller than his graceful six feet two. In the tradition of synagogues everywhere, children dart about and men pull one another closer to whisper stories at length—though one would be deceived to think they could not at any moment put a finger to the precise spot in the ancient text which the elders, droning and mumbling before the Holy Ark, have reached. But Lipski keeps his head in his prayer book. He seems a man unto himself.

In an unremarkable three-story town house just ten minutes away on avenue de Boetendael, a winding and leafy street in a good section of town, Lipski's wife, Tanya, and the servants are making a last check of the long dining table. Extended to seat twenty-two people, it now sticks out from the dining room almost into the foyer. The crystal and silverware must be spotless and the flowers as fresh as they should be. In this house, the Rosh Hashanah dinner is one of the major events of the year.

Among the guests who soon begin to arrive are some of the most accomplished members of the small Jewish community—no more than twenty-five thousand—here in Brussels. They include scholars, businessmen, and musicians. None are more accomplished, however, than the host himself. Abram Lipski is among the leading structural engineers of Belgium. Just this morning, he stood at the side of the king, Baudouin, at a ceremony dedicating the new municipal subway system, of whose tunnels and stations he was primary designer.

Like the rest of the older generation at this table, Lipski was born in Eastern Europe. Like them and twenty generations of their forebears, he had seemed consigned at birth not only to poverty but to the scorn of gentile neighbors. That, and whims of violence. If, as a child in Lodz, it had been suggested to Lipski that one day he would grow up to stand, by invitation, at the side of a European king, he surely would have roared with laughter. So would the gentiles of Lodz. It would have been one of the few things on which they could agree.

But the miseries of a childhood in Eastern Europe were nothing compared with what he would endure here in otherwise hospitable

Belgium under the Nazi Occupation. Of sixty-five thousand Jews in the country before the war, almost half were lost. Some at this table had managed to survive within the borders of Belgium despite the thoroughness of the hunt. Beyond any other of their achievements, then, none are more remarkable than this: their bones did not rise in vapor out of a smokestack at Auschwitz and neither do they lie decomposing amid the human rubble of some unnamed killing ground in the east. On this evening, they are still able to wish each other the traditional Hebrew greeting:"*Le-shana tova tikatevu*"—"Happy New Year."

Almost the last to arrive are Raphael Lipski, son of the hosts, his wife, Selma, and their three young boys. Tall and erect, with black hair and sharp black eyes, Selma is not the sort of woman who will ever enter a crowded room unnoticed. Head up, as remote as a favored thoroughbred among the admiring bettors, she seems to move in a field of her own proud energy. Courtesy might have suggested that she say a word or two to me, the foreign stranger seated to her left. But she does not.

It is while the plates are being removed after a first course of homemade gefilte fish that David, the oldest of Selma's three sons, comes wandering over from his place beside his father to whisper something in her ear. He is a slender, dark, and fine-boned child of perhaps eight years, already carrying himself with the confident and dignified grace that marks him as his mother's child. As he leans toward her, I notice a small pin on the breast of his white shirt. It is fashioned into the Hebrew word *zechor*, meaning "remember!"

"Where did your son get that pin?" I ask, knowing of only one place it was likely to have come from.

For the first time, Selma Lipski's large black eyes fall on me with full attention—showing at once their capacity to engulf as well as to ignore.

"He got it in Israel," she answers, "at a place in Jerusalem called Yad Vashem."

Her three sons had been to Yad Vashem the previous spring. Like thousands of other tourists, they had walked through the Museum of the Holocaust, stared down at the slabs in the Hall of Remembrance bearing the names of the camps, and, at the end of an hour or so, had stopped at the snack bar and gift shop beside the parking lots where the *zechor* pin was purchased. But her sons had also done what few others have had the honor to do. They planted a tree on the Avenue of the Righteous. It is a tree in honor of Henriette Regina Chaumat, a woman who had died just a year earlier at age seventy-seven. During the Occupation, Madame Chaumat had stepped forward to become the unlikely but absolute keeper and preserver of the infant Raphael, who, at three, was even then a candidate for deportation to Auschwitz. What Selma Lipski does not say here at the dinner table is that she herself has become by her own choice the chief keeper and preserver of memories of the late Madame Chaumat.

Raphael Lipski (family and friends call him Raffi) is seated or, rather, gently slumped—across the table within reach of his three active sons. He is as fair as Selma is dark, with thick blond hair and a high pink flush on his cheeks that would normally belong to a child just in from the cold. His eyes are a Delft-like blue, transparent and untroubled, and if the capacity for purely adult mischief were not in them, they would also be considered childlike. What Raphael Lipski shares fully with his wife, beyond their powerful good looks, is a palpable glow of well-being which seems as if it could issue only from a person on whom fortune has bestowed, since birth, exclusively what is good and comfortable in life. That is why the story Selma has to tell seems so incongruous. No sooner had her husband reached the age of three, in the summer of 1942, than he became a warm bundle in line for deportation to the east. For the next two years, his one precarious hold on life was through this person unrelated to him, this stranger who put herself in more danger by keeping him than if she were hoarding contraband, this Madame Chaumat.

Speaking in throaty French with brief excursions into English, ignoring the others now as she had earlier ignored me, Selma explains that Madame Chaumat was not the only one to be honored with a tree on that morning in April 1976. Right beside it, a second tree was planted in honor of the two poor but brave couples who had, during that same period, hidden Raphael's parents in the house they shared at Ghent. One of those couples and the surviving member of the other had stood watching on the windy knoll that is the new section of the Avenue of the Righteous while the three sons of Raffi and Selma Lipski took turns filling in dirt around Madame Chaumat's tiny carob tree. Had she lived another year, she surely would have planted it herself. Then the boys handed the spade to the old people. One after another, they took turns shoveling fresh earth around a tree of their own.

Eleven people had, at Abram Lipski's expense, flown together from Belgium to Israel for that ceremony. They had driven all over Israel together in a rented minibus. There had been Selma Lipski and her three sons; the senior Lipskis; their younger son, Alex, born after the war; the three older members of the Flemish families; and a mother's helper for Selma. In short, everyone who had a connection, direct or indirect, with those days had gone on the trip—except for Raffi Lipski himself. He had appointed his children to plant the tree for Madame Chaumat.

Selma Lipski anticipates the next question. No, her husband had not been too sick to make the trip with everyone else. No, he had not been faced with some unspecified great emergency. Nothing at all had prevented him from going to Yad Vashem. He had simply stayed home. This is not easy for Selma to explain—especially to a stranger. Each time she grasps for the words, it is as painful as listening to an engine which turns over and over, straining to catch the spark, but never quite connecting. All that she can say, finally, by way of explanation, is that her husband is very, very *sensible*.

The word is not an evasion, but it is hardly a total explanation. Any amplification must depend on knowing much more about Madame Chaumat, about the events and emotions that have worked on Raffi Lipski with such force as to keep him from going to the Avenue of the Righteous to plant a tree for the woman who had saved him. The only thing that seems clear from his wife's fore-closed explanation is that he failed to make the trip to Yad Vashem not for lack of caring, but because he cared too much.

At the end of the meal, Selma beckons Raffi to her side of the table. Twining the tips of her graceful fingers with his, leaning close, she explains to him what business has brought this American to Belgium. At this moment, relaxed and well fed, he does not seem much interested in admitting such a dark and serious topic to the end of this particular evening. He seems much more interested, in fact, in developing the finger play with his wife. At tactile range, there is a subtle but effortless erotic quality to this couple which, as eroticism will always do, supersedes all other interests. But then, quite unexpectedly, Raffi stops the playing and looks closely at the guest.

"My father wrote a last will and testament during the war," he says. "It is quite unusual, I think. Would you like to see it? Come—we'll go upstairs now."

Leaving the others to sip coffee and brandy, Raffi takes my arm. We go through the living room, into the hall, and up the stairs past the family living quarters, to his office on the third-floor premises of the engineering firm in which he and his father are the principals. Like the offices of engineers everywhere, even prosperous ones, this one belonging to Raffi Lipski is lackluster.

"Please, sit there at my desk," he says, going to rummage at the bottom of a file cabinet. It takes him several minutes to come up with a faded brown envelope, which he hands to me unopened.

"Read it at your own speed," he says. "I'm going back down-stairs. If you need any help, just call. You might have to. The language is remarkable, but it isn't all perfect." Raffi shut the door and left me in silence.

The will has been typed, single-spaced, on three pages bearing the letterhead "A. Lipski, Ingénieur, A.I.G., Ingénieur Conseil, rue du Patijintje 24, Gand." Though the text is true to the dry and, in places, obtuse style of testamentary language, this will deals not with the disposal of wealth or property, but with the disposition of

A. Lipski's then only begotten son, Raphael. It has been executed at Ghent on August 31, 1942. After Abram Lipski's signature, there is a statement by his wife, Tanya, affirming that her husband's wishes for their son are also her own.

Raffi Lipski comes dashing up the steps every few minutes to help me through the thornier parts of the French text. At the end, he says, "Not all the parts are equally interesting. But don't you think it is an amazing document that my father found it in him to write? . . ."

He sits on his desk, a big, golden man of thirty-seven, rereading the fine points of his disposition. The situation seems so far removed from present-day reality that he might have read it dispassionately, as he would an historic document, as a curiosity. But when Raffi looks up, the humor, the satisfaction, and the apparent complacency that have played in his eyes all evening are stricken away. Instead, I am looking into the anxious eyes of a lost child, which well up now with tears.

"You must pardon me," he says, "but on this subject, I am very . . . *sensible.*"

As quickly as the tears have come they are blinked away. Raffi points to a portion of the text dealing with his education. His father requests that he be taught to read the Bible in the original Hebrew, "with particular attention to the Prophets."

"You see that?" says Raffi. "Well, I must tell you that as I grew up after the war, my father monitored all my studies, but I never heard from him again about paying special attention to the Prophets. That's what you call human nature, yes?"

Raffi smiles as delightedly as if he had sneaked out of a dull classroom unnoticed. In his eyes, the seraph and the imp dance together, which is to say that even with the tears banished, they are still the eyes of a child.

At 8:30 on a Tuesday evening, four days later, Abram Lipski climbed the stairs to his own office opposite his son's. He had set aside this evening to tell the story of how he, a Polish Jew, came to Belgium, how he found the best, and how his family survived the worst, and by whom they were saved. It is a story, Raffi says, which, though it ends happily, has never ceased to haunt him.

Lipski was born in 1911 in Lodz, a word which he still pronounces, with anything but love, as in "trudge." It was then an industrial city of some six hundred thousand souls, of whom perhaps one third were Jewish. There were Jewish captains of industry in Lodz, but not in Lipski's family. His father devoted his days to the study of Scripture and his mother was a housewife. The family lived in a poor section of the city among few other Jews. "At first I was sent to the local school," says Lipski. "Then, when I was fourteen, I made a big effort to go to a particularly good Jewish school in another part of the city. Even the Polish government, which rated all schools for academic standards, put this one in the top class. Here I learned to speak and write Hebrew, as I do still. I also studied Latin—quite a rarity in Poland. About one third of the classes were conducted in Hebrew, the rest in Polish. I was a good student, especially in mathematics, and when I graduated, I decided that I wanted to study to be an engineer.

"Now there was only one problem here. As I was a Jew, I could not go to the university in my own country. It is true that a tiny handful of Jewish students who had the right connections politically could get into the university. There were Jews serving in the national assembly, for example, representing their all-Jewish districts. Their children had a chance. But my family had no such connections, so I had no chance at all. Just the same, I took the entrance examination for the famous Politechnika Warszawska, the engineering university in Warsaw. But I did this primarily to prove to my mother that if I wanted to go to university I had no choice but to emigrate. In this I was successful. I did very well on the exam, and I did not get into the university. You had to do well in a measure that was not available to me.

"I should say that about this time something happened which had a heavy influence on my life and my psychology. My brother David, who was six years older than me, had gone to Israel—then still called Palestine—to be a *halutz*, which in Hebrew means 'pioneer.' In those days, to put an acre under the plow, first you had to clear an acre of stones. For a year, he worked on a border kibbutz, called Ein Ganim. But this was not enough for him. He got together a group of about a dozen *halutzim*—this is the plural for pioneer—and applied to the government to start a new kibbutz. While they waited for the new land to be allotted to them, David continued to work at Ein Ganim. One day he cut his hand on a sharp stone. It was a small cut but it got infected. Well, this was before penicillin, and even though they took him to Hadassah Hospital in Jerusalem, he died. This was in 1928. He was buried on Har Hazeitim, the Mount of Olives. And even though he was only twenty-four years old, he was already well known in Israel. If he had lived, he would have been a leader of the new country. This was accepted by all who knew him. He was also the chief of our family. I was not of the same capacity.

"My family was Zionist, and probably we would have all followed him to Palestine. But when he died, that was the end. My parents considered that they had given enough for Zionism.

"So instead of going east to Israel I went to a student clearing house in Lodz which offered information on all the universities of Europe that admitted foreign students. Actually, at that time the closest desirable university city was in Prague, which was then a real intellectual center. Quite a few Polish students even went to German universities then. I looked through all this information just as you would look through a menu at a restaurant. And I picked the University of Ghent, which was said to have a good engineering faculty. By mail I applied for admission, and by return mail I was accepted. It was as simple as that. And then I boarded the train for Belgium. In the whole country, I did not know a single person. And I did not know a single word of French or Flemish."

Lipski arrived in Ghent in the fall of 1931, a tall, fair man of nineteen, taciturn by necessity and determined to be frugal as well as studious. It was the first time he had been out of Poland, or even much beyond the environs of Lodz. Even by the standards of a Jew from worldly Warsaw, he would have been a provincial. Yet it is not what Lipski saw, but how he was himself seen that most powerfully astonished him.

"For the first time in my life," he explains, "people called me a Pole. Yes, I had a Polish passport; yes, I had a Polish name; yes, I spoke Polish as a mother tongue; yes, my family had lived in Poland for centuries. Centuries! But I was not a Pole to the Poles. I was a hated Jew: 'Jew—get out of my way. Jew—what are you doing on this street? Jew—see this knife? I'm going to cut off your beard.' In this atmosphere I grew up.

"Let me tell you a small story to show how deep this poison ran. In order to get to my high school, I had to take two trams on which, every morning, I met a Polish boy my own age. We got to be friendly and we talked a lot. Of course, between a Jewish boy and a Christian boy, this friendship never went beyond the tram. Anyway, one day he says he has a serious question for me. He hesitates, but I see he is very curious. Finally, he asks: 'Abram, is it true that at Passover, you Jews use the blood of Christian children to make your matzoh?'

"I answered him as best I could by explaining that according to Halachah, the code of Jewish law, it is forbidden for a Jew to eat an egg if the yolk has so much as a drop of blood in it, even the tiniest fleck of red. No matter how poor a woman was, she would throw out such an egg, even if it meant she would not have another to eat. Could he think, then, that Halachah would allow the blood of Christian children to be mixed with the flour of the matzoh? This was the most persuasive answer I could give him. But if he had to ask such a question, then I am certain he had already made up his mind about the answer. It was the answer he got from his family, his friends, his priest. Do you know what they call it in Polish if you spill a bottle of ink and make a stain? They call this stain a Jew: 'Look, you have made a Jew.'

"So this is how we were regarded in Poland—as something worse than dirt, a stain, something evil. To come out of a country poisoned by hate to a country of . . . normal people . . . this I shall never forget. In one stroke, I was treated like a human being who happened to be a Pole, a Pole who happened to be a Jew. Thanks to my Latin, I was able to learn French quickly. Within a month I was already able to manage simple conversations. And within a month, too, I knew I would never go back to live in Poland. If I had any doubts about that, they were erased in the summers when I went home to Lodz and saw the scrawls on the walls that I had grown up with: *Kill the Jews!* The slogans were the same, but the paint was fresh. In German, there is a word, *Stief-mutter*, which means a sort of evil stepmother. Well, Poland was my real mother and acted like the *Stief-mutter*. Belgium, which owed me nothing at all, acted like the most loving of mothers."

Lipski quickly fit into a close cadre of student friends—a mingling of Belgians and emigrés, like himself, from the eastern regions. Upon graduation in 1935, he was chosen for a year's apprenticeship to a prominent engineer on the university faculty. "In this way," he says, "I was able to earn my life." After that year, despite the hard times, Lipski always managed to have a job. At night and on weekends, he worked with another emigrant engineer, Ovchi Lempert, in a consulting practice of their own. In the summer of 1936, Tanya Lempert came by train from Bessarabia to visit her brother. He introduced her to Abram. They were soon engaged, and in 1938 they were married. Raphael was born the following year.

"This was a child like you cannot imagine," says Lipski. "Beautiful like an angel. In the park, people would stop just to look at him. I know I am the father, but believe me, this was a wondrous child." Up until Raffi's first birthday the Lipskis could hardly have been happier. Abram was able, despite the times, to "earn a life" for his family. They lived in a simple but comfortable apartment in Ghent, surrounded by a warm circle of friends. Nobody, of course, could ignore the shadow that Hitler was casting over Europe. But it seemed especially difficult to perceive that the shadow would become so dark and so enveloping that it would soon settle down over them even here in peaceful and hospitable

Ghent. Above all, Abram and Tanya Lipski did not realize that as vulnerable as they themselves might be, none was more vulnerable than their cheerful, beautiful, and beloved Raffi.

It was not entirely their own fault if the Jews in Belgium, like Abram Lipski, did not see the shadow settling. Had Hitler not told the world that, having taken the Sudetenland, he would be satisfied with his acquisitions of territory to the east? Even if he wasn't, surely he would honor his own standing guarantees of the neutrality of Belgium. Even when his forces thrust across the western borders on the morning of May 10, 1940, sweeping aside all such guarantees with them, it could be honestly said that for the time being life was no worse for the Jews than for any other citizens of the occupied lands. This was not wishful thinking and certainly it was not the result of chance. According to the special orders (*Sonderbestimmungen*) written in secret a full seventy-eight days before the invasion of the west, the soldiers of the Sixth Army under von Reichenau were warned "not to bring up the racial question. . . . The fact that an inhabitant of the country is Jewish is not a reason of itself to take particular measures against him. . . . Do not touch the Jews in occupied territories."

According to the Nazi schema, the French-speaking Walloons of southern Belgium as well as the French themselves were considered to be, racially speaking, "Romanic" peoples, just one step below the Aryans. Under the conquering Reich, they would be accorded some sort of independent national status, unlike certain of the "subhumans" (*Untermenschen*) of the east. Consequently, the citizens of France and Belgium were to be treated as human beings and for a brief time, astonishingly, so were the Jews of those countries. That period of grace lasted for six months. Then, on October 28, 1940, the German military commander of Belgium, Alexander van Falkenhausen, issued the first edicts against the Jews. The order requiring all heads of households to enter the names, ages, and sex of their family members in a new register of Jews may have seemed, at the time, far less onerous than the order that banned Jews from the "sensitive" professions like teaching, law, and journalism. In retrospect, however, it was more ominous, since it told the Germans where, in the black of night, to come pounding on the door, whom to look for, and who might be missing.

Lipski registered his family according to the German order of October 28, 1940. Like their brethren in France and Holland, most Belgian Jews did the same. Still, even at this early date, a handful chose to take the chance of not registering. These were, in the main, highly mobile young adults, active on the political left, who could change their names, move to a new address, and get false papers to match. But such risks were not for Lipski. He was not, in the first place, politically active, and now that he had a son as well as a wife, disobeying a German order would have been foolhardy. Moreover, even though all members of the family looked "Aryan," Lipski and his wife had only to open their mouths to betray their Eastern European origins.

Finally, it did not seem to make sense to Lipski to contemplate disobeying the registration order because he was not affected by that other, apparently more debilitating order of October 28 which banned Jews from "sensitive" professions. Engineering was not in that category, and, luckily, Lipski's main client was a Christian—a relationship that also would have been forbidden in reverse. So Lipski continued to go to work each morning and come home each night just as he had done before the invasion. But now he, too, carried that disquieting ID card. Instead of the block letter "J" as prescribed in Holland, this one was stamped in Flemish and French, *JOOD/JUIF*. After a respite of ten fine years, Lipski was once again in a land where, for purely negative purposes, being a Jew came first.

He adjusted as best he could as, decree upon grey decree, the Nazis continued to squeeze harder. In the springtime of 1942, he and Tanya put on the "star of six points, colored yellow with black borders, the size of the palm of the hand, inscribed with the black letter 'J,' to be affixed to the left side of the chest, securely attached." Very little seemed to have been left to chance in this order of May 28 except, perhaps, whether a child like Raffi Lipski was supposed to wear a star the size of his own palm or one the size of his father's. Tanya Lipski remembers, with gratitude, that upon seeing her star, many men on the street removed their hats and in the crowded trams a seat would quickly be given up to her.

A yellow star might cover the heart but the heart went on beating. Unfair as life might be, it also went on. People managed because they had no choice but to manage. Lipski, in any case, suffered less than many other Jews of more substance. He had no visible personal assets for the Germans to "aryanize." As a full-time consulting engineer to a factory in Ghent owned by Christians, he managed to continue earning a living when other Jews could not. Lipski even received a certain kindness when, early in the summer of that year, he applied to the local Wehrmacht commander for permission to send his wife and son to a tiny village thirty kilometers from Ghent where Raffi would not suffer so much from his asthma. The commander, named Dietsz, confirming Lipski's estimate that he was "not such a bad sort," readily agreed to the request.

Each morning of the summer, Lipski rose alone. He made his own breakfast and went to work. Other Belgians did much the same, of course, having sent their own families to summer residences. But for a Jew to continue functioning more or less normally had to be considered a minor triumph. If Lipski had been an optimist, he might even have believed that he had outlasted the German schedule of deprivations and humiliations against the Jews of Belgium. Optimistic Jews in France and Holland could have believed likewise. The catch, of course, was that one had to assume the Nazis would behave within normal human boundaries. But, though he had told nobody, Lipski no longer believed that. He had no way of learning that the genuinely unthinkable was already taking place at Auschwitz and other points east. But without knowing exactly what was in his nostrils, Lipski had caught a whiff of the gas.

That is why, even as he put the best face on the situation and continued to carry on, Lipski had already taken the first precautionary and indirect step away from obedience to the conqueror. That step had been hidden within the request to send his family to the country. "It is true that Raffi had a touch of asthma," Lipski explains. "But this was not the primary reason that I sent him off with his mother. I did it because I wanted to eliminate them from our registered address. I felt that to be at home had become dangerous."

Early that summer, the Germans had begun sending a certain number of young Jewish men to work camps in Calais and northern France. After a furor had risen in Holland a year earlier over the deaths of four hundred young Jews who had been "working" at Mauthausen rock piles, the Germans had learned to kill with more stealth. The call to hard labor, in any case, was not limited to Jews. In all the conquered countries, the Germans were regularly throwing out the net for strong young men whom they could put to work. Lipski was prepared to voluntarily answer a work order, not because he wanted to, obviously, but because implicit in it was the threat that if he did not obey, his family would pay the price. That is why he did not hesitate to cut into his limited budget to buy a superior pair of boots and other clothing that would hold up under hard labor.

"I felt—well, this is what happens in war and this is the sort of hardship I will have to undergo, so I might as well be prepared," explains Lipski. "I would have done anything, and they could have done anything to me, if it meant saving my wife and my son."

As the summer of 1942 ended, Lipski was still working and still waiting for the call to forced labor. It never came. But then, in the last week of August, he heard some news from Antwerp, thirty miles away, that made him doubt whether even his earnest offer of work for the Reich—or any other offering, for that matter— would placate the Nazis or preserve his family from them.

Until this time, Belgian Jews, like Christians, had been called to hard labor by written order, delivered either by Nazi or Belgian police or, in certain places, by messengers of the Association des Juifs en Belgique (AJB), an official but captive Jewish umbrella organization of the sort that the Nazis used wherever they had to deal with substantial Jewish communities. Along with its more miserable tasks, the AJB was charged with maintaining orphanages, hospitals, old-age homes, and other civic services for the captive community. Its counterpart in Holland had even managed, for a time, to persuade the Nazis to pay wages to the forced laborers from its community—albeit at rates lower than the Christian scale.

The AJB, and organizations like it, represented one way in which the Germans attempted to put an administrative face on their barbarism. The arguments will go on forever as to whether prominent members of the Jewish community should have agreed to be part of it. In fact, they had no alternative. In the worst of all possible worlds, they did what they could to make ever greater misery more orderly and perhaps, therefore, more bearable. Certainly their efforts postponed for a while what now happened in Antwerp.

Of all the prewar Jewish communities in Belgium, the one in that busy port city had been the largest and most prosperous. Inevitably, it was the one toward which the Nazis were most oppressive. For two years, they had ruthlessly extracted what spoils they could from local Jewish businesses. But until this last week of August, people had not been violated at home. Now, in the hour before dawn, came the pounding on the doors. Whole families were roused and given a moment or two to collect a few belongings. Then, filing out in single column, guarded front and rear by Gestapo agents, the families were led away to "furniture" vans which took them direct to the Dossin barracks at Malines. There they would have to wait no more than a few days before a train could be filled up to take them to Auschwitz.

These forays thrust a new and dreaded word into the consciousness of the Belgian Jews. The word was *rafle*. It meant, abstractly, a violent and greedy taking. But now it had a very specific meaning that began with the sound of trucks rumbling up in the night. With the *rafles*, the Nazis had reached the limit of what they could do to the Jews within the borders of friendly, civilized Belgium. Ironically, this last step was made very easy by the first step. To find out where to go on a *rafle*, the Nazi teams had merely to look in the register of October 1940, in which every Jewish family was entered by name, age, sex, and home address.

Lipski could not know where the victims of the Antwerp *rafles* were to be taken. But he did not need to know the specifics in order to affirm the suspicion which for him, he says, had now become inescapable: "If the Germans were taking the ill, the elderly, and the infants, this was not to put them to work at hard labor. This was for something else."

Lipski could be thankful that he was able to have this revelation in Ghent instead of Antwerp. This small and still peaceful city could hardly gather enough Jews for a minyan, let alone a *rafle*, and the fact that his family was at that very moment legally tucked away in a country village showed that the local German commander had a heart. Just the same, in light of the Antwerp events, Lipski decided to take some major precautionary steps. The first was to type out a last will and testament. By temperament as well as by training, Lipski was a rationalist, a planner, a methodical man, and these qualities do indeed shape the will. But it is also colored throughout with a moral fury that has nothing to do with being rational, planned, or methodical.

Lipski goes directly to the question of who shall be guardian (*tuteur*) of Raphael in the case that both he and his wife are not alive or are otherwise unable to "manifest" their will. Lipski has divided the potential guardians between two lists. List A consists of four residents of Ghent who are authorized to be entrusted with the care of the child at any time up to the end of the war. At the top is Tanya's brother Ovchi Lempert. Then come two Christian women with whom the Lipskis were friends. Fourth is Joseph Bayart, the child's pediatrician. Lipski empowers each of them to dispose of "all my money and property" on behalf of Raffi. If that should not be enough, Lipski requests that the "definitive" guardian reimburse the "provisional" guardian for the difference. "It goes without saying," writes Lipski, "that I will make good the deficit myself if I survive. . . ."

List B consists of ten nominees for "definitive" guardianship once the war is over. It begins with Jonas Braverman, husband of Lipski's sister Ruchla. He was born in Lodz, but here his last known address is listed at 275 Seventh Avenue, in the heart of the Manhattan fur district. Then comes Ovchi Lempert from the top of List A. Third is Mordechai Lempert, another of Tanya's brothers, who was still back in Kishinev, Bessarabia. Fourth is Lipski's sister Ruchla, a teacher who apparently did not make it to America with her husband, since her last known address is here listed as Novolipie 13/3 in the Warsaw ghetto. Fifth is Ruchla's twenty-two-year-old son, Imanuel Braverman, a student who until 1939 had lived in Lodz but whose last known address was listed in the will at a post office box in Komi, Russia. Sixth through tenth are all blood relations of Lipski or his wife, all with last known addresses in Poland or Bessarabia.

Lipski has ranked the ten prospective "definitive" guardians according to his careful estimate of their ability to do best by his child. Because his assessment had more to do with where they lived than who they were, he also provided an easy way for anyone lower on List B to go instantly to the top. They would have only to make their home in "Eretz Israel (Palestine)." Lipski wrote that clause six years before the creation of the modern State of Israel. Given the nearly two thousand years since the last such state, six years is hardly a breath in time, of course. But given, too, that this will was being written by a hunted man in the dominion of Hitler, it is almost eerily prescient that Lipski could speak of such a prospect at all—let alone with confidence.

To one looking over Abram Lipski's shoulder as he worked, it might have seemed that List B was unnecessarily long. But here again Lipski was prescient. Though full-scale deportations had only just begun that summer in Western Europe, he sensed that life for the Jews had reverted to the law of the wild. So, like a fish that lays a surplus of eggs out of which only a few or even one might survive, Lipski has overdrawn his list of *tuteurs* in the hope that at least one might survive to raise the child according to the wishes of his parents. Amid such an enveloping pessimism, incidentally, it is easy to overlook the rather astonishing fact that the only person whose survival Lipski's text takes totally for granted is his helpless son.

It has taken half the will to dispose of the question of guardianship. Now Lipski explains how he wants the child raised. First comes the requirement for a "Jewish education as profound as possible in the religious, philosophic, and, above all, the national senses." As for the "hope—so ancient yet so alive—of the Jewish People to return at last to its Country to rebuild a spiritual and material existence—that should also be his hope. He should contribute to its realization according to his means." Lipski is also anxious that these feelings, once instilled, be kept in perspective. Thus, "a non-Jew who is a just man and a good, hard worker should always be held dearer than a Jew lacking in those qualities."

Next, Lipski disposes of the parties who have caused him now at age thirty-one to write this will in such a spasm of pessimism. "I hope that if not I, at least my son will live to see the rightful punishment of these crimes which those hateful persecutors have perpetrated on us for almost ten years and which actually seem now to pass any imaginable limits. We are placed at the head of a long list of subjugated peoples who have the great honor, heavy as it is, to embody both their sufferings and their hopes for liberation. The men (do they deserve the name?) who have made a calling of abusing us are, down deep, more naïve than ferocious or cynical in imagining that they can do anything against our spirits even as they snap now like dogs at our bodies, not having been satisfied at brutally destroying the fruits of our labor.

"But if by the worst imaginable turn of ill luck," Lipski cautions, "justice does not triumph soon and forcefully, my son shall never despair of Her. And never should he be jealous of evildoers because of the material benefits, which may seem quite permanent, derived from their crimes. The justice of a cause which one defends or personifies is within itself the principal recompense. I have faith that, in the final count, this recompense will not be the only one."

Pushing aside the possibility of any such "ill luck," the father now turns to the day when his son must choose a profession. That choice, "apart from his predispositions and capacities, should be made before any calculation of income—this always being uncertain anyway. The profession should not allow him to provide for his needs; it should give him the joy of working and of rendering service to his neighbors and of being productive. He shall energetically defend his legitimate interests." Lastly, having dispatched the weightier and grimmer concerns, Lipski asks the guardian to encourage his son to "practice the most diverse sports, thereby developing his agility, strength, and all else that is favorable to his well-being."

His will in order, Lipski took at the same time a further precaution on his own behalf. He no longer slept at home or anywhere else on a regular basis. Luckily, he had a wide circle of Christian friends, many of whom welcomed him with a place to sleep in their own homes. Lipski did not let any one bed get too warm. If there was to be a mini-*rafle* in Ghent, he wanted to keep down the odds that the Gestapo could find him. It was a wise decision. One morning late in September, he was walking home for a quick change of clothing before work when, just a block away from his door, he was stopped by some neighbors.

"I didn't know these people personally," he says. "But they knew me. 'Take care,' they said. 'The Gestapo is waiting for you.' I thanked them for their advice. Then I turned around and walked back the other way."

At that moment Lipski made—or, rather, had made for him—a seismic shift in his family's adaptation to life. "Until this time," he explains, "we had lived a legal life. We had obeyed the occupier. As long as we were living on the surface, we had to obey. As long as I had a wife and child, any other life had been unthinkable. But now I knew that if we were to survive, we would have to disappear—dive below the surface. And we could not reappear until the Germans were gone. I did not know how we could do this. I only knew we had no choice. Now, because we know what did happen in those times, it seems as if to hide was a natural thing. But frankly, then it was a fantastic decision."

Lipski's most urgent task was to spirit his wife and child out of the tiny village where the Germans had recorded their presence. His first impulse was to go after them himself, but he was pulled up short by the realization that it was no longer safe for him to be seen on the streets of Ghent. He had to start thinking of himself not as an oppressed man walking free but as a fugitive. Now he needed help. Ever since the *rafles* had begun in Antwerp four weeks earlier, many of Lipski's friends had offered to help in whatever way they could if the worst should come here to Ghent. Now Lipski drew upon these promises.

By eight o'clock that morning, an employee from his office named Jean Vigeno was already off and pedaling furiously with his own wife on a tandem bike to collect Tanya and Raffi Lipski. They made the trip in just over an hour. It was fast enough to beat the Gestapo. Tanya Lipski, a shy woman but always firmly calm in a crisis, whispered in her son's ear to be good, and handed him over to Madame Vigeno, who took him back to Ghent on the train. Then Tanya herself joined Jean Vigeno in pedaling back to town. That first night, the family hid together in the attic of Vigeno's mother. But in the morning, they were asked to leave. "She was an old, poor woman who had a lot of compassion for us," explains Lipski, "but she was afraid."

For the next twelve days, the Lipskis played a sort of desperate and macabre game of musical chairs, darting furtively from one friend's home to the next. They did not play the game by choice. But the behavior of Vigeno's mother had become a pattern. "People saw us being hunted," says Lipski, "and in their human hearts they had a first movement toward compassion. But then, after a day or two, it was pushed aside by a more powerful impulse. They were afraid." Lipski does not make this judgment with reproach. These people owed him nothing, and while nobody could say for sure what would happen to a Christian family found to be harboring Jews, the prognosis was not good. In any case, those friends who kept the family for even one night still showed more courage than certain other friends, who were now afraid even to open their door to the fugitives. Ironically, these were often the same friends who, just weeks earlier, had most fervently sworn to be there when they were needed.

In this late summer and early fall of 1942, there were about sixty-five thousand Jews trapped in Belgium. For two years, most of them had done their best to stay alive by trying to meet each new and more oppressive requirement of the Germans as best they could. Now, separately but simultaneously, all over Belgium other Jews were making the same momentous decision that Lipski had made. If it was no longer "legal" for them to be alive, then they would move under the surface and commence an illegal life. Each family that survived would have a different story to tell—or if they did not survive, a different story would be told for them. But there were certain basics common to illegal life everywhere. For foreign-born Jews whose tongue would betray them, it was usually necessary to be physically hidden. For their children whose native language was French, however, it was only necessary to provide a new identity. In this situation, it was easier and more logical to preserve a family in parts rather than as a unit. The parents, for example, might be hidden in the attic or cellar of a private home, while their child, furnished with a new name and suitable life history, might be "placed" with a farm family or in a convent orphanage where his particular misfortune would go unquestioned amid the general misfortune. It would be left to a severe and unrelenting test of his parents' stealth, luck, and the kindness of strangers to decide whether the child's assumed and temporary status would become permanent and genuine.

Removing the children from even the closest-knit family was, above all, a matter of safety. Adults could be trusted to maintain total silence and stillness as necessary in an attic hideaway, for example. But a child might pick exactly the wrong moment to start screaming. In this period there were, in the wreckage of the deeply religious Jewish community of Eastern Europe, rabbinical courts convened in secret to decide if it were God's will to smother a baby when its crying threatened to expose a whole family in hiding—crying that may have been set off by the thump of Gestapo boots on the floorboards. Though it was a beloved tradition for religious men to argue the finest and most theoretical points of rabbinical codes, this particular situation was not theoretical.

For Jews born in Belgium, or for those who could pass as natives, the key to sustaining life was not bread but the paper that would identify them as Christians. Luckily for them, the Belgian underground, with members well sprinkled throughout the municipal bureaucracies which the Nazis allowed to continue functioning, quickly developed the essential capability to produce high-quality birth, marriage, and—most precious of all—baptismal certificates. A great number of those civil certificates were issued, or were purported to have been issued, from the city hall of Nivelles, where a fire had wiped out public records a few years before the war, making it impossible to check a certificate "against the books."

But a German or Polish Jew who had only recently fled his homeland could take slight comfort in his possession of even the most authentic-appearing papers. Stopped by the Gestapo in a random street check, for example, he would not be persuasive in identifying himself as, say, a certain "Jean-Paul LeFlaive." So Belgians of recent vintage like Abram and Tanya Lipski were forced to try to hide physically rather than attempt a masquerade which they could not carry through convincingly. But for Raffi, born Belgian and speaking his first words in French, the situation was different. For perhaps the first time in history, this child and thousands like him were far safer having been removed from the embrace of parents and deposited in a house of strangers.

For two weeks following the Gestapo's dawn raid on their home, the parents of Raffi Lipski had trundled him from one family of Ghent Christians to another. Only when he was safely settled would they worry about finding a hiding place of their own. They would have been happy to leave Raffi in one place, but a three-year-old boy, adorable and "easy" though he might be, was still an enormous responsibility and a nearly total drain on his guardian's time and energy. That is why Lipski was having such trouble in finding for Raffi—to use his odd phrase—a "final solution."

Still, on the twelfth day of their life beneath the surface, Lipski dared to hope that at last he had found a family different from the others. "These were people," he explains, "who professed such love for Raffi that they almost tore him away from us by force. They promised to keep him for as long as necessary. But then, after just two days, we got a message from them. They also turned out to be afraid."

With this last and unexpected setback, Lipski was up against the fact that he had just about run out of friends and even friends of friends whom he could reasonably ask the favor of providing a haven for his child. It was only then that he realized, quite abruptly, that his thinking need not and could not be limited to guardians in the shape of full-scale families. Out of that thought sprang another. In the circle of friends he had entered when he first came to Ghent—a circle where he had been startled to find acceptance not as a Jew but as a human being—was the woman named Henriette Chaumat. Of her background, he knew almost nothing except that she had been born in Paris and that when she was still very young she had cut off all ties with her family and moved to Ghent. She was a singular, highly independent, impeccably stylish, and quite beautiful woman. As long as Lipski had known her, she had been the mistress of a prominent physician in Ghent.

If she had no use for a husband, she seemed to have even less use for a child. She was, apparently, the highly satisfactory center of her own life. Nobody seemed a less likely candidate to accept delivery of a walking, talking, defecating, and otherwise totally demanding package. Still, Lipski had a hunch, and one night early in October he stole up to her small apartment in the center of Ghent to broach the question. Henriette Chaumat looked at him steadily. Unlike so many others, she neither gulped nor drew a fearful breath.

"*Bien sûr,*" she answered unhesitatingly. She would take the child.

More afraid to move by daylight than to disobey the Jewish curfew, Lipski arranged for the transfer to take place the following night at ten o'clock on a tramway platform near the home of Madame Chaumat. Too ashamed to face him after their professions of love for the child, the family now relinquishing Raffi sent him via an intermediary. Wrapped in a blanket against the chill of the early fall evening, Raffi was handed over to his father in silence. Lipski had assumed his child would be asleep at that hour. But Raffi's eyes were anxious and as round as buttons.

"*Papa, papa,*" asked the child, "*pourquoi tu es venu?*" ("Papa, why have you come?")

It was a question that startled Lipski and to which, as he dashed with the swaddled child through the streets of Ghent, he could think of no suitable response. Why, indeed, should it seem strange for a child to find himself in the arms of his own father? But the child was correct. He sensed, even if he did not understand, why it was no longer normal to expect to be in the care of his parents. They had told him as much. So now that his father had reappeared, it could only mean that once again something was very wrong. Raffi repeated the question, as small children will, over and over: "*Papa, pourquoi tu es venu?*"

"For those two long previous weeks I had thought of nothing but questions of where we would find safety," says Lipski. "But now as I was running with my child and he was asking me this question, suddenly questions of my own began to strike me with terrible force. What kind of people would make a man run through the streets like this with his child so that the child would not be murdered? Did this ever happen to anyone else in the history of the world? Could these men be made of the same flesh and bones as I? . . ."

Lipski dashed up the two flights to Madame Chaumat's apartment. Winded, he kissed his son and gave him over. The door shut. Outside, keeping to the shadows, Lipski slipped back to his own hiding place and his waiting wife. He still could not think of an answer to give his son.

The place to which Lipski returned that night was a small storage room in the home of friends whose support had, for several days now, shown no signs of wavering. With the transfer of Raffi safely completed, it actually seemed that for the first time since their flight had begun two weeks earlier, all members of the family were reasonably secure. But it was a security that would be short-lived. Despite the care he took in slipping in and out of the house, he had apparently been spotted by a neighbor who knew that he was a Jew.

So far, Lipski had been lucky with neighbors. If it had not been for those who had warned him as he was walking home the previous month that the Gestapo awaited him, he and his family would have been in an infinitely worse situation than they were now. In all the occupied countries, the files of the local police as well as of the Germans were filled with letters from citizens who knew or else suspected that Jews were hiding, say, one flight up or perhaps in the house across the street. Concierges, in particular, were legendary for missing not so much as an extra heartbeat within the premises they managed. If such information proved correct and resulted in the deportation of the "fingered" Jews, the informants were often rewarded by the Germans.

Sometimes, however, the malevolent neighbor tried first to get his reward from the victim—in exchange, of course, for silence. That is what this neighbor wanted from Lipski. But meeting the terms of his blackmail was out of the question, not simply on principle, but because the dwindling remnant of Lipski's savings was unalterably set aside for the maintenance of his son and, as available, for his wife and himself. There could be only one response to the neighbor's demand. The couple would have to vanish.

Once again Lipski felt he had drawn to the bottom of his reservoir of helpers. But now it was Tanya Lipski who had an idea. If Madame Chaumat seemed like an odd choice for keeper of their son, Tanya's idea of a candidate for their own keeper seemed just as improbable. She was thinking about a short, plain-spoken, hard-working woman named Hermine Van Assche, whose husband and daughter the Lipskis had never met. Before the Germans had come, Hermine had been the family maid.

Very early the next morning, October 12, Lipski rode alone on the tandem bicycle into a poor section of Ghent where he had never been. On Melkerijstraat, a narrow lane of narrow homes, he knocked at the door of No. 8. If there was any confidence in his knock, it was only because this had been Tanya's suggestion. She was normally content to let him make the major family decisions. But when she did volunteer a suggestion, he had learned it was best to listen. She had instincts he did not, and they were rarely wrong. It did not help, however, when Hermine herself opened the door and, seeing her former employer, began to tremble with what he took to be fear. For an instant, he thought she would simply shut the door on him. But even as she trembled, she reached out for his arm to bring him into the house. With a surge of relief and gratitude, he realized that she was not trembling out of fear but because she had been confronted, here in the grey of dawn, with a man she never expected to see again.

"I must explain," says Lipski, "that two families shared this little house. There was Hermine and her husband Ceril. Then there was Ceril's sister, Zulma, and her husband Pieter Henry. Each couple had a child—the Van Assches, a six-year-old girl and the Henrys, a tiny baby. It was lucky that Hermine answered the door, because, of all these people, I knew only her. In fact, the others had already gone to work, taking the children to grandmothers, and Hermine herself had been on her way out the door. If I had been five minutes later, it is possible that for us the rest of the war would have been totally different."

For the first time, Lipski spoke to Hermine in a capacity other than employer. He told her about his family's flight for the last two weeks, right up to the current predicament. Then he asked what he had come to ask. Might there be a tiny spot in the house where he and Tanya could stay for a few days until they could make other arrangements? At the very least, Lipski suddenly realized, he would need a place to stay until dark. It was now just after eight o'clock, and with the bustle on the bright morning streets he could not risk being recognized by yet another potential blackmailer. But on this point Lipski did not have to worry. Hermine was happy to have him stay the day. As for herself, she would also be happy to have him and Tanya stay longer. But she could not speak for the others. It was her brother-in-law who made all final decisions in the household. For the moment, Hermine sat down and wrote a letter to the others, who would be home before her, explaining the situation. Then she was gone. For the rest of the day, Lipski sat quietly behind closed shutters, in the darkened front room of the house, and waited to see what their fate—or today's fate, anyway—would be. Lipski was glad when he thought of how generously he and Tanya had treated Hermine during the time she worked for the family, and he only wished that it was her husband, rather than the other man, who was the decision-maker in this household. It turned out to be, once the family had convened that evening, a most extraneous wish.

"For as long as you need," said Pieter Henry, a short, bristly-haired man who spoke only Flemish. "I am pleased for you and your wife to be our honored guests."

It was only after Lipski returned that same night with Tanya that he learned that Pieter was a man who meant exactly what he said. Until an upstairs storage room could be cleared out for them, they would sleep in the best room in the house—the bedroom of Henry and his wife. Flabbergasted and even appalled at the prospect of heaping dislocation upon an act of grace, the Lipskis tried to refuse. They could easily go up immediately and clear away a corner of the storeroom. But Henry would not allow it.

"This man saw himself first and foremost as a patriot," explains Lipski. "To him, since we, as Jews, were the enemy of his country's enemy, we were his friends. And since, on a purely personal level, we had been good employers of his sister-in-law, he also welcomed us as personal friends. 'For people like you,' he said to us, 'it gives me pleasure to show my respect and to offer you what I can.'"

Lipski does not say what he was thinking about as he fell asleep that night. But he might well have reflected on the curious and unexpected happenstance that while many friends had dispensed a variety of kindnesses during these weeks of flight, only a stranger had offered him and Tanya his own bed. It had been only four nights ago that he had dashed through the darkened streets with his son, wondering how men could be so incomparably brutish as to bring him to such a moment. But now, in this bed of honor, he could also marvel that in the matter of simple decency, men could vault as high as they slither low. They seemed able to do either, moreover, with equal unexpectedness and for equally little reason.

It was an easy fifteen-minute bike ride from the poor section of Ghent where the parents of Raffi Lipski were hidden to the elegant central district where the child now lived in a second-floor apartment with Madame Chaumat. From the time he was handed over that night in October until the following April, Raffi did not leave the apartment. Madame Chaumat needed very nearly all this time to perform a most difficult and delicate task. The child had to have certain basic facts of his life extracted from mind and heart, and others implanted. Abram and Tanya Lipski were no longer his parents; they were simply people who had loved him but who had died in an accident of war. They had been replaced by his aunt—"Tati"—who loved him just as much. He was even lucky enough, she told the child, to have a brand-new name. Gone was Raphael Lipski. In his place was a boy named Nicholas Loubet. Hearing this, the boy scratched his head full of blond curls and stared at the woman as if she were out of touch with reality. Madame Chaumat found herself wishing he was not so happy and secure in the old facts. She wondered if even her formidable and usually triumphant will power would be enough to tear out those old facts. Over and over, she would take him in her lap, or call to him from the kitchen, and drum into him the new facts.

"You are no longer Raffi. You must never use that name again. When I call Nicholas Loubet, only then will you answer. I am your Tati, and you are my Nick. . . ."

"I don't want to be that person. I am Raffi Lipski—"

"*Non, chéri*, nobody will know you by that name. They will know you and love you only by the name I am calling you. Nicholas Loubet. Nick. Nick, Nick, Nick, Nick."

It was well into the winter before Madame Chaumat began to feel that her work, in all its maddening repetition, was finally taking hold. The child at last began to answer to his new name. With pleasure, she heard him call out her own name as well—"Tati, may I have a biscuit?" . . . "Tati, when will the war be over?" Most gratifying of all, references to his real parents had altogether ceased. For a while, Madame Chaumat had begun to wonder if a strong-willed forty-five-year-old woman might not actually be beaten back by an angelic three-and-a-half-year-old in a battle of wills. Now she rested easily, until, one evening in December, she heard a small voice coming from the room of what she had thought was a sleeping child. Curious, she stole to the half-open door and peeked in. The child was sitting up in his bed with a small tan teddy bear in his lap. He spoke in the low tones reserved for a true confidant.

"Teddy, Teddy," he was saying, "I am going to tell you a secret. A secret just for us. Everyone thinks my name is Nick Loubet. Well, that is not my name. My name is like my papa's. But if anyone finds out, we will both be punished. And do you know how? By spanking . . . like *this!*"

The boy turned the teddy bear over and, in quick but light strokes, spanked its backside. Then, setting it back upright, he patted the toy soothingly. "Remember, Teddy, you are the only one who knows the secret and you must never, never tell anyone else. . . ."

Madame Chaumat was startled. She had greatly underestimated the child. In their test of wills, she had not, apparently, won at all. He had merely allowed her to think that she had won. But he had not, either, made a full disclosure to the teddy bear. It was true that by revealing that his real name was not Nick Loubet, he had let out a portion of a highly important confidence. But only a portion. Raffi had not gone so far as to reveal what his name actually was. He had only said it was "just like my papa's." Turning away from the door of his room, Madame Chaumat could feel a new appreciation for the wisdom of this child.

Raffi Lipski's singular beauty, which caused even people in a hurry to pause in the streets and parks, now became a potential problem. It would be improvident to allow him to play or be strolled outside lest he be recognized. Even if the gamble was taken, there remained the delicate question of just what Madame Chaumat could say, even to unsuspecting persons, about where she had acquired this child. Other single women, with more typical and visible family connections, might have claimed him as a nephew with much more credibility than she, whose independence from all such ties was well known. Most of her friends and neighbors, of course, would not have dreamed of causing problems, no matter what they suspected the truth to be. But it was the one viper in the bag of garter snakes, so to speak, against which she had to be on guard. So all that fall and winter the child remained in the apartment. He was not even allowed at the window. For one who, like Henriette Chaumat, believed in the healthful virtues of fresh air, it was a maddening situation.

That is why, early in April 1943, both Madame Chaumat and the Lipskis agreed, through their intermediary, a neighbor named Louisa, that it would be best for "Tati" and "Nick" to relocate in a small village near the city, just as Raffi and his mother had done a year earlier. They picked Astene, a pleasant hamlet not far from Ghent. Here Madame Chaumat could more reasonably put forward the story that Nick was her nephew, in her keeping since his parents had died in the war. But as she began to receive regular visits from the doctor whose mistress she had been for many years, she knew that even here in Astene her story would soon be discredited. In its place, the villagers would congratulate themselves on discerning a far more plausible—and tasty—story. This boy, obviously, must be the love child of the doctor and Madame Chaumat. Sure enough, shortly after the doctor's first visits to her small apartment, she began to notice stares, whispers, and once, when she turned around in the bakery, a smirk from the girl who had just given the child a *baguette* to carry. So the villagers had a love child in their midst. To the extent that this version of the child's origins kept him twice removed from his real identity, Madame Chaumat could not have been more pleased.

Back in the small house on Melkerijstraat, life was also taking a shape which, if it was not ideal, still allowed for a level of survival that was beyond complaint. On the morning after they had slept in their host's bed, the Lipskis set to work preparing their two attic rooms for an occupancy of unknown duration. Their first task was to block out every speck of light from the ample windows that faced both east and west. They would learn to miss sunshine, moonlight, and even the sight of rain pattering and glistening on the old tile roofs of the surrounding houses. But a view out meant a view in, and that was out of the question. Nobody had used the attic for years, and any sign of movement now by day or, worse yet, even a dim sign of light by night would have made the neighbors curious. Still, furnished sparsely with a few chairs, a makeshift bed, a desk, and a few lamps, it was not at all a bad hideaway. An essential feature was a ladder leading to a trapdoor in the roof. On the first moonless nights, Lipski had worked out a rooftop escape route to the next block. He had even taken Tanya, highly dubious, out for a dry run. If the Gestapo ever came knocking, they would steal off with the agility of cat burglars.

"A more delicate problem than hiding from the world outside," says Lipski, "was hiding from the world inside. Silly as it may sound, it was this charming six-year-old girl from whom we had to hide. One word to her friends on the street about the funny new people living in the attic and it could get back to their parents and then . . . who knows what then? That is why, unless the child was asleep or out of the house, we could not come downstairs or move around except in stocking feet. So I devised a simple electric bell system between us and the world downstairs. We had the bell, and they had the buzzer. One bell meant come downstairs—usually they had food awaiting us. Two bells meant come down, but only if we felt like it. Three bells required us to maintain absolute silence.

"You needed ration cards to buy food at this time, of course. For this there was a lively black market, and I had made arrangements. But the food still cost money. I was a lucky man, because all during the Occupation, I had the opportunity to continue earning a life for my family. This was thanks to the manager of the rubber factory, a certain George Buysse. He was my principal client. He could easily have fired me after the Germans took over—they would have loved that. But he kept me on, claiming that I was essential to the ongoing operations. Then, once we went beneath the surface in September 1942, I could no longer appear at my office. At this moment, our number-one worry was not to be caught. But if we were to survive more than a few days, then I had a new worry. How could I support my family? If I had been working for ten years, I might have had enough savings to carry us for a long time. And I also might have made a much earlier decision to go underground. But I had been working less than four years, and we had a baby and no savings. Now that I could no longer show up at the office, I assumed I no longer had work. But Buysse told me not to worry. He would take me off the books but continue to pay me for work which I would do at night.

"For almost two years I worked like a ghost, drawing up construction plans and handling account books. He could have hired a hundred others to do such a job. But he gave me the work and continued to give it to me for the two years we were fugitives. Without it, we would have been lost. Because, you see, these people who hid us were very, very poor. Even Madame Chaumat, despite appearances, had next to nothing. Yet they gave us what money cannot buy—courage and kindness. To have asked them for anything that cost so much as a centime would have been intolerable.

"I want to tell you just one more thing about the manner I was treated in my work. Every few weeks, I would have to review the work with Buysse. We did this at his home—a very large, handsome house located on the factory grounds in Ghent. I always slept over and left early enough so that I could be back in my own hiding place before dawn. This was because I could not leave for the meetings before dark, nor could I return too late lest a German patrol ask what I was doing out on my bike so late. I had false papers, of course, but if they wanted to look me over more closely, I would have been in trouble.

"Anyway, whenever I could, I picked the most rainy, miserable nights to go out, since the chances of being stopped were smallest. So, coming into this beautiful home, my boots were usually covered with mud. Now there were several servants here who could clean boots. Madame Buysse was always at the door to greet me, and she had but to give the word. Do you know how, in ancient times, the wealthy Chinese kept a long fingernail to show they did not do manual labor? Well, this Madame Buysse could have had ten long fingernails. But she took a brush and pail, and while her husband and I went over our work, she cleaned my boots. It was a gesture, a symbol, that until I die I shall never forget.

"The behavior of the Buysse family was an exception to my own finding that the wealthy were—despite their sympathies—more cautious about helping Jews like us than the poor. They had more to lose if they were caught. Poor people like the Henry and Van Assche families, on the other hand, were more willing to take the big risk because they did not worry about losing what they did not have. Being poor, of course, did not give them or anyone else the slightest reason to take on such a responsibility as hiding Jews. To take this step took courage, a pure heart, and a pure motive. In all the time we were hidden Henry and his household never wavered. Sometimes, at night, when we were listening to the BBC, I would try to tell him how badly we felt at being such a long-term burden and danger to him and his family. But he would not listen to that.

"'The only thing I am dreaming,' Henry would say, shrugging off my apologies, 'is for the day to come when I can see you and your wife walk free.'"

· · ·

Henriette Chaumat passed the remainder of the summer of 1943 as uneventfully as could be expected for a highly distinctive bachelor woman bonded to a beautiful and precocious child of suspicious origin. In this small town of Astene, the stares, speculations, whispers, and smirks never abated. Yet she was pleased to endure it all as long as the truth was not discovered. Then, one fine August morning when she and the child were out strolling, she heard from behind the one word that could slice through her like shrapnel.

"Raffi! Raffi!"

She turned around to see two women rush up to the child.

They knelt to touch him, but she pulled him away.

"What are you saying? You've scared my Nick."

"Why . . . this is Raffi Lipski from Ghent—the son of the engineer! Who would not know him?"

"You are mistaken. This is my nephew Nicholas Loubet."

Without further conversation, Madame Chaumat hurried the boy home. She was a woman used to making any and all decisions—even those that would cause others to flinch. But this was a situation in which even she could not contemplate making a decision on her own. Indeed, she was not even clear as to the options. She was certain only that the covenant made between her and the Lipskis when she took the child would now have to be broken. They would have to meet face to face. Through their faithful intermediary, Louisa, the meeting was arranged for the following evening at her apartment. While Louisa stayed upstairs with the child in Madame Chaumat's own apartment, they would decide what to do about his having been recognized.

"This was exactly the sort of chance discovery we had tried to prevent by sending the two of them out of Ghent," says Lipski. "It was bad enough that somebody should recognize Raffi and pronounce a name that had taken so much patience to banish. Still, if these had been people we could trust, I would have been less concerned. But of all the people to have recognized the child, these two women were potentially the most dangerous. They were not the problem themselves. They were merely a pair of sisters who knew the girl friend of Tanya's brother. It was their brother who was the problem. He was the mayor of Astene, and he was a Black Shirt—a Belgian Fascist. Next to delivering my child into the hands of the Gestapo, he was the worst person into whose hands Raffi could fall.

"As a student, and later with my wife, I had enjoyed wonderful evenings of camaraderie and good food in this apartment of Madame Chaumat. But there was no pleasure this time. There was also no clear-cut solution to our problem of what to do about Raffi. In the first place, you cannot imagine what it was, in these times, to find a new hiding place. On short notice it was impossible. Still we would have found something if we felt the danger was too great. But the period of greatest danger—those hours after Raffi was recognized—had already passed. If these sisters were going to tell their brother, I believed they would have done it then. They had come to Astene, surely, to visit him, and they would have had the opportunity to give Raffi away. The fact that nothing had been heard from them confirmed my own instincts about the nature of these sisters. They knew my wife and me, they knew Raffi, and many times they had shown affection for him. I felt in my bones that they would not bring harm to him now. So, all things considered, we decided it was best for him to stay put for now with Madame Chaumat in Astene. Just the same, I wrote these sisters a letter that evening. I can no longer tell you the exact words, but here is the substance: 'We know you have discovered our son. His life is in your hands. But don't suppose for a moment that if you give him over to your brother any one of you will go free. I make you responsible. I hope you have enough heart not to kill an innocent child. But if that happens, you will pay.'"

The three adults were so deep in debate that night that they did not notice at first when the front door was pushed open. Then Abram and Tanya Lipski looked up and, for the first time in almost a year, they saw their son. He stood quite still, dressed in a tasseled bathrobe. Stricken by the surge of their own feelings, they did not know what to say, or what to do, or even what name to call him. But it was the child who spoke first.

"*Bonsoir*, Monsieur Théophile and Madame Elza," he said evenly, calling them by the names of the couple that Tati had told him she was coming to meet in Ghent. "Have you heard the news on the radio? Kharkov has fallen!"

"This is marvelous news," said Madame Chaumat. It was indeed. Eight days earlier, the Germans had at last been pushed back, over a terrain of corpses, from Stalingrad. And now the historic city of Kharkov . . .

". . . But tell me, *choupette*," she said, using her own name of endearment, "what are you doing down here?"

"Louisa has fallen asleep on the couch. But I was awake."

Still the parents could not move or speak. It was their son and it was not their son. To pick him up, kiss and hold him, would have been more than wonderful. It also would have been destructive of all that had been accomplished in a year. Rooted to their seats, they remained silent. But, as their son had done first, Madame Chaumat now saved them the need to do anything at all.

"This was a very singular woman," says Lipski now, "and even though I knew her very well, she remained unpredictable. She took pride in her own self-discipline and she took pride in the self-discipline she had instilled in the child. Now she did something I could never imagine her doing, and yet which was totally in character. She made a test."

"Come here, Nick," said Madame Chaumat. The boy left his station at the door and walked to her side. "Give your hand to Madame Elza." The boy extended his hand and made a bow with his curly blond head.

"Now tell me the truth, Nick, do you think that Madame Elza looks like your mother?"

"Madame Elza is not so beautiful as my mother," said the boy proudly. "My mother was the most beautiful woman in the world."

"And what about Monsieur Théophile? Does he not look like your father?"

"My father, he was much more handsome and much, much bigger than Monsieur Théophile."

"But, Nick, you can see that Monsieur Théophile is very handsome and also very, very tall."

"Ah, but my father was so tall that . . ." The boy turned around and pointed a chubby finger triumphantly at the door. "My father was so tall that he could not even go through this door!"

"And can you tell Monsieur Théophile and Madame Elza what has happened to your daddy and mommy?"

"My daddy and mommy are dead. They have been killed in the war. A bomb came down on top of them. They were lying like this"—the boy rocked back with his eyes closed, hands at his sides and fingers straight, his small features flattened out—"and now they are buried in the ground. But their souls have gone to heaven."

A silence lay on the room. Then Madame Chaumat said, "You've bothered us enough. Now say good night to Monsieur Théophile and Madame Elza. Then give Tati a kiss and go right upstairs to bed. If Louisa wakes up and finds you have gone off without telling her, she will be very angry."

Unconcerned and even saucy at this prospect, the child extended a hand to his parents. Then he reached up to kiss Tati noisily, and ran out the door.

"This story which I have just told you," says Lipski, "*ce n'est pas du roman*—it is not out of a novel. This child who was so courteous, who told us about the fall of Kharkov and also about how we looked when we were dead . . . this was my son who had been so abundant and natural in his love. When we came back to our hiding place that night, for the first time I broke down. My wife was stronger. She did not cry."

Nearly a year passed. In the attic on Melkerijstraat, Lipski bent over a makeshift drafting table and, on miserable nights, delivered his work to George Buysse. Tanya Lipski read one book after another, did sewing, and waited. Years later she would look over at her husband and say, with a mixture of affection and sarcasm,

"Living all that time in an attic with a wonderful husband like mine? It was a pleasure. He is so easy to live with. . . ."

The northward progress of the Allies following the June 1944, invasion of Normandy, which Lipski had followed so avidly on the BBC by pressing his ear to the radio, reached Belgian territory by early August. But it was not until September 6 that they liberated Brussels and Ghent. On that day, almost exactly two years after he had first knocked on this door fearful and nearly hopeless, he and Tanya raced out. They had only one mission in mind. On their tandem bike they set off toward the village of Astene to recover their son.

The nature of the welcome that they would get from the child was, however, problematic. For these two years he had been well drilled with the information that his parents were gone forever. To all appearances, the drill had been successful. These two persons now puffing away on the tandem bike, as he had made abundantly clear in their surreal meeting that night in Ghent, were nothing like his parents. They were "Monsieur Théophile and Madame Elza."

They found him among a gaggle of children who were being permitted to swarm, as if it were a toy, over a newly arrived British tank. "He saw us even before we saw him," says Lipski. "And what should he be shouting as he ran toward us?

"'Papa, Maman . . . Papa, Maman!' And how he hugged and kissed us as warmly as we hugged and kissed him. This was our loving Raffi, restored to us as before. And he talked to us as if it had only been overnight since we had been separated. We never heard again about Monsieur Théophile and Madame Elza. Now you may ask the natural question—did he know we were his real parents that night at Louisa's apartment a year earlier?

"I can only answer that we didn't know then and we still don't know now. Perhaps, being a five-year-old, he had not yet put any boundaries between what is real and what is make-believe. Only he knew the answer to that in his child's mind. Now that he is a man, that answer has also been taken away from him. There will never be an answer. All we can say is il a *joué le jeu*—he played the game."

Despite their jubilation and their hunger to have the child for themselves, however, the Lipskis did not forget that Raffi was more used to living with Tati than with them. And it was not only Tati. There was her friend, the doctor from Ghent, who had given school lessons to Raffi on weekends and provided fatherly companionship. So the Lipskis instituted a two-home program, in which the child only gradually was shifted over to living full time with them. "In all that time," explains Lipski, "Raffi had hardly been out of her sight for a moment. So at first we took him only on weekends. Then three days a week, and then, finally, we reversed the process and sent the child to Tati only on weekends. So he never lost her. Seven years after the war, when our second son, Alex, was born, she came to live with us as one of the family. She played a large role in raising him. But it was Raffi who was her masterpiece."

Abram Lipski has been carrying on a near monologue for over three hours. Though he has grown hoarse, his English has become stronger. His son Alex has brought up sandwiches, cookies, and cold drinks. They have all been eaten, but not by Lipski. Only now does he permit himself a sip of sparkling water. His story has a happy ending and it seems as if he ought to be pleased. He is, after all, able to enjoy comforts, honors, and, most important, a family intact. But in his face there is no repose. Instead, his eyes are hollow and his handsome face sags. But it is not the kind of sagging that comes with fatigue or age. As on an overloaded bridge, it comes from too much weight pressing down.

"You will pardon me if I repeat myself," he says, "but I cannot believe what happened in this war had a precedent in human history. Yes, I know that in the heat of battle it has happened that everyone was killed—not just the healthy men, but the women, children, and old people. I can see, too, that if they choose me, an adult, for the enemy, then I will have to flee for my life. But to seek after a child, like a bandit seeking after a rich man? To make me run like a fool in the street with the child in my arms so that it will not be killed by other men? This was like a *cauchemar*—a waking nightmare. How could this be? And still I have to say that next to what the others went through, that was nothing. Because the others went through the most awful hell that can exist to their deaths. . . ."

Lipski knows that what he has to say isn't news and that he has returned to this statement repeatedly this evening. But he can't help repeating it because he can't come to terms with it. Now it is almost midnight and Lipski has at last fallen as silent as the rest of the house. He sits that way for quite a while, those questions seemingly fastened to his mind. His pale-hued eyes look my way but really beyond. They are disconcerting and even a bit frightening because what he was spared is what they see, and always will.

In that Rosh Hashanah week, Alex Lipski keeps a promise to take me to the house on Melkerijstraat in Ghent, forty miles from Brussels, where his parents had been hidden. Alex is thirteen years younger than his brother Raffi but, quite apart from that gap in their ages, it would be difficult to tell that they are brothers. Raffi is big, blond, and relaxed. Alex is slender, dark, and intense. As we set off for Ghent in his sports sedan, Alex snaps into the dashboard a cassette tape of songs by Jacques Brel, Belgium's national torch singer. He sings along, throwing himself into the songs in a keening, intense tenor. His brother, driving into town for an ice-cream soda the evening before, had been more inclined to mumble sleepy Hebrew lullabies.

Though Alex Lipski has always gone with his family on New Year's visits to the home where Pieter Henry and his family moved after the war, he had never been to the house in the attic of which his parents had been hidden for two years. French is the language of Brussels, but here, just an hour's drive away in Ghent, the people speak only Flemish—and that with a vengeance.

That is why Alex has brought along his Aunt Flore, who speaks Flemish. The fourth member of the group, whom we have picked up in Ghent, is Zulma Henry, a stocky, handsome woman of about sixty-five. It was her sister-in-law, Hermine, who had worked for the Lipskis as a "day woman" and her husband, Pieter, who had authorized their preservation.

Now, on this pleasant Tuesday morning, we all stand a bit uncertainly in front of the house on Melkerijstraat. This neighborhood was not the best in the war days and it is not the best now. Red and yellow late summer roses bloom on a trellis over the door, but the dark brown shutters on all the windows are closed. Alex pushes the buzzer. Several minutes pass before a suspicious concierge finally comes to the door. In Flemish he tells us coldly that he is not empowered to allow anyone inside—not even for the briefest look around. But at the insistence of Aunt Flore, he agrees to see if his boss is available.

More time passes before a pale young man dressed in a business suit appears at the door. A few words are exchanged uncomfortably in Flemish and then in French. He is not very communicative in either language, but only, as it turns out, because he is an Englishman named John Smith and he would much prefer to speak his native language. His London-based electronics firm, together with a local partner, has recently converted this house into an office and warehouse for the distribution of phonograph components. He is straining hard, at first, to understand just why this mismatched group of strangers would want to visit such an unremarkable house. Even when it is explained to him that the attic had been a hiding place for the parents of Alex during the war, he remains dubious. But he does agree to give us a brief tour of the premises. The living room, containing crates and only a few stray pieces of furniture, is quite forlorn. Seeing nothing familiar, Zulma goes to an out-of-the-way spot under the stairs.

"Here is where Monsieur Lipski put the bell system," she says. "One bell—come down. Two bells—come down if you please. Three bells—danger. When an unexpected knock came at the door, we always rang three times before answering it. But in all that time, the wrong people never came. We had to be particularly careful when my husband brought home coal in a hand wagon from a cache we had in the countryside. Nobody could understand why we used so much coal."

The group troops up the stairs, past the second-floor quarters where the two couples had lived, to the top floor. It is divided, as it was then, into a small and a large room. Both rooms are swept by clear light from east and west, making this the most pleasant space in the house.

"These are the windows which my father always said were the most tightly sealed in Ghent," says Alex Lipski. Now they look out, once again, on a jumble of old tile rooftops. It was a vista which, after the first hours of their twenty-two months here, Abram and Tanya Lipski never saw.

"Here they had a kitchen," says Zulma, pointing to a spot where a hot plate had been, ". . . and here a fire, there a bed, here a chair, up above a ladder to the roof, in front a place to walk."

John Smith stands to one side, visibly perplexed by this recital. "You say your parents were hidden here during the war?" he says, finally, to Alex.

"For almost two years."

"Pardon me, but I don't quite understand. Why were they hidden here?"

"They were Jews," Alex Lipski fired back, staring at the man with a trace of impatience.

"Oh . . . I see," says Smith. "I'm sorry, I didn't realize. . . ."

Downstairs, Zulma stops for a moment on her way out the door. "Do you see this spot?" she says. "Once my husband came home on a warm night and he found the door was already open. And here was Monsieur Lipski, listening to a broadcast of the BBC. This was always dangerous because the Germans forbade it. But here the door was open wide. My husband said to him, 'If you leave the door open like this, the Gestapo will invite themselves in, and then we won't have you anymore.'"

"That's my father for you," says Alex Lipski. "He would seal up the windows the tightest in Ghent, and devise an excellent bell system, and then he would listen to the BBC with the door open. That's him all right!" Thinking about this, Alex lets out a loud delighted and unexpected laugh.

Luckily, Pieter Henry was more attentive to security than the man he was hiding. He took care, for example, not to bring in supplies except by night, lest his neighbors notice that his household was consuming heavily. And his ability to keep a secret was absolute. Tanya Lipski tells the story that once, in strictest secrecy, Pieter's brother had confided to him that he was hiding a Jew in his house. In the spirit of fraternal competition, that made this brother quite pleased with himself. But Pieter merely gave him a dubious look.

"Aren't you afraid?" he asked.

"No," said his brother with pride.

"If I had a Jew in my house," said Pieter solemnly, "I'd be scared."

It is only a five-minute walk from this modest house to the even smaller house on Komerijstraat where Pieter and Zulma Henry live today with their daughter, recently divorced, and her two small sons. Now that Pieter has a bad right leg, even a short walk is no longer feasible, but as the others return, he is at the door waiting, the two grandchildren peeking out from either side of him. He is a short, stocky, almost gnomish man with bristly brown hair. Peering through thick eyeglasses, he welcomes me with an immediate and four-square smile. If this is the same smile that greeted Lipski, not only a stranger but a fugitive, thirty-four years ago, it must have seemed worth more than gold.

Small as it is, the living room has been furnished with large stuffed chairs, an ample sofa, and a big-screened television set. The fabrics are big, happy florals and the rug is a rough, warm rag weave. The only objects which set this snug and simple living room apart from others are on the mantelpiece. There, in a leather case, is the medallion of Yad Vashem. Beside it, in a plexiglass frame, is the certificate that designates Pieter and his wife, Zulma, as Righteous of Nations. Next to them is a large, upright, alert-looking, stuffed red squirrel.

Pieter Henry is not a man of expansive philosophical sentiments. When he is asked why he, a stranger, was willing to hide
Abram and Tanya Lipski, he rears back as if the question hardly
needs asking. "They were people and they were in trouble," he
says. "Besides, I was a soldier once, and I know what it is to have
no place to sleep properly. So when Hermine, my sister-in-law,
came to me to ask if we could hide them, I said why not?"

But many others, including good friends, had also felt a first
rush of sympathy for the Lipskis and their son. Yet when they
heard the Gestapo trucks rumbling close by at night, that sympathy
was usually extinguished by fear. Pieter, on the other hand, had
hidden them in an already crowded house, bringing them food
and coal, taking away their refuse, for almost two years. Had he
not become scared like the others? Had he not felt, at some time
in those two years, that he had done enough?

At these questions, Pieter draws himself up straight—slightly
slanted, actually, because of the bum leg. "Yes, of course there were
times when we were scared," he says. "But we didn't mind. This is
part of being a patriot. I come from a family of patriots." Pieter
hobbles to an oak cabinet over which hangs a cage holding a small
yellow canary. From a back drawer he brings out a bronze medal
which, at first glance, looks identical to the one from Yad Vashem.
But this medal is struck with the likeness of King George above the
inscription "*Rex Britanniae omni Rex in India.*" On the back is
inscribed the name Emile Henry.

"This is the medal my father got from the British in the First
World War," says Pieter Henry. "He was a sharpshooter. And he
also hid an underground chief. One day this man was captured
by the Germans, and they found a piece of paper in his pocket
on which were the words 'Emile Henry.' So they began looking
for two people—Emile and Henry. They never found such people,
and they never found my father. So you see my father was a
man of deeds before me. It is my family tradition. So when
Hermine asked me to hide these people, I did not think it
unnatural."

Alex Lipski listens closely as his Aunt Flore translates Pieter's rough Flemish. He does not say much himself. He continues to listen, on the way back to Brussels, as Flore reaffirms that it was the man's *Kinderstube*—his upbringing from childhood—as a patriot that led him to save the Lipskis. "This was a patriotism that he drank with his mother's milk," says Flore.

But now Alex shakes his head vigorously. "I don't think that was really it," he says, "even if Pieter did keep talking about patriotism. It is not an act of war to do what they did. It was just an act of human feelings."

Raffi and Selma Lipski like to call their home "the kibbutz." It is a rambling, floor-through apartment in a three-story house on Avenue Hamoir, several minutes' walk from the city observatory. This neighborhood of large houses is, in truth, an unlikely place for an outpost so down-to-earth as a kibbutz. It is a more exclusive neighborhood, certainly, than the one a few miles away where the senior Lipskis live. But Raffi and Selma have a point. While Brussels remains a city of formality—dinner invitations are written correctly, maids and butlers serve correctly, and guests dress correctly—the style in all such matters is, at their house, explicitly casual.

The apartment is furnished comfortably but plainly. Nobody tries to keep the premises pristine. Guests needn't call far in advance. A few hours' notice will do. But when you arrive, be prepared to be accepted without ceremony. Selma will not hesitate to serve a pot-luck dinner on the formica table in the kitchen—something most Brussels matrons would no more do than serve in the bathroom. But above all, Raffi and Selma call their home the kibbutz because here members of the Jewish community from anywhere in the world who are sojourning in Brussels will always find a welcome.

On this particular evening Raffi Lipski sits on the living room couch after a late dinner with the textbook for an accounting course in his lap. He is in good humor tonight. For the last year he has been confined to a most uninteresting diet due to danger-ously high cholesterol. But this week he has been given a clean bill of health. If anything, the bottom seems to have dropped out of his cholesterol count. Raffi has celebrated this milestone, just now, with his first liberated dinner. With Selma's approval, he has eaten salami, sausages, a hard-boiled egg, several kinds of creamy cheese and ice cream—all the delicacies that the Jewish and Belgian elements in his palate conspire to love. Now, after applying himself only very modestly to his accounting lesson, he puts aside the textbook and begins to talk about Madame Chaumat. Selma joins us after putting the three boys to sleep. Her hair is pulled back with a ribbon, showing off her big, dramatic ears.

"You should talk to my wife about this woman," says Raffi. "She knows more about her than I do. More than my father, too."

"It is true," Selma says matter-of-factly, sitting down on the sofa beside her husband. A long-fingered hand slips across his shoulders. "The reason I know a great deal about Tati," Selma continues, "is because she used to come here on Sundays for the noon meal with us. Afterward, my husband would retire for an hour's nap. And I would stay with her in the kitchen. Then I would ask her about everything that touches on this husband of mine—his reactions, his moods, his attitudes. If he goes into a bad humor with no direct explanation, I want to know why. Normally he is a man of wonderful disposition, and there must be a reason, even if it is hidden. If he can't stand somebody or something, why? It is no secret that we are formed as adults out of our lives as children. So while Raffi napped, I inquired into his early life with Tati. If he slept an extra half-hour, we talked an extra half-hour. In this way, I learned as much about Tati as about my husband.

"This was a difficult but remarkable woman. She was white-haired from an early age, slender, and very dynamic. And though you would see a severe, arbitrary, and hard exterior, she had a pure and warm heart inside. I think this exterior was put on like a shell as the result of a traumatic and bitter childhood in Paris. She told me once that her parents did not want her. They had wished for a boy. She never got along with anyone in her family, and when she was only eighteen, she severed all ties and came here to

Belgium. And this shell that she came with, she never shook off. But she always remained, too, *une vraie femme parisienne*. Until the day she died at age seventy-seven, she never wore a dress that was not of beautiful fabric and cut. Her shoes were always classic but totally stylish. And though she never had any money to speak of, whatever she bought for the house was in exquisite taste and would not have looked out of place in the quarters of a princess. If she bought silver, it was plain silver, but of the most impeccable quality. If she bought a vase, it was a vase of subtle but elegant shape. You hear it said that we have fine linens here in Belgium, but you would be hard put to find linens of such fineness in the homes of most Belgians. And though everything she bought for herself or for her house was meant to please her, it was also meant to please the men in her life. She was a real mistress—"

"Not mistress," says Raffi. "You mean housekeeper."

"Mistress, too," insists Selma. "*Tout pour l'homme.*"

"I don't deny that she had a need to please the men in her life," says Raffi. "But she also had a compulsion to dominate people as much as she could. And this contradictory attitude led her to be unable to live with any person older than . . . two years! When my brother Alex was that age, for example, I remember once they got into an argument, and she said, 'Who is the master here?' "

Selma draws back and gives her husband a look of incredulity. "Raffi," she says, "you don't think that I have arguments with my children? Do you think that I don't say to the child, 'I am your mother and I have my reasons?' Is that so bad?"

"All I can say is that this was a woman who never lived with anybody because she could never get along with anybody. Even my mother. Tati lived in our home as a member of the family when my brother was an infant. She could have stayed forever. But when she left the house and went back to Ghent, it was because she could not get along with my mother. Notice I did not say my mother could not get along with her. When Tati left, she herself said, 'Your mother is a wonderful, fine woman and I have nothing against her. It is just that I cannot stand her!'

"I will tell you a story about Tati that shows just how strong a person she was. This goes back to the war, when she and I were living in Astene while my parents were hidden in the attic of Pieter Henry. One morning she was riding her bike in town and she had a little collision with a German soldier who was also on a bike. Well, it really was nothing, and nobody was hurt. But in the exchange of words that ensued she did not feel that he had been a proper gentleman. Now this is a woman who can ill afford to draw attention to herself and, therefore, to me. She should have breathed a sigh of relief that nothing more came of the incident. But what do you think she does? She goes to the local head-quarters of the Wehrmacht and demands to see the commanding officer. She makes a formal complaint to him personally about the behavior of this soldier. And do you think she goes to do this alone? Not Tati. She takes a child along in her arms. This child is me. While she describes the incident to this commander, I am playing around his office. They had only to take a look at me with my pants down to see that I was circumcised according to Jewish law. But I must say that this was one prohibition Tati drilled into me right away—I must never, never make 'peepee' in the park.

"The next morning came a thump on the door. It was an officer of the Wehrmacht standing there with a soldier in tow. 'Is this the man who behaved rudely toward you?' he asked.

"'Yes,' said Tati without hesitation. And they went away.

"Again, on the following morning, that same officer appeared. This time he wanted her to come with him. Well, you can imagine how people who harbored Jews grew nervous even at the passing in the road of a German truck. So this request—I should say this order—ought to have been enough to give anyone a heart attack on the spot. Anyone but Tati. She simply picked me up and went with the officer in his jeep. We were driven to an airfield.

"'I have something to show you,' said the officer.

"There, far on the periphery of the airfield, was this soldier, with a full pack on his back, walking on his knees. He had to walk around the airfield like this three times. It was his punishment for having had the misfortune to bump into Madame Chaumat and not to say he was sorry."

"The reason my husband knows this story, by the way," says Selma, "is because I repeated it to him after Tati told me. It is not a story that she ever told his parents. I don't deny that she was a strong person, but she never tried to dominate me. From our first meeting, thirteen years ago, we got along fine. That was in Switzerland, where I was vacationing with my family. Raffi was working at the time in Lausanne. Madame Chaumat was also there. At that time, Raffi had gone out with quite a few girls, but he had only just met me. And he brought me around to see this Tati, whom he was always talking about. After this introduction, she said to him, *'Elle est bien'*—she's okay. Of course, she only told me this much later.

"From that time onward we got along with much pleasure and no problems. And it has been the same for my children as for me—which is not to be taken for granted. Like all children, mine have their dislikes. They would rather not, for example, have guests at the dinner table. Not even their grandparents. They like to have the attention for themselves. But with Tati there was no such problem. They do not yet understand what happened in the war—not exactly, at least. But they did sense that she was someone special, deserving their best feelings. And even though she was more difficult with them than others in their lives, they were less difficult. In time, they will learn how right their instincts were.

"Our relationship with Tati is not typical. We know many young adults here in Belgium who were hidden during the war. Otherwise they would not be here. But after the liberation their parents came back—if they survived—and said their heartfelt thanks to the savior and took back their child. If the parents did not survive, then perhaps an uncle or cousin came to take the child. Either way—*c'était fini*. It wasn't that the parents were not grateful. It was just that the wartime life had been artificial and now they went off to resume an old life or start a new one. But my husband's parents never completely took back the child. They went on keeping Tati as part of the family as long as she was alive—not only the existing family, not only the second son born seven years after the war, but the next generation, who are my own children."

"It has been the same with the people who saved my parents," says Raffi. "Each New Year's Day they go to the home of Pieter and they exchange presents. This has occurred without interruption for more than thirty years. You might say that this is only right and natural. But, as my wife says, this kind of continuity is exceptional. And when the daughter of Pieter and Zulma was married, where do you think the wedding took place? Right in the house where you came last week to eat Rosh Hashana dinner."

Raffi's eyes flickered and closed while he spoke. The accounting textbook, which had lain open on his stomach, is now shut on the floor. "If you will excuse me, I am going to take a five-minute nap," he says, and even these words are carried under by sleep.

"This is my husband for you," says Selma. "In five seconds, he can fall asleep. In five minutes, he can wake up refreshed. Come, I'll show you some things we've stored in the pantry that belonged to Madame Chaumat."

As she sweeps out of the living room with her long stride, Selma pulls up short at a shelf of books. "Do you see these old cookbooks? They were hers. French women were not in the habit of using cookbooks, so in this sense she was quite progressive. See how she has marked the margins with her own notes? Here she has written out her own recipes for a seafood soufflé . . . for a fruit tart . . . and a recipe for rabbit pie. She hoped to improve her cooking, but believe me this woman did not need a book to produce superb food. As a young woman in Ghent, she often had my father-in-law and other poor students over for dinner. They did not eat caviar, but according to him they ate food which would be the envy of people who ate caviar. As poor as she was herself, she always set out a splendid table. She also knew every mushroom in the forest, every berry in the field. She and Raffi would make expeditions all around Astene to gather these delights. Others ate poorly during the war, but those two never lacked for anything."

Selma continues to the pantry, where she climbs up on a stool to reach a high shelf. "Look at these things from her kitchen." She hands down a set of earthenware soup bowls, splash-glazed in chocolate brown and hand-thrown in the rustic style that is in vogue today, but somehow fresher and finer. Down comes a large tureen of blue-and-white porcelain, aswirl with butterflies and flowers done in the swift, sure strokes of the watercolorist. Then comes a fat teapot, then a set of wineglasses etched lightly with flowers, then four candlestick holders in the shape of a squirrel, a woodchuck, a hare, and a fox. Once, reaching too far, Selma almost comes crashing down off the stool. But if she shows any concern, it is only for the beauty of the things that belonged to Tati.

"We have nearly all her possessions," says Selma, finally coming down off the stool. "All but her clothing. Whatever she wore, as I told you, was beautiful and stylish. But it is one thing to use objects which belonged to the dead, and another to wear their clothing. So I gave all the clothing to charity. She's been dead now for just over a year. For us, it was quite sudden, though she had not been feeling well for several months. But she would not admit it to herself and she hid it from us. Many old people go to the doctor at the drop of a hat. But she was too independent for that. She insisted that whatever was wrong, she could take care of it herself. Perhaps if her friend the doctor were still alive, she would have allowed him to make an examination. Well, eventually, one day she found herself too sick even to move. So she let us take her to the hospital. She seemed to rally quite well there. But then, one day when Raffi and his father were out of the country on business, she died. It was funny, but when I got to the hospital, the nurses gave me all her personal things unquestioningly. Raffi and I had visited so much they just assumed we were her children. After I arranged for the funeral I went back to her apartment to take care of things there and also to see if she left a will. She had never uttered a word about this because, I think, she didn't want to worry us. All that I could find was a handwritten paper from fifteen years earlier. Well, I am a person more animal than rational, and my instincts told me that this was not the only will. So I called a notary whom she knew. Sure enough, he did have a will from her, made out only a month earlier. It was a good thing I found it because it turned out that she did not want to be buried at all. She wanted her body donated to science."

Selma goes next to a chest in the dining room and brings out a small jewel box. It contains a strand of small matched pearls, a white diamond in a plain setting, and a silver pin in the shape of an airy naiad, exquisitely tooled in the art-nouveau style. Beneath the jewel box is an album. It is filled with snapshots that appear to be from the flapper era, with stylish people posing contentedly at the seaside, in a park, beside a fountain. The men are sharply dressed in fitted jackets over baggy pants, and they wear white Panama hats. Then there is a young woman, perhaps not yet out of her teens, in some of the photos who is reedy, dark, and erect. Though the men smile gaily or languidly, she looks directly at the camera neither smiling nor, despite the evident good times, even hinting at a smile. In her long, straight dresses she is elegant, severe, and compelling. You would not think to call her beautiful because, with her, beauty is not the point. If she is on intimate terms with any man in these snapshots, it does not show.

"You should not get the wrong idea from my husband about one thing," says Selma. "He may be right that Tati could not live with a man. But that doesn't mean she lacked excellent invitations. When she was just nineteen and newly arrived in Belgium she was proposed to by a young man who was heir to a sugar factory in Tirlemont. He was handsome and wealthy. For a poor young girl, this was a dream. But she refused him. When she told me about this, I was very relieved. '*Heureusement pour moi*, Tati, that you did not accept,' I said to her. 'Otherwise you would not have been in Ghent to save my husband.'

"My own wedding was a very big affair. It was held here in the Great Synagogue of Brussels. At the end of it all, when it came time for me to throw my bouquet, I saw all the bridesmaids standing before me. And I thought, Whom shall I throw it to? A silly question suddenly seemed terribly important. Then—I don't know why—I decided, I won't throw my bouquet to any of the bridesmaids. I will throw it to her. It happened quickly and I didn't think any more about it. Not until I was going through the belongings in her apartment on the day she died. And at the end of this album, pressed against the back cover, I found the bouquet. She had pressed and dried it, preserving every petal of those six yellow roses." Selma holds them out now, still bound by a yellow ribbon. "And this was a woman," says Selma, "in whom you might easily think there was not a tiny grain of softness."

It is almost midnight by the time Selma has finished showing off the cookbooks, kitchenwares, jewels, albums, and other memorabilia of which she, by common consent, is chief curator and fiduciary. Even Abram Lipski would not deny her that role. He has neither need nor desire, in any case, to preserve a single object from those days. He carries it all within. Now, quietly, Selma comes back to the living room, where Raffi still lies on the couch, napping. He is thirty-seven years old. In the year of his birth, 1939, the Germans began to draw up the secret plan—this was, to be sure, only one detail in a much blacker and grander plan—for the first walled ghetto since medieval times. It was to be in his father's hometown of Lodz. They would make it into a slave-labor camp for one hundred and sixty thousand Jews, replacing those who died with fresh deportees from outside. It went on like this for five years. Then, just as Raffi Lipski and his parents were being reunited in Ghent at the end of summer, 1944, the slaves of Lodz were advised that they would be "transshipped" to new work camps in Germany. But the trains went only as far as the gates of Auschwitz. So ended the generations of Jewish citizens, not as ink stains—the name by which Lipski had heard Jews called as a child—but as bone ash and vapor.

Selma goes next to the back bedrooms where the three boys are sleeping. Like all young boys, they sleep in anything but normal positions. The oldest, David, lies on his back in his underwear, his arms flung back, a shock of dark hair covering his eyes, his mouth open. His pillow is on the floor. This has been yet another perfect autumn day turned into a perfect autumn night in Brussels, and a bit of moonlight filters through the trees outside the bedroom window, falling on the dresser top. There it catches the silver of the pin which the boy had worn on his breast to his grandfather's Rosh Hashana dinner. *Zechor*: it means remember those who disappeared, one by one, million by million, into the dark. But for David and his brothers, it also means remember those—Tati, Pieter with his bum leg, and the others—on whose account they will wake up to the light.

EPILOGUE, 1999

In November of 1998, Abram and Tanya Lipski had been dead for more than a decade, and the three sons of Raffi and Selma Lipski were married men. Two of them were awaiting their firstborn children. Raffi at age fifty-nine, with his blue eyes, flushed cheeks, and halo of silver hair, retains the angelic look of his childhood—as well as a striking resemblance to his father. He and Selma and their old dog now live in a large house—too large says Selma—in a wooded section of Brussels favored by diplomats. As one enters, there's a graceful armoire on the left and an oriental carpet on the floor, both of which were willed to the couple by Madame Chaumat.

While most of the wartime generation of the Henry and Van Aasch families have died, Raffi and Selma carry on a warm relationship with Zulma and Pieter Henry's daughter, who as a schoolgirl had kept the secret of the guests in the attic despite the fears of Abram and Tanya that she was too young to understand the consequences.

And the shadow of long-ago events hangs over the Lipski family despite their good luck then and since. In a startling judgment, Selma says that she always felt her husband and his parents were born at exactly the same time.

"The same time?"

"Yes," explains Selma, "because they all had to be hidden in 1942. That was the event that shaped the rest of their lives." It has also shaped Raffi's brother Alex, although he was born after the war, as Alex revealed

when he spoke of his son's battle with cancer of the lower leg. After months of debilitating chemotherapy, radiation, and surgery, the cancer persisted. Doctors called for a doubling, even tripling of chemotherapy and radiation, even though the ten-year-old was weak. The intensified regime could have been enough to cure him—or to finish him off. Alex compares the situation to "being on the election ramp at Auschwitz. You had to go to the left or to the right. But not down the middle."

The boy withstood the new treatment. It killed the cancer, not him. "As my father had to fight for Raffi," says Alex, "I had to fight for the life of my son."

Sietske Postma and Family

On a June morning in 1941, a twenty-year-old Dutch woman named Nurit Hegt went with her mother and her sister Reina to the town hall in Amsterdam where, by Nazi order, they were to be issued identification cards marking them as Jews. By then an entire year had gone by since the Germans had conquered Holland. But for those Jews who chose to be optimistic there was still time to take comfort in the belief that if only they would fulfill each German wish to the letter, nothing too awful would come to pass.

Nurit, however, was not an optimist and her instincts told her that no level of compliance would save the Jews from the worst. She was not, moreover, the type to keep her feelings under her hat. Even though Reina was older by three-and-a-half years, it was Nurit who had always been the independent and headstrong one in the family. Since the death of her beloved father when she was sixteen, Nurit and her mother had argued frequently. Now, with her mother's impending marriage to a man Nurit did not like, the arguments were worse than ever. At that very moment, seeing that in the town hall there were two lines for ID cards— one for Jews and one for everyone else—Nurit suddenly found herself in a new exchange of words.

"I was quite blond then," she explains. "I looked exactly like a shiksa. Nobody would ever take me for a Jew. So when I saw these two lines, I said, 'Mother, are you crazy? Why should I get into the Jewish line? I don't look Jewish. My name doesn't sound Jewish.★ I am not circumcised, like a boy. Who will know the difference?'"

Nurit would have qualified as a good crossover candidate in more than her "Aryan" looks. She came from a family of barely observant Jews who, on her mother's side, had been Dutch for three hundred years. Generation by generation, the old orthodoxy had been lost until only a few traditions remained. At Passover, the family still gathered for a Seder. On Sabbath eves, a white table-cloth was still spread, and as a child, Nurit had been highly displeased at a prohibition against riding her bicycle to her grandparents' house on that day of rest. Though Mr. Hegt had once brought in a private tutor in Judaism for his daughters, those lessons had lasted less than a year.

So it was only those few ongoing symbols—the Seder, the white tablecloth, and the bike ban—which still outwardly identified this family with their religious heritage. They were more Dutch than Jewish. At that very time, Reina was engaged to a Christian boy. Though her mother drew the line at this level of assimilation, Nurit herself didn't mind. In fact, while she now had a Jewish boyfriend named Kurt, before him she had dated a Christian boy herself— until *his* parents had objected. She fancied that if the right fellow came along, she might well do it again.

But when it came now to Nurit's impulse to cross over to the "Aryan" line, her mother would not hear of it. "You are a Jew and it is forbidden for a Jew to go to the other line," she said. "You are

★Nurit's given name was Noortje—classic Dutch. She took the name Nurit in Israel. It is the Hebrew word for a desert flower.

also one of the family. If you do such a thing, not only will you be in danger but we will be in danger."

"Then maybe I won't live at home anymore," Nurit said to her.

More than thirty years after this exchange, Nurit's own daughter—also barely twenty and unmarried—would strike out on her own and, on a bookstore clerk's meager salary, manage to keep her own little apartment. But in orderly, stolid Holland in 1941, an unmarried daughter did not move out so easily. A child living at home, moreover, felt compelled to obey her parent. So, despite her instincts, Nurit remained in line until her turn came to be issued a detailed, two-part ID card. On each half was her photo, a set of fingerprints, her signature, the signature of the issuing officer, and a register number. Dominating both halves of the card was a large letter "J."

By accepting that mark most Dutch Jews, of course, were ensuring their own end. Of about 110,000 who registered, three quarters would be murdered within three years. For Nurit, this same act would change her life in a very different way—not only the outward events but also her interior life as a Jew. Given her feelings just then, however, if those changes had been previewed for her she almost certainly would have hooted in disbelief.

Nurit Hegt would have hooted as well at any preview of what the Germans had in store for her. And in this she would have been joined by all Dutch Jews. No Western Europe Jewish community had firmer roots than theirs. Thanks to the long-standing Dutch penchant for tolerance of those who could bring them prosperity, Jews who were expelled from Spain and Portugal in the sixteenth century had found a safe haven here. They had names like Belmonte, Teixeira, Laguna, Fonseca, Pardo, and de Pinto. A bloc of directors of the East India Company, chartered by the Crown to make money in the New World, were Sephardic Jews. Having been authorized to settle first in Rotterdam, the Jews soon established communities in Amsterdam, Groningen, and The Hague. By the late seventeenth century, they were being joined by the first trickle of "Ashkenazi" Jews arriving from Germany. These newcomers were mostly paupers, and the well-to-do Sephardim looked down on them in much the same way that, several hundred years later, the German Jews already entrenched in American cities would look down on the newly arriving Jews of Eastern Europe.

The Dutch Jews cultivated a close relationship with the House of Orange in the seventeenth century—even to the extent of officially celebrating certain royal birthdays in their synagogues. When the Dutch state nearly went bankrupt in 1748 and again in 1750, it was the financier de Pinto who reorganized the debt and averted catastrophe. The royal secretary wrote to him that "you have saved the state." Members of the royal court were often entertained at the city or country estates of Sephardic grandees, just as later European rulers would avail themselves of Rothschild hospitality. Yet, despite such apparent chumminess, the Dutch Jews were officially barred from all but certain lines of business. They were forbidden from entering most professions except, principally, medicine. The inevitable result was a galaxy of noted Jewish physicians. The Jews, it must be said, seemed happy enough to prosper in their authorized commerce and—particularly in the case of the Sephardim—to keep their society closed and, in certain instances, to hold to traditions too archaic even for the Dutch. The town records of Amsterdam, for example, show that in 1712 the burgomaster refused the application of Benjamin da Costa to marry his cousin Sara Suasso because neither had yet reached the age of twelve years.

Though carefully regulated in commerce and, by their own choice, at a cultural distance from the society around them, the Dutch Jews were never ghettoized, and their civic rights never ceased to expand. When the Enlightenment brought fully franchised legal rights for the first time to many European Jews, their Dutch counterparts were already well ahead in the game. William III, stadtholder from 1672 to 1702, had seen to it, for example, that the wording of oaths required for certain professions was adjusted to be acceptable to Jews. In the nineteenth century, the Dutch government recognized and even extended financial aid to a full range of Jewish educational and benevolent institutions. By the beginning of the twentieth century, Jews were workers, traders, teachers, doctors, lawyers, and journalists very much in proportion to their numbers. And the once supreme Sephardic Jews had, as a group, all but disappeared. They had no way to replenish themselves as the still-arriving Ashkenazim did. The two groups, which once would not deign to share a synagogue, were now thoroughly intermarried. Nurit herself was the product of such a union. Her father's name—Hegt—was pure Ashkenazic. But her mother's maiden name was Rodrigues-Lopez, and that side of the family could trace itself back a dozen generations or more to the expulsion from Iberia. Nurit was to be the only survivor of that maternal line.

In Holland, as in France and Belgium, the Germans at first circled around the Jewish question with stealth. In all three countries, the first summer months after the Occupation in 1940 were allowed to pass quietly. Certain Germans even hinted that Jews would be treated like other citizens.

When the first anti-Jewish measures came, they did not even mention the victims by name. One, taking effect on August 5th, was a ban on *shechitah*, or ritual slaughter—"koshering"—of edible animals under Mosaic law. With what seems now a macabre sense of irony, the Germans called this new law Avoidance of Cruel Practices in Slaughter. Another law, enacted August 20, gave the newly appointed Reichskommissar of Holland, the Austrian Artur Seyss-Inquart, the right to dismiss civil servants at will. Then, on October 18th, the Germans got down to real business. They ordered an "Aryan attestation" form sent out to all education departments in Amsterdam—Form A to be signed by Aryans and Form B to be signed by Jews. This required, obviously, a legal definition of who was who. Seyss-Inquart simply followed, with only the slightest changes, the Nuremberg racial laws of 1935. On October 22, it was decreed that all Jewish businesses had to be registered—the first step toward expropriation and looting of assets. By the following June 1941, all Jews carried the big black "J" on their identification cards. In July came the decree that Jews must wear the yellow star on their breast. Dutch Jewish children were commonly told by their elders that though this step was meant to humiliate them, they must regard it as a badge of honor.

In the beginning, the Dutch Jews did not take all this lying down. When Dutch Nazis raided their neighborhoods, working-class Jews fought back so vigorously that on one occasion a uniformed attacker was fatally mauled. One of the first frontal attacks in Holland against the Germans occurred in Amsterdam at a Jewish-owned ice-cream parlor called Koko. When a German patrol entered the place one evening in early February 1941, a jury-rigged ammonia gun behind the counter was set off in their faces. Though no serious injuries occurred, the Germans saw fit to put one of the co-owners— a German refugee named Ernst Cahn—before a firing squad. In addition, they sent four hundred young Jewish "hostages" to Buchenwald and then on to Mauthausen. Roused to a protest of their own by this action, Dutch workers led by longshoremen went on strike all over Holland, shutting down ports, factories, and even the Amsterdam trolley cars. The German army commander in Holland, General der Flieger Christiansen, proclaimed martial law in the northern provinces and warned of the death penalty for those who continued to strike. In three days the strike was broken and the "guilty" Dutch cities of Amsterdam, Hilversum, and Zaandam were forced to pay fines of eighteen million guilders.

As for those four hundred young hostages, they were set to work toting rocks out of a pit at Mauthausen—work so brutish that, despite their youth and good health, many soon began to die of exhaustion and others hurled themselves headfirst into the pit, causing German complaints that the rocks were being splattered with blood and brains.

As an employee of the post office, Nurit Hegt had felt the effects of the first really nasty German measures before the end of 1940—a full six months before she stood in line to get her Jewish identity card. Along with all other Jewish civil servants, she had been banished from her job. Once again, to their credit, the Dutch did not knuckle under without protesting. A small blizzard of letters was generated between Dutch and German authorities over the persistent question of how such an action could be squared with Dutch constitutional guarantees of equal treatment for all citizens. And once the banishment of Jewish workers became a fait accompli, Dutch administrators dickered endlessly over whether this was to be termed a mass "dismissal" or a mass "suspension." They succeeded in providing partial pay for their former co-workers until, late in 1941, the Germans cut that away as well. Dutch educators were notably bold in standing up for their banished colleagues. At Leyden, for example, Dean R. P. Cleveringa of the Law Faculty delivered a ringing defense of the distinguished Jewish jurist Professor E. M. Meijers. Calling the German action "beneath contempt," he went on to contrast "power based on nothing but force" with "this noble son of our people, this man, this father to his students, this scholar whom foreign usurpers have suspended from his duties . . . a man who, as all of us know, belongs here and—God willing—will return to us." Lest his words vanish into air, Cleveringa had forty-eight copies of his speech run off for posting—an act which earned him eight months in prison. But, considering that many others who spoke up for the Jews ended in death camps, his punishment was astonishingly light.

In truth, Nurit took the loss of her job with mixed feelings. She had never wanted it in the first place. In fact, she had never wanted to do most of the things she had to do since becoming a teenager. As a child, for example, she had always been highly musical and loved to play the piano. Her father had been ready to send her, after high school, to the conservatory. "I hoped very much to go myself," she says. "At the time, I was going to an academic high school, which I liked very much because I was able to study many languages. But then my father became sick and he told me that after the term ended I'd have to be taken out of school to work in the family business. So I left the school, which I loved, for work which I hated. But I loved my father too much to say no. At that time, you didn't say no to your father anyway. My grandfather had also been working in the business. And now my father said to him, 'Listen, you're seventy-five years old and now, while you still have good health, you have the right to retire for a few years of leisure with your wife.' But my grandfather didn't see it this way. He saw me as the one who had caused him to be pushed out of the business. So, on top of everything else, he started to have it in for me. 'You are the one who is keeping me from working,' he said. And I was the one who didn't want to be working in the first place! My sister would have preferred to study Dutch literature—she was smarter than I—but she did not mind working in the business. I learned to do the books very quickly because I hated to sit very long at my desk. I couldn't keep still. I kept getting up to help the workers move crates in and out of the warehouse. But the thing I liked best was taking the cash bag to drop it off at the bank. It got me out into the streets where I could breathe the fresh air and walk!

"My father died when I was sixteen. Times were hard for us but even so, my mother and sister still wanted to send me to the conservatory. But I could no longer consider it. It would be much too expensive and, besides, I could never have respected myself if all the rest of the family were working in our grocery warehouse while I was off in the academy playing the piano. I knew I didn't want to be a teacher, and suppose after all that expense I didn't make it as a performer?

"So I went right on helping my mother and sister run the business. But then my mother started up with this man whom she would later marry. He had been the husband of my father's sister, who had also been very sick and who died soon after my father. He was the postmaster in a town in the south of Holland. As children, all the cousins went there in the summer because he had a big house with gardens. I liked it there very much. But even as a young girl I never liked him. Then, when his wife got sick, he did something that revealed his character. My mother had said to Father, 'You know, she has her four children who need to be cared for—I really should go down there to help her for a few days.' We had a maid, anyway, so it was no problem. Even though Mother had never separated from my father even for a day, she decided to do this out of her good heart. . . .

"But she came back sooner than we expected and she was crying. It was because of the way this man had treated her. He said, 'What are you doing here? Who needs you?' And he sent her home. Well, my father was very angry. My parents were never the type who talked about other people in front of us children, but I heard Father telephone his brother-in-law. He was very, very angry. And after that I could never have respect for this man. Yet he was the one my mother later married.

"So this man saw me lugging crates and doing general heavy work at the office—which I did only so I wouldn't have to sit. And on weekends I was always running off to do all sorts of sports—especially rowing. And he said to my mother, 'She is getting too much like a man. I'll help her get a job at the post office.' So I ended up in a training course for teletype operators at the central post office in Amsterdam. Since I already played the piano, my fingers were among the fastest. The job was to start on October 1. But then at the end of August I got a call from my new boss. And he said, 'Miss Hegt, I need you to work a month early. Please come in on Monday.'

"But I was supposed to crew for a race that Monday. The others were counting on me. So I said firmly, 'No, I am in a competition on Monday.'

"When my mother heard that, she grabbed the phone from me. 'My daughter will be there,' she said. And again I said loudly, so that he could hear, 'No!' But in the end I had to report to work anyway and my crew couldn't even enter the race because I wasn't there. I was very good at my job but I hated it. So you see in my whole life circumstances pushed me to do things against my will."

Compared with what was shortly to come, the preliminary steps taken in 1941 seemed bearable—especially since the civil service still managed to pay some sort of stipend to workers like

Nurit. The great exception, of course, was the deportation to Mauthausen of those four hundred youthful Jews. Both victims and killers, incidentally, seemed naïve, each in their own way, about this pilot project. Those young Jews had willingly, even defiantly, acknowledged they were Jews when the Germans picked them up randomly on the streets of Amsterdam. They laughed and joked as they boarded the trains which would take them out of Holland. They expected to be home soon enough.

The Germans, for their part, did not yet bother—or think they had to bother—to keep the enslavement, brutalization, and murder of these youths a state secret. They even sent home death notices to the families of the victims. This caused problems they had not foreseen. The Joodsche Raad, or Jewish Council, founded early that year on German orders, protested the deaths to the Nazi command. How could so many young, healthy men be dying? This protest was a useless exercise, of course. But the Joodsche Raad also protested through the Swedes, who customarily mediated the problems of Dutch citizens in the Reich and of German citizens in Dutch colonies. The Swedes demanded that the Reich Foreign Office allow them to inspect conditions at Mauthausen but were stalled indefinitely while Gestapo Chief Heinrich Müller was told to give the camp the appearance of being civilized. Since the four hundred Mauthausen Jews were never heard from again, it appears that the Germans did away with the rest of them silently. When the Dutch church leader Dr. J. J. van Dijk complained about the deaths of those young men, the Nazi Generalkommissar Schmidt answered, "Is it our fault that they choose to jump off mountains?"

For the great proportion of Dutch Jews, life for the time being was a web of ever more tortuous, but still not untenable, restrictions, announced in nearly every issue of the *Joodsche Weekblad* (Jewish Weekly), the official organ of the Jewish Council. Then, in the spring of 1942—just prior to the first large-scale deportations—these restrictions became all but paralyzing. On March 21, Jews were forbidden to ride in cars with the exception of ambulances, vehicles in service to the Reich, and hearses. On May 8, Jews were ordered to wear the yellow star, even if they should be leaning out a window of their own home. On May 29, Amsterdam authorities were told not to issue fishing licenses to Jews anymore. On June 12, the *Joodsche Weekblad* announced that Jews were now prohibited from "every form of outdoor sport including rowing, canoeing, swimming, tennis, football, fishing, etc. . . ." Jewish housewives were forbidden to shop in non-Jewish shops except between the hours of three and five o'clock in the afternoon—presumably when the best fruits, vegetables, and meats would already have been bought by Christian housewives. Some storekeepers, however, are reported to have put aside choice items for their old customers. One woman, no longer able to shop for flowers at her favorite florist, continued to receive a bouquet daily in secret. The Germans had already deported Christian storekeepers for smaller courtesies than that.

On June 22, 1942—the same day as Amsterdam Jews were having their bikes taken from them—Adolf Eichmann told Karl Rader-macher, the Jewish Affairs expert in the Foreign Office in Berlin, that all was ready for the first of the large-scale deportations that had been envisioned in the famous Wannsee Conference on January 20. One hundred thousand Jews were to be shipped eastward to the killing centers from France, Belgium, and Holland. The Dutch quota was forty thousand. Four days later, at ten o'clock on the Sabbath eve, key members of the Jewish Council in Amsterdam were called to the office of Ferdinand aus der Funten, Chief of "Jewish Immi-gration" in Holland. He told them that all Jews between the ages of sixteen and forty years should be prepared for deportation. By now, after the Mauthausen debacle, the Germans had learned how to play the game. These Jews were merely to form "police-controlled labor contingents." And why, asked the Council members, "police controlled"? Aus der Funten replied that in the camp environment police could best look after the safety of the Jews.

Now began a degrading, unrelenting, and finally useless scramble on the part of the Dutch Jews to keep the names of their families and friends off the official deportation lists which the Jewish Council was required to submit to aus der Funten at an average rate of nearly fifteen hundred persons per week. A maze of special exemption lists sprang up—notably the Bolle list, named for the General Secretary of the Jewish Council. Those who could prove their indispensability to the work of the Jewish Council—as many as eight hundred Dutch Jews per day—were issued the precious stamp that said, "*bis auf weiteres freigestellt vom Arbeitseinsatz*"—exempted from labor service until further notice.

Aus der Funten was more than willing to entertain the Jewish Council's endless requests for exemptions and cutbacks in the process of delivering deportees. He even showed deep concern. Professor D. Cohen, co-president of the Council, tells of going to visit aus der Funten on the morning of August 6, 1942, to protest a special hunt, to commence that very day, for an extra quota of two thousand Jews. By now, after more than a year and a half of almost daily dealings, the two men were intimates.

> I found him [aus der Funten] in his room in a state of great—it struck me and it still strikes me—genuine agitation. He explained that the raid had been ordered simply because too few Jews were reporting for transportation and that the trains simply had to be filled. But, looking at me, he added, "Believe me, Herr Cohen, it is the last thing I wanted." I then took both his hands and said, "But, Herr Hauptsturmfuhrer, then please don't do it." He turned to the window, as he always did when trying to hide his tears, and then back again to tell me, "Herr Cohen, I have no alternative!" I pleaded with him again, but he simply repeated his words.

The raids continued unrelentingly through the winter of 1942 and the spring of 1943. Just as unrelentingly, aus der Funten and the Jewish Council kept up the surreal game of juggling the names of the ever-diminishing body of Jews in Holland. As the able-bodied people scrambled to get themselves and their families off the deportation lists, it was inevitably the disabled who were drafted. On January 20, 1943, aus der Funten traveled into the countryside near Apeldoorn to lead a raid personally on the world-renowned Jewish mental hospital there. More than a thousand patients of all ages, ranging from the imbecilic to the schizophrenic, were hauled off to waiting trains. It was emblematic of the whole affair that a young girl who refused to wear clothing was seen being taken into the winter air wearing nothing but her strait-jacket.

The next institution to be raided was the Jewish Invalid Hospital in Amsterdam. Even when the Gestapo hunts were at their most savage, this had always been an untouchable haven. Since volunteer workers as well as the regular staff had so far been safe from deportation, some people were even reported to have paid for the right to be volunteers. But on March 1 this hospital too was raided. It is a sign of the remarkable and perhaps bizarre determination of the Jewish community to go on as before that just two days before the raid, the patients were scheduled to see a fully staged operetta.

Three days later came the first of a series of raids on the only other Jewish hospital still in operation, the Nederlands-Israelitsch Hospital. There, among the nurses who were forced to ready their patients for deportation, could be found the former teletype operator Nurit Hegt. As a child, she had once wanted to be a nurse. Now, being no more anxious than anyone else to be deported, she knew that by working in this capacity she had the best chance to keep her life fastened in Amsterdam. By that spring of 1943, however, she realized that nursing would only postpone her deportation. Her beloved sister Reina had been hidden by her Christian boyfriend with a family in Rotterdam. Her mother, resigned to doing as she was told, continued to live at home with her detested stepfather. But rather than stay with them, where she was more likely to be picked up in a night raid, Nurit was sharing a small room with three other nurses at the hospital. Still, from the day of that first raid on March 4, 1943, she knew she was not safe even there. She also had a good idea what it was that she was not safe from. "I had already heard rumors that we were going to the gas chambers," she says. "Many people did not want to believe it. But I believed it. Out of all those young men who went to 'work' at Mauthausen, why didn't we hear a word? Then when they put the nightly curfew on us in 1943 I would hear the Gestapo banging on the doors of homes in the Jewish quarter not with their hands but with their boots. And then you heard them shout, '*Raus! Raus!*' Sitting in my little room, I was so frightened. I knew the truth. We were all to die."

Even as she remained on a supposedly "safe" list of nurses (not all nurses qualified) that spring, Nurit decided not to wait for the day when no list would keep her safe. She would try to hide. But where? Through whom? "I decided to try first by asking my sister's boyfriend if perhaps he could arrange to hide me near my sister in Rotterdam. But he said to me, 'You are too Jewish.'

"That was a funny thing for him to say, because my sister was the one who looked Jewish—dark like Anne Frank.

"'No—I don't mean your looks,' he said. 'I mean your gestures.' He meant that I talked too much with my hands. Supposedly, in a Jewish household, you were always talking with your hands.

"'Then I'll put my hands behind my back,' I said. But that wasn't the issue. The issue was that he was looking for an excuse not to help me."

One evening not long after this disquieting exchange, Nurit received an unannounced visit from a certain Mrs. Levison, who was a friend of her mother's. She had come to ask Nurit what kind of ID card she carried.

"One marked with the 'J,' of course," she answered.

"Then I will buy you one without the 'J,'" said Mrs. Levison. She was soon back with an ID card in the name of one Franciska Slujk. It was genuine, except that now Nurit's own photo was pasted onto it and imprinted with a counterfeit stamp.

"I wanted to pay her for it," says Nurit, "but she wouldn't hear of it. Later I found out that it had cost two hundred guilders. That was a lot of money—more than I could have gotten together. This Mrs. Levison is a splendid person. Today she lives near Tel Aviv."

A few evenings later, Nurit was visited by one of the male nurses on the hospital staff. She did not know it then, but he too was connected with the underground movement. Why, he wanted to know, was her rucksack neatly and fully packed in the corner?

"Because if they come to take me away suddenly," she answered, "I want to be all ready."

"With a face like yours?" said the male nurse, shaking his head. "That would be a pity." To which Nurit adds, "So you see, to my sister's boyfriend I looked too Jewish to help and to this nurse I looked too much like a shiksa not to help!"

Soon came the next in a parade of evening visitors who, by a process that remains shadowy, would each take a part in enabling the survival of Nurit Hegt. One woman, a stranger, was a Christian member of the underground who specialized in finding hiding places for Jews. For Nurit she had arranged a place with a family in the small city of Ermelo in the central province of Gelderland.

"You will be going to a family that has agreed to take in a student," said the woman. "But I think they will also agree to take you." In this declining hour of their fortunes, the Germans were scouring the land for young Christians who could be sent off to forced labor in the Reich. They were particularly pleased to grab those students who had refused, earlier in the Occupation, to sign the so-called "Aryan attestation" that had gone out to all students and teachers.

Early the next morning, feeling not free but frightened, Nurit removed the yellow star from her breast and walked from the hospital to the central station, where she took a train to Ermelo. What she found there did not exactly have the markings of an idyll. "The woman who greeted me at the door had four small children and a husband who was very sick. I saw the situation at once—she needed a housekeeper and nursemaid and so she decided to take in a student. That was okay with me. But as we talked, I watched these young children. And I decided I did not want to take the responsibility for what might happen to them if the Germans uncovered me in this household. Their parents could have been sent to a concentration camp for harboring me. So, at the end of the interview, I blurted out the truth."

"I must tell you," said Nurit, "that I am a Jew."

As Nurit expected, the woman was taken aback. "I will have to discuss this with my husband," she said wanly. As Nurit left, she knew she would not be returning.

Grim and fearful as the atmosphere was in the ghetto hospital, Nurit was relieved to be back. She was even glad, in a way, to put back on her yellow star. If, on her foray to Ermelo, the Germans had inspected her ID with its pasted-over photo and counterfeit stamp, she knew they would have found it wanting. She would certainly have been put in the punitive barracks at the Westerbork concentration camp to await the next train to Auschwitz. Here in the hospital she remained safe for now. That is why, when the woman from the underground returned with the prospect of a new hiding place in the south, Nurit was less than enthralled.

"Thank you," said Nurit, "but I don't trust my luck to travel all the time on the train. If they pick me up, it's all over. But if you could find a family willing to hide me knowing in advance that I was Jewish, that would be different. I would go in a minute."

"You are not supposed to make it hard for me," said the woman. "In any case, I am supposed to be concentrating on finding hiding places for children rather than adults. But I feel something special for you. I am going to find you a place."

The first to be taken away in those March raids on the Nederlands-Israelitsch Hospital had been the oldest and sickest. Then, with the patient load reduced, the Germans decided to slim down the staff accordingly. But when they came to take away those nurses who, unlike Nurit, had no place on the exemption list, they did not find them. Tipped off the day before, they had slipped away into the night. As long as candidates for deportation had presented themselves compliantly, the Germans were willing to hold to a certain etiquette, sham though it was. They could even act regretful at the measures they were ordered to take. But the escape of the nurses put a new face on things. On June 10, a Gestapo force marched into the hospital breathing fire. Nurit had never seen so many. Everyone— doctors, nurses, male nurses, and kitchen staff—was ordered into the courtyard. If the missing nurses were not delivered up quickly, they were told, then those on the exempted list would take their places. "You should have seen how they strutted around in their jackboots," says Nurit. "I stood there with my knees shaking. . . ."

Though she could not have known it, Nurit's underground contact had arrived at the hospital gates at that very hour with a new and firm offer of a hiding place that met her needs. Thinking better of sticking around at that moment, the woman returned the next day.

"Tomorrow morning you go into hiding," she said. "In the north." She took the rucksack away with her so that Nurit would have to carry only a small bag.

That evening Nurit's mother came to visit her in her room at the hospital. It was the eve of her twenty-second birthday. Her mother was not pleased with the news.

"'Don't go,' she said. 'Come with me when we are called. We will work hard and we will be together.'

"But I said, 'It's not true, Mother. It won't be work. They are killing us all!'

"'No,' she said. 'It's not true. Stay with me because you are the only one left from Father.' She meant that since my sister had already gone into hiding she had no more children of her own except me. But I said no. Later, I thought about how thoughtlessly cruel a child can be to her mother.

"I didn't have any money then, of course. So when Mother saw she couldn't persuade me to stay with her, she gave me what she had with her—eleven guilders."

Her mother had not been the first to beg Nurit to stay. Just a few days before, the hospital director had delivered a stern lecture to all the nurses. "He was very angry with us," she says. "He wanted to know how we could run off when there were so many sick people to care for. But we were young and we wanted to save ourselves."

So, on the dot of six o'clock the next morning, Nurit hurried out of the hospital. Though he was awake, the concierge looked away. He did not have the heart to stop the girls he saw slip out each morning. Holding her small bag close, and again with no star on her breast, Nurit, not daring to look left or right, headed through the streets that were forbidden to her. But she was unmolested. At the central station she went, as she had been directed, to a spot between two postboxes. There Nurit found a second nurse, who had slipped out of the hospital fifteen minutes before her. Almost immediately they were joined by the woman from the underground. She told them to follow her onto the train—but not to talk to her or sit near her. In an act of bravado that was startling even to themselves, the two girls chose to stand beside two Dutch SS men in uniform. For the next two hours, they chatted away as they rolled northward past endless ditch-bordered fields grazed by big, blimp-bellied, mottled black-and-white Friesian cows. They debarked at Leeuwarden, the provincial capital. For lunch, they selected the restaurant of the Oranje Hotel, which bore a sign saying "*VOOR HONDEN EN JODEN VERBODEN*"—Dogs and Jews Forbidden. It was a warning that the Germans insisted be posted all over Holland long after the majority of Dutch Jews were dead and the rest in hiding.

Only when lunch was over did Nurit hear where she was to go. By local bus, she would be heading for Ferwerd, a well-scrubbed little village of some three thousand well within reach of the North Sea fogs. There she would be met by the town doctor and given a final set of directions to her hiding place.

Alone now on this last leg of the trip, Nurit could have used some sort of friendly welcome. But the doctor, a tall, severe-appearing man, did not have so much as a smile for her. His instructions were simple. She was to walk thirty paces behind him down the main street of the village. When he paused to look at his pocket watch, she was to knock at the door of the house directly on the left. She would be expected. Nurit understood the need for such precautions even in a village as serene in appearance as this one. While no Germans were stationed here, the citizenry was bound to include some German sympathizers. It was, after all, a mere fifty miles from Ferwerd to the border of the Reich itself.

Nurit followed the doctor past a bakery, a sports store, and several taverns. Seven doors past the town square he pulled out his watch. After he had gone on, she went to the door and knocked. Nurit, although on the whole strong-willed and fearless, was now shaking as much as she had when, just two days before, the Gestapo had hauled the staff of the hospital into the courtyard for a dressing-down.

The young woman who opened the door was slightly taller than Nurit and perhaps five or six years older. Her features were strong and her deep-set eyes were somewhere between green and grey. They looked at each other for a moment in silence. But thirty-five years later they both agree on what was said.

"My name is Franciska Slujk," said Nurit. She was regarded with a silence that she felt she must fill. "I don't have any money . . . today is my birthday!"

"My name is Sietske Postma," said the other young woman, closing the door behind them. "In this house you don't need any money."

For some reason, as they stood there staring at each other with an unavoidable touch of mutual embarrassment, they both laughed. And for the next two years the facts as established in that introduction remained unchanged. There, in the home of Sietske Postma, her father, Djoerd, and her young brother Renze, Nurit Hegt—or, rather, Franciska Slujk—would not have any money, nor would she need any. And while the last of the Dutch Jews, the rest of her own family included, were killed by the Germans, while nearly all of Holland suffered hunger and other deprivations, here in this small town in stern and unsmiling Friesland—"the Cold Land"—hardly a day or even an hour would go by when Nurit and Sietske would not find themselves laughing.

Djoerd Postma was a woodcraftsman who built wagons and tools for the local farmers. His father and grandfather had done exactly the same thing. His wife had died when Sietske was just eleven years old and her brother Renze was four. In 1937, when she was twenty-one, Sietske had finished her training to be an elementary-school teacher. Just as her father came from a line of woodcraftsmen, she came on her mother's side from a line of teachers. But it was a hard time to get a job. Those few that became available inevitably went to men with families to support. Sietske had little choice except to help her father in the shop and keep house in place of her mother.

Neither Nurit nor the Postma family had the least idea how she had been selected to arrive on the doorstep of No. 9 Hoofdstraadt. She would never know all the details. To be sure, nobody else knew the whole story either, since it was a standard security procedure of every underground movement to keep members in the dark about everything except what they needed to know to do their job. Still, certain facts relating to the dispatch of Jews to Friesland were obvious. In the first place, while the big Dutch cities and even the more populated countryside to the south were held closely under the German thumb, sparsely settled Friesland was only lightly policed. To this day there are more Friesian cows than Friesian people. With many farms placed well off the main roads, it was feasible to physically hide foreign-born or "ethnic-looking" Jews who could not afford to show their faces in public. And with all those cows the Friesians could feed extra mouths with a surplus of dairy products even when, toward the end of the war, many citizens of Amsterdam and the other cities were starving.

So, all things considered, it was not surprising that those concerned with saving Dutch Jews looked to Friesland. In town after town, the word was passed up from Amsterdam to the local underground chieftains. Can you find us people who would be willing to hide Jews? In Ferwerd, both the town doctor and one of the several pastors were the contacts. In each case, they had to make a discreet canvass. They preferred not to approach families with small children, who might give the secret away in school or on the streets. They could not, obviously, approach a family that might be collaborators, or in close proximity to such a family. They could not, above all, approach a family which might falter under the ongoing burden. The penalty for harboring Jews, as announced by the Germans, was to share the fate of the Jews. All these factors having been duly weighed, the doctor and the pastor decided to ask Djoerd Postma if he would be willing to hide someone. But, as his daughter remembers it, the approach was roundabout.

"It was the pastor who came to us first," says Sietske. "That was a few months before Nurit came. And he asked us if we might take somebody.

"'Yes,' Father said.

"A few weeks later the pastor came and asked, 'What about a girl?' And my father turned to me and asked, 'What about a girl, Siets?'

"'Yes,' I answered.

"Still later the doctor came and asked, 'Will you have a Jewish girl?' And my father asked me, 'How is that looking to you, Siets?'

"'Yes,' I answered. 'A young girl would be nice—maybe nine or ten years old. . . .'

"A few days later the doctor came back and said, 'How about a girl twenty-three years old?'

"'Yes,' I said. 'Yes . . .' If I had said no, my father would not have taken her in."

Those exchanges between the pastor and the doctor and the Postma family were spoken in plain Dutch. But exchanges between underground units in Ferwerd and the south were encoded. When the request came up from Amsterdam to hide a Jewish girl, for example, the doctor and the pastor answered with a question of their own: "Was the medicine for internal or external use?" A foreign-born or overtly Jewish-looking girl could not risk being seen in public. The suspicions of anyone sympathetic to the Germans would quickly get back to the Gestapo. Such a girl would best be hidden on an isolated farm. She would have been a medicine for internal use. With her luminous, Sephardic dark looks, Nurit's sister Reina would have been such a medicine. But Nurit, with her blond hair and button-small features, looked as if she might spend her Sunday mornings teaching a Lutheran confirmation class. She could comfortably promenade on the streets of a village like Ferwerd knowing that the insular Friesians would take her for a city girl from the south, but not for a Jew. She was, in short, a medicine for external use.

Sietske herself, however, might well have been surprised to see standing at the door a girl whose basic looks were not so different from her own. Nurit was the first Jew she had ever seen. She was supposed to be exotic. And though Sietske did not subscribe to it, the belief was still widely held in Friesland, as in so many other places, that Jews were born with a pair of horns.

Given four days' notice of Nurit's arrival, Djoerd Postma had built a narrow bed for her, enclosed in a long pantry on the right side of the front room. Sietske slept in an identical bed on the other side of the room. Djoerd himself slept in the rear of the building where his shop was located. Renze slept alone upstairs near a rear window leading out over the adjoining rooftops. If the Germans came in the night looking for strong young men to send off to labor camps, he would be out that window before they ever got up the stairs. Not that Renze was afraid of the Germans. He worked at a farmer's dairy depot a mile outside town. Each evening he brought back a supply of milk for local use, and he never tried to hide, as other boys did, from the Germans he met on the road. Rather, he bid them a bold greeting. Many in the town, in fact, wondered if he was not himself a National Socialist. But the truth was that while he took precautions against being spirited away in the night, he was not a young man who had any inclination to grovel before the occupiers or scurry like a rat into a hole until they had passed by.

Although Nurit did not, in fact, know what made her announce her birthday on the Postma doorstep, she knew very well why she had declared in that first breath that she had no money. Jews who were lucky enough to find Christians to hide them took it for granted that they would have to work in some way for their hosts. On more than a few Friesian farms, Jewish boys previously familiar only with the pavements of Amsterdam were working from dawn to dark in the flat, fertile fields. Jewish girls were scrubbing, sewing, and caring for children. From her own first hours in Ferwerd, Nurit declared herself ready to help in any way she could. She tried to help her new "cousin" with the dishes and the cleaning, but her offers were always politely declined. She tried to do what she could in the shop—if only to sweep the floor of wood shavings—but the broom was taken from her hands. Though Renze's boldness with the Germans scared her, she even offered to help him tote the milk. He declined this too. All the Postmas were polite but resolute. This was not at all what Nurit had expected and she was perplexed. Finally, when they were all together at the dinner table one night, she asked them, "Why won't you let me work?"

"We didn't bring you in to be a maid," answered Djoerd Postma.

Brief as it was, it took some time for the fullest meaning of this answer to sink into Nurit's head. In later years, when she thought about it, she was ever more amazed. This family had known even better than she how utterly vulnerable and helpless she was as a stranger and a fugitive in Friesland. They knew she had to do whatever they told her to do. They knew other Jews were working hard—even like slaves—as the price of being hidden. And they knew that Nurit would, like those other Jews, do whatever they told her to do. That was precisely why they did not want her to do anything. They wanted her to understand that they had brought her in not to be a maid or any other kind of worker. They had done it simply because it was the right thing to do. And the more Nurit thought about this, the more she realized that by a stroke of unfathomable luck she was now a member of a most remarkable family.

Other demonstrations of their extraordinary nature soon followed. One day, for example, the minister came to the Postma home to discuss a problem with Nurit. Having observed her going about the village now for a few days—as an "external medicine," her instructions had been not to be the least bit reclusive—he had decided that she was passing very well as a Christian girl, with one exception. Nurit thought that he would say she was talking too much with her hands, but it was her feet the doctor was worried about.

"He claimed that Jews walk flatfooted like a camel—including me. 'You must be careful about every little thing,' he warned, 'because in the next town an SS man is stationed.' I had already heard about this German. He made his patrols on a bicycle with an attack dog running alongside. Whenever he headed for Ferwerd, the gentile boys—except for Renze—all hid. They didn't want to be taken away for forced labor. This SS man had a mustache and that's what they called him—'Watch out! Mustache is coming!' Whenever we heard this, Siets and I took a walk across the fields to the dike. For those two years, Siets never let me go anywhere unless she was by my side.

"Anyway, this doctor said to me, 'You have to get shoes with heels so you won't be walking flatfooted. Because this Mustache is always checking girls from behind to see how they walk. And if he saw you right now walking down Hoofdstraadt, he would say, "She is a Jew."' The doctor scared me very much. But it was summer and I had only brought my sandals to the north with me and I had no money to buy a real pair of shoes. Siets had a ration coupon which entitled her to one pair of shoes. She was planning to get herself a new pair for the winter. But without any hesitation she said to me, 'Come, Franske, we'll get a pair of shoes for you.'

"Of course, this business of Jews walking like camels is so much rubbish," Nurit says now. "Once I saw Prince Klaus, consort of the Princess, when he was visiting here at Nahariya. And how do you think he was walking? Flatfooted like a camel—or, according to this doctor, like a Jew! Take your pick."

Though Nurit may not have come from a wealthy family, she certainly owned a pair of shoes with heels. She had a full wardrobe back in Amsterdam. But she had purposely gone into hiding carrying only summer things in the certain belief that within a few months—by early fall at latest—Germany would be vanquished, life would return to normal, and she could return to her family at home. "When you are young you just don't think ahead so far, that's all," she now says, shrugging off that monumental miscalculation.

Even before the end of that August 1943, the first chill winds had swept off the North Sea, blowing across the low fields and dikes, previewing the new season for Nurit, and mocking her skimpy clothes. Yet there was no sign of the war's ending. What she needed now was an acquisition even more major than a pair of heeled shoes. She needed a winter coat. But no matter how much she shivered she was determined not to say a word about it to Sietske. She did not have to.

" 'You take my coat,' she said. 'I will go to Dokkum' "—this was a town ten kilometers north—" 'and buy fabric to make myself another coat.' So I got my shoes and I got my coat. And let me tell you, this fabric that she bought to make her new coat was not as good, and certainly not as warm, as the one she gave me."

Lest this relationship between Sietske and her new cousin become unnaturally idyllic, the two of them soon put it on the right track by having their first spat. The first and the worst. It was set off on one side by, of all things, Nurit's musicality and on the other by the fact that, despite her imperturbable exterior, Sietske Postma was highly sensitive to minor but thoughtless cruelty.

"It happened one evening when some friends of Siets had come over to her house," explains Nurit. "Young people were always coming to her place. She had a sort of harmonium in the living room that she did not play so well herself. But I was always playing a little jazz or "Plaisir d'amour" or something. And when these people came, they gathered around the harmonium to sing the popular songs. Whatever they asked Franske to play so that they could sing along, I would play. Then, one time, Siets sat down and started to play. And I said, sarcastically, 'Ah, Siets, you are playing very beautifully. . . .'

"At that moment she looked up at me and I saw that she was very angry. 'That was an ugly thing to say' is all that she would say. But she kept looking at me and her eyes instead of being their normal grey were flashing green. That is how they get when she is very angry. For more than a day, she would not talk to me.

"Perhaps you can imagine how I felt. Things had been so good until then. I felt so lost. I didn't know what to do. Even Uncle, who did not pay much notice to what went on between us girls, sensed something was wrong. But it was Renze who was the one who knew what to do. Back from work, he turned to his sister and said in dialect, 'I can see that Franske has been crying. What has happened?'

"'She angered me,' said Sietske.

"'Are you not ashamed?' asked her brother. 'Here is this girl who was forced to flee her own home. She has to be in this strange place without even her own name. And she is our guest. How can you carry on this way? If you make her so unhappy that she is forced to leave, then I promise you that I will leave with her.'

"Renze said all this in fewer words than I just did. That is how Friesians are. But it was enough. Siets and I both apologized for what we had done to each other. From this incident the most important thing I learned was the fineness of Renze."

Nurit would wear Sietske's coat, which she thought she was borrowing only briefly, all that first winter and the next, and, before ever leaving Ferwerd, she would be breaking out her light-weight clothing for two more summers as well. For this city girl the simple country life became routine. Once her hosts were assured that she did not think they had brought her in to be a maid, they even allowed her to help with the chores, modest as they were in a family without infants. The two young women took long walks daily, usually out toward the dikes; if no fogs rolled in, they could see the North Sea, which, reversing the color of Sietske's eyes, was green when it was calm and grey when it was angry. Among the buttoned-up Friesians of this town, it was widely noted how often and with how much pleasure in each other Sietske and her cousin Franske from Amsterdam could be heard laughing.

If the surface of daily life was cheerfully serene for Nurit, its undertone was pure bleakness. Though she had no proof, she did not delude herself about the fate of the Jews back home. If she could have convinced herself otherwise, she would have done as her mother begged her and waited for the boot thumps on the door calling them to the transit camp at Westerbork, where they would wait again for their assigned seats on the train to the east. Though her hosts were touched by none of this, they saw the truth as clearly as Nurit. Soon after her arrival they made her a proposal. Why not bring her mother up to them to be hidden?

Nurit explained the problem. Her mother, born Rodrigues-Lopez, wore her heritage on her face. In Seville, she would look like everyone else. In Ferwerd, she would look like a Sephardic Jew. But Djoerd Postma had already taken that into account. He would build her a little room in the attic. She would be snug and comfortable. On dark nights—better yet, on moonless or stormy nights—she might even be able to go out for a walk.

Via the underground mail service, Nurit passed on this invitation to her mother. The answer was quick and firm. She could not leave her second husband. Her responsibility was to stay with him. But even if she had felt free to leave Amsterdam, she could not impose that responsibility on the family who was already so good to her daughter. If she was discovered, they would all be deported. She would wait her turn to go to Poland and work hard when she got there. On an August day in 1943, just a few weeks after writing this letter, she and her husband answered the thump on the door.

To be a full-fledged member of the Postma clan, Franske quite naturally had to be a pious adherent of their stern Dutch Reform faith. Three times each day she bowed her head at the table while Uncle thanked God for the meal they were about to eat. On Sundays, wearing her best clothes, she walked to the big brick church on a knoll behind the village square where she raised her voice in hymns to God and Saviour. It ought to have been easy. If there is any one fact that is clear about the young Nurit Hegt up to the time she knocked on the Postmas' door, it was her neutral-tilting-toward-negative feelings about being a Jew. First and foremost, she felt herself to be a Dutch girl, and being a Jew only made her less Dutch without giving her anything in return. It made her unhappy.

"My first boyfriend, you know, was a gentile," she explains. "I was eighteen years old and crazy about him—or at that age so I thought. And he invited me to a dance. I bought a new dress. And then, at the last minute, he said to me, 'My parents found out that I'm going with a Jewish girl and they hit the roof! They threatened to throw me out of the house if I see you anymore.' I was stunned. That was the first slap in the face I got for being a Jew. My mother wasn't so unhappy about it. That meant that she had only *one* daughter going with a non-Jewish boy. And she said to me, 'So why don't you find yourself a nice Jewish boy now?' But I told her they didn't appeal to me. They all looked the same with their curly hair. . . ."

Once the Germans had commenced their campaign to vilify the Jews in the eyes of the Dutch, Nurit's feelings on the subject were only exacerbated. "You can imagine," she says. "We are pushed into a corner. You are Jews, they tell you. You are mosquitoes. We must annihilate you. And if you are a young girl like I was, not at all religious, you ask yourself, 'For what? Why was I born a Jew?'"

Given these feelings, Nurit might well have been pleased—maybe even delighted—at finding herself thrust into a devout Christian family in a devout Christian village where, as she observed, "everyone was always clasping their hands and praying." Those people had no problem accepting her. Unexpectedly, however, she had big problems accepting herself. "As a child, I'd learned what gentiles believed about Jesus," she says; "that we Jews were guilty of making him hang on the Cross and that he was the Messiah—neither of which we believed. But I had never before been faced with these beliefs directly. Now I sat at the Postma table three times a day while Uncle prayed and read the Bible out loud. And I found that I couldn't stand it. Yet I couldn't ask them to stop all this reading and praying to Jesus. I was thankful to be a guest in their house and at their table. So even though I still hated being a Jew, I closed myself against Jesus. It was the same at church. They did not press me to go with them on Sunday mornings. But I felt I had no choice. If I stayed home, people would have become suspicious of me. That would have put the family under suspicion as well. So I sang the hymns as loudly as any other girl. But mentally I shut out the name of Jesus even while it formed on my lips. So you see I had to hypnotize myself to be just like them on the outside. This forced me to find my true self on the inside. Until then I had thought that maybe I would become a Christian. But now I said, 'No!' At last I felt my Jewish blood start to run. . . ."

Soon enough, Nurit had a chance to test this new pulse. One day in the middle of that winter of 1943–44, the minister came to pay her an unexpected visit. She was glad to see him. Unlike the severe and unsmiling doctor, the minister was a friendly man. But she was taken aback by the question he now asked her.

"'Franske,' he said, 'shall I teach you the catechism so that you can become a Christian?'

"Straight out of my heart, I said, 'No!'

"'Why not?' he asked.

"'This I cannot do because of my parents.' My father was dead and my mother was already gone, of course, but I felt an obligation as strongly as if they were still with me. 'I am a Jew and I am proud to be a Jew,' I said to the minister.

"He did not ask me again if I wanted to learn the catechism. Perhaps he respected me because I was so forthright. He was a very good man who had three children of his own—two of whom were retarded—and he was also hiding a Jewish child. The area was full of Jews. But not all the children could go to school, because they looked too Jewish. So this minister would visit them in their hiding places to give them their lessons, just as the children were getting them in regular school. This he took upon himself."

In that winter Nurit not only discovered that she was a Jew, but also, to her even greater surprise, she uncovered in herself nothing less than a Zionist. She even knows the precise date and place of that epiphany. It was February 6, 1944, and she was standing in the Postma kitchen washing dishes. "Suddenly my right hand went up and it was as if God had lifted it and said, 'Nurit, you are going to Palestine.' Yet before this moment I was in no way a Zionist. I was against it. When my friends in Amsterdam had talked about it, I had asked, 'Who goes to Palestine, so far away, and why?'

"That evening Siets and I went walking out on the dike. And I said, 'Siets, today I got my religion back. Here in your house you have not only saved my life but you have allowed me to get back my Jewish feeling. I am proud that you brought me in and I hope that I can give something back to you in some way.'

"I have told many people since then about that revelation. They have not all believed me. But when I told Siets about it that night on the dike, she believed me, understood me, and supported me.

"'If I were you,' she said, 'I would also want to go to Palestine.'"

Fired by her new faith, Nurit soon had a chance to test it in the unlikely role of proselytizer. In April 1944, she heard whispers that another Jewish woman of her own age was being hidden right in Ferwerd with a family active in the underground movement. "I'd like to meet this girl," Nurit told Sietske. "After so long I feel the need to meet one of my own."

Since this was a potentially dangerous expedition, Nurit thought it best to venture out for the first time alone, not under the protective wing of Sietske. If the unexpected should occur, better that one rather than both of them be caught. But Sietske's response was both direct and predictable: "We will go together, just as we always do."

They went that evening to the house where the young woman was said to be in hiding. The eldest son of the family came to the door. Nurit came straight to the point.

"I know you have a Jewish girl in this house. I would like to see her."

"What makes you think we have such a person here?"

"Because I myself am a Jew."

Declaring herself to a stranger was decidedly risky. But the risk was well calculated. "We knew he had been working in the underground," explains Nurit. "If he should be a traitor and turn us in, I had a few things I could tell on him!"

The young man took them in to meet the girl without further questions. Her name was Eina DeHaas—an old and honored Dutch-Jewish name. Unlike Nurit, Eina came from a traditional Jewish family long settled in a small town in the center of Holland. "In those provincial communities," says Nurit, "you cannot turn up your nose at your religion the way you could in Amsterdam. Your neighbors are observant and God-fearing themselves and they don't appreciate it if you don't heed your own religion—even if it doesn't include Jesus. But now this Eina told me something that shocked me.

"'I have three brothers, all of them hidden,' she said. 'Two of them wish to become Christians. And to tell the truth I have decided myself that it is the best thing to be.'

"How is that possible for a girl whose Jewish background is so solid?" asked Nurit.

"'It's brought me nothing but suffering to be a Jew,' answered Eina with strong feeling. 'When I am a Christian, all that will end.'"

With prodding, Nurit discovered that Eina had not come to her decision independently. Her host family was actively pressuring her to convert. They were assisted, in turn, by a young pastor in the town whom Nurit did not know. "They may encourage you to become a Christian," said Nurit, "but in their private hearts they will never accept you as anything but a Jew. That is what you were when you were born and that is what you will be when you die. So don't even bother trying to assimilate. I know. I have been down this same road myself only a short time ago."

When Eina's foster parents and the young pastor joined the discussion, Nurit directed her anger at them. "Why are you trying to make a Christian out of this girl?" she demanded.

"Because Jesus is the Christ, the Messiah, and your Saviour, too, if you will only accept him," said the pastor.

"He is not the Messiah to us. But right now it would not matter if he was. Do you realize how unfair it is to put this kind of pressure just now on a young girl? We Jews are being sent off to the slaughter and you want to pluck away yet one more? Would you convert us now when we are a hunted people—when this Eina is on her twelfth hiding place and she is exhausted and confused? Try to convert us after the war, if you must. But, please, not now."

Nurit remembers that for the duration of this scolding Eina stood mute and quaking. "From the way I spoke," she says now, "you would not guess that on the inside I still felt afraid and lonely. But I was so mad I didn't care anymore what happened to me."

If the voice of Sietske Postma was absent from this colloquy, it was only because her mouth remained shut. "Even without a word," says Nurit, "I felt that I had her support. Back at home, I said, 'Siets, I must try to turn this Eina back to her own faith. Somehow I'll convince her that she is doing the wrong thing. But I don't want to talk to her at her house or even at your house. I will walk with her out on the dike—just the two of us.'"

Out of respect for the delicacy of this mission, Sietske at last allowed her ward to go out the door unattended. A cold spring rain was falling. But if Eina had wanted to protest that she would rather be under a warm roof than on the chilly dike, chances are she could not have gotten a word in edgewise, so busy was Nurit putting forth the proposition that, converted and even baptized, Eina would remain a Jew.

"What's more," adds Nurit, "I told her that even though I had never met them, I already hated her two brothers who also were bent on converting." While she would have no trouble standing by the rest of her statements that day, this last one Nurit would, years later, have to swallow. And though her method of persuasion was neither gentle nor subtle, it must have worked. Eina now lives as a Jew with her own family, not in Holland but in Israel.

In the midst of her nascent fervor, Nurit had once told Sietske and her father that when the war ended she would shout from the rooftops that she was a Jew. But quite suddenly, for a few interminable moments of one bizarre day, she wondered if when that day came, she would be in any position to shout. It was in that same spring of 1944, when the Germans had grown ever more desperate to find young men to support the war machine at home. In Friesland they were not above surrounding the churches on Sunday mornings to pluck away the most desirable specimens. For the first time in their lives, young men stopped going to church. Without their tenors, baritones, and basses, the traditional Lutheran hymns now issuing from those churches—music which seems to carry endlessly in the clear Friesian air and Sunday quiet—must have sounded uncharacteristically sweet and high. Since the Germans could no longer find young men by surrounding the church, on this particular day they decided to surround the town.

"Everyone in Ferwerd was united and alert to any movement by the Germans," says Nurit. "When Mustache was on his way from the next town with his police dog, the word was already flashed well ahead. We could deal with Mustache. But this time a neighbor came to us and said, 'Since Renze is away at work, I know you have nobody who the Germans might want to take in your house, but take care just the same. Four hundred Germans are all around us. . . .'"

Nurit, finding her normal presence of mind no longer intact, could only wail, "What will we do, Siets?"

"Jump into your bed and pretend you are weak and sick," she answered. "I will darken the room."

Nearly a year of serenity had lulled Nurit into supposing that she had permanently left behind in the Amsterdam ghetto the explosive thud of jackboots on the door. Now, with the covers pulled up tight around her, it was there again, her own heart thumping with it. Then they were inside—eight men, sixteen boots. Nurit's pantry door was flung open. A strange face—a Gestapo face—peered into her own.

"What's the matter with this one?" the German demanded of Sietske, who was busily pushing a broom.

"She is a sick one. Very sick."

He gave Nurit a continuing look of appraisal. "*Gute Besserung* [Good health]," he said then, and tramped upstairs to join the others who had a few questions for Uncle.

"Where is your son?" was the first question.

"He is away working."

"Working where?"

"In Hamburg."

When they came back downstairs, the German who had appraised Nurit said to Sietske, "If your brother is in Hamburg, then this girl must be his fiancée. Right?"

"*Nein!*" piped up Nurit before she could think better of it. Later she would call herself an "idiot" for her truthfulness.

"Where are your papers?"

"Papers . . . papers. Siets, where are my . . . papers?" She was speaking in a feeble and unfocused voice, as if she were indeed the family idiot. If this man had then chosen to be suspicious and pursue the matter, one more Jew would have been bagged. But he was merely impatient and a bit disgusted with the girl in the bed.

"Let your cousin do the housework—not you," he said to Siets, who continued to sweep furiously. And he stomped out.

Earlier, in the winter of 1943, Reina Hegt in Rotterdam had also found herself in sudden contact with the Gestapo. In her case, however, the slight but irrevocable tilt of fate went the other way. One evening near year's end, she ventured out of the apartment where she was being hidden to attend a clandestine birthday party for yet another hidden Jew. Just a little earlier, as a birthday present to himself, the celebrant had taken a stroll in public. He had been spotted. When Reina arrived at the place where he was being hidden, she sensed that something was wrong. As she backed away from the entrance to the building, a Gestapo agent took her arm. Unlike Nurit, she had no chance to avoid deportation even for a short time. Before boarding the train bound for Auschwitz, however, she did manage to get off a letter to her sister. It was passed out of the camp by Kurt, the young man whom Nurit had dated before the war, and delivered to Ferwerd by the prompt and highly reliable underground postal service. Only a few weeks earlier, Nurit had sent a letter by the same service to Reina at her hiding place in Rotterdam, gently upbraiding her for not corresponding more often. Among the few remains of Nurit's venerable Dutch family still in her possession in the town of Nahariya in Israel is that last letter. It is addressed "Dear Sprat." That was Reina's childhood nickname for her sister because she had been as quick and as agile as a little fish.

Just as they had kept their tightest hammer lock on the Dutch contingent of Jews among those of Western Europe, the Germans held fast to Holland until the last weeks of the Reich. They did not vacate Friesland until late in April 1945, long after they had been driven out of France and Belgium. And so it was in that month that Nurit kept her promise to herself. She told whomever she saw that she was not Franciska Slujk but Nurit Hegt—a Jew! She did it gladly. Indeed, there was no one else left in her family to do it.

The one person who Nurit thought might still be alive on that liberation day—and to whom she had a more than casual connection—was the young man named Kurt. He was a German-born Jew who had come to Holland in the mid-1930s to work for the cause of Zionism. He had rung no bells in that area with Nurit but a youthful romance did begin. Being foreign-born, Kurt had been sent to the Westerbork camp very early in the Occupation. That seniority was useful. Like many other German "founders," Kurt was able to set himself up in an administrative job from which he could maneuver to defer his own trip to Auschwitz. He had not been able to save her mother or sister, but Nurit nursed a hope now that he might have saved himself.

On a borrowed bike, Nurit pedaled for eight hours straight to Westerbork. In the chaos of the camp, she found him. He was among the thousand Jews still on hand when the Germans ran off. But any thought of salvaging this last chance at even a fragment of a happy ending would have been misplaced. "I was thrilled to see him," says Nurit. "But I felt instantly by the way he greeted me that he had another girl now. It was just an intuition. But it was correct. After two days he asked me to go away.

"'I want to be with you,' I said. But he was firm and cold. This episode was one of the worst shocks of my life. Because, you see, he was not only my first Jewish boyfriend but also my first real boyfriend. For two years I had waited for him and I assumed he would wait for me. I was a young girl and very loyal."

Not being one to shy away from hard questions, Nurit had, predictably, confronted Kurt with the hardest and perhaps the unfairest question of all. With all his pull and savvy in camp operations, could he not have done something to save Reina? "He answered that it was all but impossible to save someone from the detention barracks and that if he was going to try to get anyone out at such great risk, it would have been me. He had expected me to arrive any day. But people did survive, especially those who, like my sister, came not so long before deportations were halted. If he had made an effort, I believe my sister could have been among them."

Though the antagonisms between Nurit and Kurt were personal, it was a fact of life at the Westerbork transit camp that the Dutch and German inmates were riddled with antagonisms whose

---

★*Year of Fear: A Jewish Prisoner Waits for Auschwitz* (New York: Hawthorn Books, 1969), pp.30–35.

basis was purely that of "national" character. In his diary of one year in that camp,* the Dutch journalist Philip Mechanicus minces no words on the subject:

> There is something smouldering under the surface between these brothers of the same race—the fact that they cannot stand each other. The Germans despise their Dutch camp companions and the Dutch hate the German Jews . . . because they are *Germans—Prussians.*
>
> It is a complicated relationship. The German Jews here play the leader, just as the German Aryans are accustomed to playing the leader wherever they are. They think they have the right to do so. The German Jew, accustomed to Tüchtigkeit and Gründlichkeit— efficiency and thoroughness—cannot endure the lack of discipline or the touch of anarchy and individualism to be found in Dutch Jews. . . . The Dutch say: "Back to 'Boschland' with them, bag and baggage; they don't belong here with us."
>
> The great question is how many even of the Dutch Jews will ever see their native land and their homes again. The future is certainly not rosy as far as the German Jews are concerned. A large proportion of them do not want to return to Germany which has given them such bitter experiences and such grim memories. But they cannot see as yet where they, as stateless persons, will be accommodated after the war. This paralyzing feeling makes them morally vulnerable and, perhaps, oversensitive. . . .

In these last few sentences of speculation over the future Mechanicus unwittingly reveals how even an otherwise clear-eyed observer could fail to face up to the reality of what would one day be called the Holocaust. Here, at the very spot where the trains were being loaded, the big question still seemed to be whether the German Jews would want to go back to Germany after they had been to Auschwitz.

With no boyfriend now as well as no family, Nurit remounted her borrowed bicycle and, minus the adrenaline that had seemed to put the wind at her back on the way to Westerbork, she began to pedal back to Ferwerd. She had not got very far, however, when a curious and highly ironic thing happened. She was halted on the road by a group of Dutch patriots who suspected she might be fleeing from some town where she had been, of all things, a Nazi collaborator!

With no yellow star at her breast, no dark-eyed, olive-skinned looks like her late sister, no ID except that of Franciska Slujk, Nurit could offer no compelling evidence to the contrary. She was taken under arrest to a nearby town where the situation threatened only to worsen were it not for the presence of a member of the Jewish underground. He asked her to recite a basic Hebrew blessing or two that any Jewish girl ought to know. Secular as she was, Nurit handily drew up the required verses from memory and was acquitted. By chance, she also discovered the presence in this town of a nurse she had known and liked back at the Jewish Invalid Hospital in Amsterdam. This young woman had been safely hidden for the duration of the Occupation, only to fall sick now. On the spur of the moment, Nurit decided to plunge into the task of nursing her back to health. And for a month that is how she filled the vacuum that was her life.

When she finally returned to Ferwerd, the Postmas invited her to stay with them for as long as she might wish. As always, Nurit was grateful and at a loss to know how to thank them. But they, not she, were meant to be Friesian villagers. She would do what she had said she would do that day she realized her Zionist vocation. So, one June morning soon after V-E Day, Djoerd, Renze, and Sietske Postma stood together on the village square and waved their goodbyes to Nurit, who boarded the bus for Leeuwarden and beyond. In her pocket was the goodly sum of one hundred guilders which Djoerd Postma had given her—eighty-nine more than she had when she got off the bus two years earlier.

The first stop was Amsterdam, where Nurit had to care for what remained of family affairs. There was no family business—that had been "aryanized." There was no family apartment—it had been stripped of furniture and occupied by others. There were no burial costs. Only a few personal and family belongings had to be collected. Getting back her own winter clothing, which she had left with a Christian girl friend, was no problem. Every item was returned. But when she went to get some family possessions left with Reina's boyfriend, she got an unexpected jolt. He did not want to give them back. "These were only a few things that meant nothing to him but a great deal to me," explains Nurit. "There was a little silver and the white tablecloth my mother used on Sabbath evenings. Why he didn't want to give these things back I do not know."

She got another jolt when she traveled to Rotterdam to see the family where her sister had been hidden. They received her coolly, even with hostility. "They wanted to know why I had survived and Reina had not. They thought somehow I was guilty for that." Many survivors of the death camps reported being treated the same way upon their return. There seemed to be a feeling that those who had survived must have done so on the backs of those who perished—a feeling compounded, perhaps, by the defensiveness of those whose own actions, or lack of actions, might in retrospect have been found wanting.

Having attended to family matters as well as she could, Nurit went to work in an Amsterdam hospital while she waited for word from a local Zionist organization that the time had come to set out for Palestine. In the interim, one day, she bumped into a woman who had been with her sister at Auschwitz. "This woman told me that when they arrived they had been assigned to a group of women who were given the job of hauling heavy stones from one end of a field to the other and back again. It had no purpose except to weaken them. Those who could no longer lift the stones were gassed the next day. This woman told me that my sister was not very strong. She said she kept herself going only because she wanted to live to see Hitler die."

Nurit is a sprightly person, not given to outward signs of brooding. It is, therefore, hard to pinpoint her mental state in those months following the war. The only clue is that she admits to having lost eighteen pounds from her already small frame—"because I was so sad."

On June 12, 1946—exactly three birthdays after her arrival in Ferwerd—Nurit was at last put into a convoy of young Jews going to the southern French coast where they would catch an illegal boat for Palestine. On her back was the same rucksack filled with the same clothes she had taken into hiding. But this time she had no illusions. If she ever came back to Amsterdam, it would be as a visitor from the Promised Land. Her Dutch sense of propriety, however, would remain intact, as she herself found out on the voyage across the Mediterranean. "It was the middle of summer and it was cloudless and burning hot. Yet we were each allotted only half a cup of water twice a day, and we had only dry biscuits to eat, which made you even thirstier. People were crazed with thirst, me included, and we even drank salt water. Many of the girls walked out on deck bare-breasted. But I couldn't do it. I just put water down my blouse. I remember how it tickled!"

In Palestine, Nurit did what many young girls dreamed of doing in those times. She smuggled guns for the Palmach—the illegal Jewish army that predated the state—knowing that the good manners of the British soldiers at checkpoints would keep them from checking under her skirts. She worked on a new kibbutz where, like so many other city-born Jews of Europe, she pulled stones out of the earth with her hands. Apart from any romantic notions, she abominated this work. But she did fall in love with a dashing figure of the Palmach named Gerard. Many of the young women on the kibbutz were jealous and a little disbelieving, since, by her own objective appraisal, "I had gained back my weight so that I was a little fat and nothing special to look at." Unlike Kurt, Gerard was interested only in her. She was happy. But then on a secret mission during the War of Independence, Gerard was killed.

Nurit was working as an army nurse two years later, in 1948, when "a very nice thing happened." It had to do with, of all things, her old job at the post office in Amsterdam which she had hated so much. "I didn't have any way of knowing it," she says, "but a very great leader of the Dutch underground had been working there. He arranged for nearly every Jew who worked at the post office to be hidden. He also saw to it that a secret cash account was established for them. Their salaries were paid into it exactly as if they had been coming to work each day. After the war, they had been looking for me to give me my share. It took five years for a letter to catch up with me at last in the Negev. Four thousand guilders were waiting for me. For the first time I felt like going back to Holland.

"When the Germans gave the order in 1940 to dump Jews out of the civil service, my colleagues in the office had been startled to see me cleaning out my desk. 'Why *you?*' they had asked.

"'Because I am one of the dirty people,' I answered bitterly.

"They were incredulous. Almost nobody knew or suspected that I was a Jew. Now it was ten years later and I was received personally by the director of the post office. He offered me coffee and we talked about Israel. He asked me if I would be interested in visiting my old teletype section. Under his escort I went. Colleagues from before the war were still there and they were as startled to see me now as they had been to see me leave. They kissed me and a few cried.

"'When you didn't come back after the war,' they said, 'we assumed you had been exterminated.' "

Nurit took her four thousand guilders and went home—but not to the Negev. She found a job instead as a nurse in a soldiers' hospital near Haifa. She even took a bite out of her fortune to buy a coffee maker, a heater, and an expensive radio for the soldiers. "They were such nice boys—all nationalities and all types. I had a lot of fun. I did what I wanted and I dated many different boys—but never if they were Dutch! But even though I acted so free, it was really because nothing much mattered to me anymore since I had lost Gerard. I was actually in a deep rut. But if you have fallen into such a rut and you are able to pull yourself out on your own, then you are very clean."

In 1950, after steadfastly rejecting any and all liaisons with Dutchmen, Nurit did the inevitable. She married one. To compound the inevitable, she picked Schlomo DeHaas, one of the brothers of Eina DeHaas who had wanted to become a Christian, and whom she therefore was prepared to "hate." Had Schlomo not had his own change of heart, she assuredly would have hated him. He had indeed tried to leave his Jewishness behind with the wreckage of the war. He went into training to be an agent for the Dutch national airline, KLM. All seemed to be going well. But then, one evening, he happened by chance to see a confidential report of his progress. He was, it said, quick to learn and readily able to deal with people. That was well and good. But Schlomo was stunned by what he read next. The report recommended that he need not be kept out of direct contact with the public, since he did not "obviously look Jewish."

That gratuitous compliment did it. Schlomo decided that escaping—or attempting to escape—his heritage was not a positive endeavor. Soon he was on his way to Israel, where he knew that the many problems he would surely come up against would not include prejudice against Jews.

Nurit and Schlomo settled in the northern coastal city of Nahariya where he operated a small bicycle shop in the center of town. They had two children—Alexi, born in 1951, and Dini, born two years later. Since Schlomo and Nurit are not, by their own appraisal, sharp business people, it was hard going with the bicycle store. At times they could afford to eat nothing but eggs—a commodity which has always been cheap in Israel. Schlomo often got up and walked around in the night wondering how better to support his family. Though their situation slowly improved over the years, he never did find a different way.

In keeping with a knack of the Dutch, Schlomo and Nurit were quick to pick up languages. But they never became as comfortable with Hebrew as they already were with the English they had both learned in school, and they tended to read the English-language Jerusalem *Post* as often as any of the Hebrew-language newspapers. Nurit read with particular interest, from time to time, reports of those who were being honored with a tree on the Avenue of the Righteous. If anyone deserved such recognition, it was the Postmas. But one doubt held her back. She discussed it, finally, with a lawyer who was connected with the Memorial Authority at Yad Vashem.

"'I stayed with a family which is very dear to me,' I said to him. 'But they only saved one—is that enough to earn a tree?' He told me that I would have to write a letter to the Committee on the Righteous, which I did. Then I was called to Haifa where the member of the Committee in charge of Dutch cases heard my story in clear terms. A few months later I got a letter notifying me that the family Postma would be honored with a tree. But when I wrote to Siets to tell her, she wrote back right away, saying, 'You—aren't you crazy to do such a thing! For what? I did nothing!'

"That's my Siets."

Despite Sietske's protestations, the Jerusalem *Post* of July 27, 1976, records a ceremony held on the previous day at Yad Vashem at which Sietske Postma, representing her late father and also her brother, was honored as one among the Righteous. According to the ritual of the occasion, a memorial service was held in the Hall of Remembrance. Then the participants walked, in the dazzling Jerusalem sunlight, to the spot where the trees were to be planted. A photo of this part of the ceremony taken by the sabra Alexi DeHaas—though not quite centered, it catches the moment precisely—shows his mother and Sietske, each wearing sundresses, their four hands grasping the shovel, one on top of the other. Though the occasion is solemn, the two women are, in perfect character, laughing girlishly and even exultantly.

. . .

If you look north from the fine sandy beach at Nahariya, you can see a fierce outcropping of bluff beyond which is Lebanon. Yet the main street of this city is one of the few spots in Israel with a look that is distinctly European. Trees in stately rows shade small stores, boutiques, cafés, and bakeries which are proudly called *konditoreis*. Horses and carriages are available for hire. The DeHaas home is on a narrow side street at the north end of town. It is a two-minute walk to the beach, but the view is blocked by a stand of slender-leafed, thick-growing oleander bushes. The tiny yard of this stucco house has been carefully planted by Schlomo DeHaas with cactus, desert flowers, and tropical fruit trees. He seems determined never to plant a thing that would survive a cycle of seasons back in Holland. Arriving for the first time at this front door on a Sabbath eve a few days after the ceremony at Yad Vashem, I waited a moment before knocking. Through the screen door, from the back veranda, I heard two women breaking into laughter.

Judging by looks alone, few in Ferwerd would have been persuaded that these two were "cousins." Nurit looks out of a small, sharp-featured face, and if they did not have humor in them, her bright, unflinching dark eyes could remind you of a parakeet's. Sietske's features are more generous. Her deep-set eyes are calm, direct, and forthright. They are not the kind of eyes you would want looking at you if you had done something wrong. She is sixty-three years old, and her hair is streaked with white.

Until just a few years ago, this house was more sparsely appointed than it is now. But then the Dutch government granted reparation payments to victims of the Nazis, regardless of religion. At first, the independent-minded Schlomo was reticent to accept such payments. But after seeing that Dutch Christians were accepting them, he finally agreed to do the same. Given the extermination of his parents and many other family members, after all, he had lost at least as much as them. These payments have allowed

Nurit and Schlomo, for the first time in their lives, to spend money as they wish. They hired a woodcraftsman of the old school to build a handsome, free-standing stairway to their upstairs bedroom. Next to it they built a new bathroom with sleek Italian fixtures. They had Nurit's piano rebuilt, and installed Scandinavian-style furniture in the living room. "It only *looks* Scandinavian," says Nurit pointedly. "It comes from right here, from Israel."

Among the furnishings which are not new is an ancient Friesian clock that has been in Schlomo DeHaas's family for generations. It has only an hour hand. In the old days, he explains, people simply felt no need to know the time to the minute. Despite all that is new in their house, Schlomo and Nurit maintain modest tastes. The food is good and plain. But this being the Sabbath eve, she has set the table on a spanking-white, starched tablecloth, just as her mother did when she was a girl.

Before and after that meal, Sietske clasped her hands and bowed her head in a moment of grace—a custom which Nurit had not regularly honored since she was a young woman in Ferwerd. In this week now ended, Nurit could look back with satisfaction on a ceremony in which her savior had been thanked formally by the nation. But at dinner Nurit began to speak about someone who would never have a tree planted for him. It was the doctor who, remote as he had been to her, she well knew was the leader of the underground movement in Ferwerd. He too had been indispensable to her survival. Yet, until a few years ago, Nurit had never said her thanks. This was not a matter of chance or forgetfulness, she now explained. "He was a strange man, this Dr. Smit. He had a harelip and also a clubfoot. That's not why I say he's strange, of course. He was just terribly stiff and cold. He had a way of making you so uncomfortable. Siets herself didn't like him and couldn't stand to be near him. But the last time I was in Holland I said, 'Siets, I must go myself and thank him now or perhaps there will never be another chance.'

"She didn't want me to go and she certainly didn't want to go herself. But when she saw that I was determined, she would not let me go alone. When he received us at home, it was no easier than we expected. He seemed more aloof and more difficult than ever. I was looking for a way to break through his shield. But nothing seemed to work. Then I asked, 'Would you like to come to visit Israel?'

"'No,' he snapped. 'Hummff. I have seen the Sea of Galilee on television now. It is so very small. When I was a child reading the Bible, I thought it was so very big! Hummff.'

"He was silent again. I whispered to Siets, 'How can I thank him? I don't know what to do.' I had brought him a map from Israel and also a little silver souvenir. But it was nothing. If his wife had been home, I thought perhaps through her I could have made a connection. I didn't know what to do. And suddenly it came to me. It was the only possibility. I took out our photos of Alexi and Dini—the same two that are on my piano,

"'Doctor,' I said, 'do you see them? It's through you. Because if you hadn't saved me, then I wouldn't have these two lovely children.'

"He got tears in his eyes. He started to cry. Siets was dumb-founded. But this was a man I had to find a way to thank—not just for myself either. He had personally hidden a Jewish woman and two children in his own house. And in his cellar he had hidden hundreds of ration cards. I asked him how many Jews he had saved altogether.

"'About twenty,' he answered.

"'And have any come back to thank you?'

"'No. Hummff.'

"So I was the only one. But it was not for lack of other survivors. Every Jew who was under his wing came out alive. But he is so difficult. After the war they didn't like him in Ferwerd, so they drove him out in favor of a new doctor. He was the sort who, even if he was awarded the Yad Vashem medal, I don't think he would accept. He was just a difficult and bitter man. Soon after I saw him he died."

. . .

Today, as when Nurit first made the trip, the way to Ferwerd from Amsterdam is by train to the provincial capital of Leeuwarden and from there by a bus that wends its way through pasturelands guarded by the grassy dikes that hold back the dreary North Sea. It was 8:30 when I arrived here one September evening in 1976. Hoofdstraadt, the main street, was deserted and there was no sound except for a low but constant wind and a friendly buzz issuing from a tavern. Across from it, in a row of modest town houses, was No. 9.

As in so many of the village houses the bus had passed, the lights were on and the curtains left undrawn. For one arriving from France, where curtains, shutters, gates, and fences shut out the world as soon as dark falls, this openness came as a pleasant surprise. The house was just as Nurit had described it but, clear view or not, inside there was nobody in sight. Only when I rang the bell did a figure appear from the rear. I was befuddled; it was not Sietske but a young and quite beautiful girl with billowing blonde hair. Yet I knew that Siets, the spinster schoolteacher, had lived alone here since her father died. Was I at the right address in the wrong town? Had there been a mix-up about the weekend for which I had been invited? What would this young woman think upon being confronted by a strange American on her doorstep?

But as she walked closer I realized who it was—though I knew her only from a photo on the DeHaases' piano back in Nahariya. It was their daughter Dini, now on her first extended visit outside of Israel. I was relieved as well as surprised to see her, knowing that she could handily translate Dutch into English. Moreover, if it was in the Friesian nature to be taciturn, it was in the Israeli nature to talk. As the door opened, I kissed a silent weekend goodbye.

While Sietske served a simple dinner she had been keeping warm, Dini explained that she was staying here, rather than with real relatives from her father's side still remaining in Holland, because she preferred to be here. "With the others, I feel such an age difference," she said. "But with Siets I am at ease and at home. We have so much fun!" With that explanation, Dini wrapped her arms around the older woman, putting her head so close that her hair fell in Sietske's face and letting out a big, throaty laugh that could have rattled the dishes.

After dinner Dini slung one leg over a big armchair and went back to reading, in Dutch, *The Diary of Anne Frank*, which she had somehow never read while growing up in a Dutch-Jewish home in Israel. She looked up after a while, her face somber and thoughtful. "My mother was so lucky. While Anne Frank was cooped up back in Amsterdam until the Gestapo came and ended it, she was here for two years that were like heaven. My father survived here in Friesland as well. But he was shunted from one hiding place to another—twelve in all. In most of them he had to work very hard. They used him badly. But he doesn't talk about it. I know the stories only from my mother. He tries not to remember it, but he is always remembering it."

Still somber, Dini put down her book and went over to Sietske. "We are the chosen people," she said, wrapping her arms around her, as if to take hold of some of that Friesian calm. "Chosen to suffer!"

In Israel once I had asked Sietske—not as a victim or an historian but as a Christian who had kept the death count down by one—if she had any explanation for how the Holocaust could have happened. Nurit had fastened her dark, unblinking eyes on Sietske, waiting as well for an answer. But Sietske only looked down at her knees, her large eyes sunk deeper into their hollows than usual, shaking her head. Though she said not a word, it seemed as eloquent an answer as any. Tonight, after watching the evening news, Sietske flipped off the television and said, "Some months ago I saw a program in which a reporter interviewed a man who had been a guard here at our transit camp at Westerbork. He now lives in Mannheim. The reporter asked if he knew at the time that the trains were leaving for Auschwitz.

"'Yes,' he answered. For once, here was a German who did not claim ignorance. But then the reporter asked, 'Did you find it hard to sleep at night?'

" 'Oh, you get used to it,' he answered.

" 'With a thousand people packed aboard each train going off every few days like that, you could sleep at night?'

" 'Oh, yes . . .'

" 'And you could sleep at night?'

" 'Yes.' "

Plainly, that interviewer had not kept asking that man whether he could sleep at night over and over like a parrot, nor had the man responded in that fashion. It was Sietske, asking now for herself a variant on the question I had asked her. The answer was no different. Here in her own house she also sat staring at her knees, shaking her head in silence.

As I stood at the window in the morning watching a North Sea fog roll in, she came over to stand beside me. "One day I stood as you are standing and I saw Nurit come to this door when she was twenty-two years old," she said. "And then, a short time ago, I stood here and watched Dini come to the door. And she also was twenty-two." Sietske flashed me a smile.

"Pretty neat, huh? Pretty neat!"

It was early and very cold when, on the next morning, I left to catch the bus for Leeuwarden and home. But Sietske, who had risen earlier to fix breakfast while Dini went on dozing, insisted on coming with me to the tiny town square to wait. We stood in a steady sea wind that shot across the dikes and the low fields— so wet that even a turbot would have felt at home in it. I could newly appreciate what a mitzvah it had been, in those days, for Sietske to have given Nurit her good winter coat.

Sietske was waving as the bus pulled away. Though I doubted that she could see me through the green-tinted glass, she continued to smile and wave vigorously until at the end of the town the bus went around a curve and out of sight. That gesture has been fixed in my mind ever since. Except for small children who, having only recently learned to wave, go on with the gesture long after their parents have stopped, few people would persist in waving and smiling when they could no longer see you. But for Sietske, it was a form of support, however small, and she was not about to put down her arm, let alone turn her back. Her nature will not allow it. If she lets you into her life, then she will stand by you, in large matters and with small gestures.

One night late the following summer in Nahariya, Nurit mentioned something Sietske had done that was both a large matter and a small gesture. Perhaps she would never even have thought to mention it if she was not about to go upstairs to bed. As she stood on the stairway, all was quiet except for Schlomo's family's ancient Friesian clock. Raspy and cranky, its single hand keeps on going as it did for generations now lost. "In Ferwerd," said Nurit, "I was always careful never to go by any name other than Franciska Slujk. And that was what Siets called me, even if we were in the kitchen together, just washing dishes. She never allowed any slip-ups. But each night, when we were in our beds and the lights were out, Sietske would whisper from across the room:

" 'Good night, Noortje.'

"This was my name from when I was a little girl, from when my family was still alive. And every night for two years she whispered this. She didn't want me to forget my own name."

EPILOGUE, 1999

At century's end, Sietske Postma, age eighty-three, still lives actively in Ferwerd. She drives a snappy red Peugeot with manual shift and no radio—"my sixteenth car" she told me by telephone in her limited but energetic English. "Three Fiats, four Audis, and nine Peugeots." Which led Sietske to another lifetime statistic: "In thirty-two years of teaching I had 780 children, ages six and seven. And not one of them my own production!" She sounded relieved at that. As for her health, Sietske said, "My eyes, my feet, my hands, my lips—all are good. Fantastic!"

Nurit and Schlomo DeHaas, almost eighty themselves, remain in their seaside villa in Nahariya. The cactii which Schlomo planted in the yard decades ago are enormous. In the living room, the one-handed clock that has been in his family for generations rasps and clanks faithfully. They are regular volunteers in a local home for retarded children.

The bond between Sietske and Nurit stays firm. They exchange visits each year, sometimes in Israel, more often in Holland. "To be with her," says Nurit, "is the only time I feel like I'm in heaven—just as it was on our first day." Something else that's the same: "Sietske never raises her voice, but I see in her grey eyes when she is angry."

The DeHaas's son, Alex, is an engineer who lives with his family near the Lebanon border in northern Israel—a place where Katyusha rockets have often struck. Dini DeHaas has settled in Amsterdam where she helps released convicts find jobs. "My mom and Sietske share something quite extraordinary," says Dini. "When I see them together my mom is always happy—only with her. Sietske is the only person with whom she is completely herself."

Raoul Laporterie

After lunch one afternoon in February 1941, Nessim and Sarah Yaeche and their three children closed up the apartment they had long occupied at 47, rue Sainte-Catherine in the heart of Bordeaux. At their fabric shop on the same street, they made their unwilling goodbyes to Sarah's parents, who would try to keep up the store. Then a waiting car took them seventy miles south through endless pinelands to Mont-de-Marsan, a bustling hill city in the otherwise flat province of Landes in the southwest of France.

The car left them on a narrow commercial street in front of a smallish haberdashery called La Petite Maison. Keeping their children close, the parents took a deep breath before entering. Once inside, they did their best to look like normal customers until they could be acknowledged by the proprietor, a fine-featured, dapper, and relaxed man named Raoul Laporterie.

There remains in the upstairs office of La Petite Maison, nearly four decades later, a photo of Laporterie taken at that time. He sports a fashionably thin mustache and a smile plays in his dark eyes as well as on his lips. It is a face you might expect to see on the cover of a theater playbill—perfect for a leading man in a light farce—rather than on a storekeeper. And, in fact, on that evening near closing time he was enacting a play of sorts—though not exactly a farce—showing the Yaeche family a coat, a hat, bolts of fine woolens which he knew they had no intention of buying. By prior arrangement, the family had come here to seek Laporterie's services not as a clothier but as what in those days was called a *passeur*—someone who could slip them across the border from occupied France into the so-called Vichy Republic.

When the last customer had been shown out the door, Laporterie took the family upstairs to his office where he banished the name Yaeche—husband, wife, three children—for the rest of the war. Since all Jews had been required to register the previous fall, the name would remain on file with the police and the Gestapo. When the hour arrived for the family Yaeche to be taken away for deportation from their home of record on Rue Sainte-Catherine, more probably under escort by French collaborators than the Gestapo, all trace of them would be gone. Laporterie would see to that. But he was not ready just yet to furnish the family with names that would last safely for the rest of the war.

For now, Laporterie sized up Nessim Yaeche as adroitly as the clothier he was—perhaps more adroitly, since to this day he would be the first to admit to more success as a *passeur* than as a clothier. Then he sifted through his own personal—and precious—file of about three dozen official French identification cards until he came to one bearing the name of a certain Jean Lafont. Born June 19, 1902. Height 1.70 meters. Hair and eyes brown . . .

"This one will do the trick," said Laporterie. And he pasted Nessim Yaeche's photo on the card. With it came a ration card, also in the name of Jean Lafont, and finally the precious *Ausweis für den kleinen Grenzverkehr*—permit to cross small frontiers. With that completed *carte d'identité* tucked into his jacket pocket, Nessim Yaeche was now officially—for today, at least—Jean Lafont. The name was not made up. None of the names in the file were. Each could be traced back to real blood and bones from the nearby village of Bascons where Laporterie was mayor. But the new Lafont did not have to worry about confronting the old Lafont—even in Bascons, where Laporterie would offer the family temporary lodging in the house of his birth. Like all the others in that file of ID cards, Lafont had long been dead.

Laporterie now turned to Sarah Yaeche. She was assigned the name of his own wife, Laure. This automatically turned the three Yaeche children into Laporteries. The two older children— Huguette and Albert—accepted their new names quietly. But when five-year-old Roger was told that if he ever used his own name again the Germans would kill him, he cried fearfully and bitterly. In that winter of 1941, most Frenchmen, including most French Jews, would have blamed his parents for overstating the case. It would be another full year before their warnings as well as the child's tears were proved to be scaled to the truth.

Then, their new identities complete, the family crowded into Laporterie's ancient black Renault parked in front of the store. They sat there while Laporterie stopped for a moment to banter with some German officers at the Café du Sport across the street. Finally Laporterie threaded the car through the narrow streets of the town and headed south on route 462. After four kilometers, they came to a halt at the bottom of a gentle slope in the two-lane road. At this spot the French nation was cut by the line of demarcation drawn by the conqueror on June 25, 1940, and closely guarded by patrols, attack dogs, and checkpoints like this one. On the north side, from which they had just come, the Germans reigned directly as occupiers. On the south, or Vichy, side, they allowed the French to conduct their own affairs, puppet-style, free of the humiliation of a visible, booted Nazi presence.

"Just act natural," whispered Laporterie as two Wehrmacht border guards ordered him and his charges out of the car. He was no stranger to these guards. At least twice each day, Laporterie commuted on this road between his store in Mont-de-Marsan and his home, about twelve kilometers on the other side of the line, in the village of Grenade-sur-l'Adour. Four more kilometers down a country road was Bascons, the smaller village where he still maintained the house in which he had been born. Bascons was so small, in fact, that the citizenry did not blame their mayor for living in Grenade. Besides, by common consent, the town never had a better mayor.

It was plain that the guards not only knew Laporterie but were glad to see him. He was, for one thing, unfailingly good-humored. He seemed to look upon them not as oppressors but as decent fellows like himself, doing a thankless job as best they could. But they had better reasons to look well upon this Frenchman. Didn't he maintain, despite the privations of war, a superior stock of clothing in his store of a type utterly unavailable in their own country? Wouldn't he carefully and cheerfully pack up their purchases to send home to their families? Hadn't he once even brought them a gift of two dozen briny-fresh oysters? Anything less than the most forthcoming treatment of their favorite Frenchman would have been merely churlish.

With Laporterie's passengers, the guards were more careful. They inspected the *carte d'identité* of each adult, being sure that the physical description corresponded to the photo and to the person. They checked the ration card and the Ausweis. They ordered the tradesman Lafont to undress in a cabin at the side of the road for a thorough search. There was nothing to find, of course. All the money and valuables that the family Yaeche had brought with them from Bordeaux, nearly all of which they would trade for sustenance and safety in the coming years, remained hidden away in the store at Mont-de-Marsan. Laporterie would bring every bit of it, hidden in various crevices of the Renault, on another day. In the meantime, Yaeche could only be grateful that the guards had not asked him to drop his drawers, thereby uncovering the only incriminating evidence he could not leave behind. Most tradesmen from French villages were baptized but not circumcised.

In ten minutes, it was done. The Renault, carrying its unflappable driver and five profoundly relieved passengers, chugged up the slope into unoccupied France. For the family Yaeche, it was the beginning of a four-year campaign to survive. For many *passeurs*—there was no lack of them along the frontier—the job would now be finished. Having collected as much money as they could or dared, they would quickly rid themselves of their clients. But for Laporterie, at eight o'clock on this evening, the day had hardly begun, and among all his concerns the least was money—except insofar as it meant replacing the funds he had taken from the family at his store in Mont-de-Marsan with an equal amount from his own reserves at home in Grenade-sur-l'Adour. From there he would drive the Yaeches down the pretty country road to Bascons, where he would install them in his own house. Then, at the village hall, his trusted assistant, Henri Dumartin, would go to work making up permanent identities for the family. They would become the family of Paul and Jeanne Grenier, thereby resuscitating the name of a loyal and lifelong villager even as his remains continued to rest in the graveyard down the road.

Finally, at the end of the evening, there was the mail to deal with. Stashed in the false bottoms of the reserve gasoline cans of the Renault, there were hundreds of pieces of mail which could not legally be sent at this time from one zone of France to the other. Only postcards, written in a prescribed fourteen-line format, were permitted by the Germans. The going rate for a *passeur* to deliver an interzonal letter was five to ten francs. Laporterie never charged anything—which is only one reason why, unlike certain *passeurs*, he emerged from the war a poor man.

Oddly enough, in the first weeks after the line of demarcation was drawn on June 25, 1940, the heaviest pressure to cross it came from the south, as tens of thousands who had fled the Nazi blitzkrieg now wished to trek back home. Even more oddly, Jews were as anxious as anyone else to get back to homes where the Germans—or more likely, French police—would, one day soon, thump on the door. After that, the flow was mostly the other way. There were escaped prisoners of war who hoped to evade recapture. There were priests and nuns who knew that the Nazis had no use for them. There were young men who wanted to cross the line and escape being drafted into forced labor. Then there were the Jews.

They came from as far away as Amsterdam, Antwerp, and Brussels. If they had been born in Germany, Poland, or other Eastern European countries where the Nazis had already come down hard on the Jews before the invasion of the west, they were, inevitably, fleeing for the second time. When the Germans wanted Jews to deport, the French first gave them these foreign-born. That was a fact on both sides of the line. Vichy France was not unyielding to German wishes, in absentia, on Jewish matters. *Liberté, Egalité, Fraternité* notwithstanding, the Vichy government was quick to enact racial laws which defined Jews—qualified them for a unique end, really—even more stringently than Hitler had caused them to be defined at Nuremberg in 1935. Special police units were formed, as in the north, to hunt Jews. Special camps were secured to hold them. Scarce rolling stock was reserved to ship the catch back to the Occupied Zone where the tracks curved east to the killing centers. When the Germans insisted that no train was to leave the south loaded with less than a thousand Jews, local French authorities generally complied, even if it meant sending out the police to scrape up, for good measure, a few dozen extra bodies at the last moment.

It took luck to survive such hunts in the south, but it took much more luck in the north. With the Gestapo looking over their shoulders, the gendarmes were bound to try just a little harder. They proved how much harder on July 16 and 17, 1942, when they rounded up some thirteen thousand Jews in a perfectly planned and executed sweep of Paris. About half were sent directly to Drancy, the camp closest to Paris. The other half—mostly women, children, and old people—were stuffed into the Vélodrome d'Hiver, an indoor sports stadium, where they were held under abominable sanitary conditions for several days before being shipped to holding camps to await the trains to Auschwitz. The gendarmes proved how diligent they could be in at least three cases, when seriously ill Jews, upon being arrested in the middle of the night, expired. As they were under orders to deliver the persons listed to the Vélodrome d'Hiver, the gendarmes wrapped the corpses in blankets and carried out the job.

So, all in all, it was better to be on the run in the environs of the Côte d'Azur than in Paris. Things were not so organized. Better yet, one always had the chance to scoot across the Italian border from Nice. The *carabinieri* showed, in general, even less inclination than the most lackadaisical gendarme for hunting Jews—even under orders. Best of all, however, was the prospect of getting across the border with Spain and on to Portugal. Except for Sweden and Switzerland, there was in Western Europe no other haven from deportation to the killing centers.

The first step to any of the above prospects was to cross the line of demarcation. To be a Jew with a legal *Ausweis*, however, was a contradiction in terms. Even for gentiles with every good reason to enter the unoccupied zone, an *Ausweis* was hard to get. In Paris, at the German administrative offices on rue du Colisée, hundreds of applicants lined up at dawn, ready to claim every variety of affliction, family tragedy, or crisis. Many came with doctors' certificates urgently prescribing "taking the cure" at spas in the south like Châtelguyon, Royat, or Eugénie-les-Bains. These requests were almost routinely denied. Telegrams announcing the death of a father or mother stood a better chance of persuading the Germans to grant an *Ausweis*. But no matter how many waited outside, only fifty cases a day were processed. Then, out of whim or spite, the Germans sometimes closed down the line of demarcation entirely. Privilege was extended to few. No less a personage than Xavier Vallat, Commissioner for Jewish Affairs in the Vichy regime, had to apply for an *Ausweis* to travel freely between the two zones. Given the ever-increasing load of anti-Jewish orders coming from Paris, it would seem that nobody needed an *Ausweis* like Xavier Vallat. But, steeped as he was in the work dearest to Hitler's heart, his application was denied. Vallat might have done better—provided his cause had been right—to apply for his *Ausweis* in the small office of La Petite Maison in Mont-de-Marsan.

Under Laporterie's shepherding, certainly, the trip across the line of demarcation had been painless for the Yaeche family. As they prepared to sleep on this first night away from home in the comfortable house lent to them by their host in that village of Bascons, they could not know how desperately other Jews would try to make this same passage in another year's time. They could not know about the killing centers. They could not, in short, know what it was they were escaping from. They only knew that the farther away from the Germans they could get, the better off they would be.

Only one cloud still hung over the family—particularly Madame Yaeche. She wished that her aging parents, Asher and Simcha Haim, had agreed to come with them. Despite her entreaties, they had insisted on staying put in Bordeaux. In a few days, Laporterie would succeed with them where their daughter had not. He persuaded them to come, under his personal escort, from Bordeaux to Bascons on a sort of trial run. But after a short time, they insisted on going back.

"Don't worry," they said. "The Germans won't want us. We're much too old to be sent to work camps. When you come home, you'll find us safe. . . ."

Today there is nothing but a slight widening of the shoulders of route 462 to mark the spot where Laporterie established himself as master of border crossings. From this spot, now as then, the land trails off into endless miles of scrub pine, underbrush, and ditches. It is damp nearly everywhere here. That is why the region was originally named Aquitaine. That is also why in old prints of the area you can see, improbably, shepherds tending their flocks while standing on stilts. To keep from sinking, the stilts are shoed with large, flattened knobs. Even now, after the tenacious application of modern methods of swamp drainage and even on what seem to be firm beds of pine needles, this is a region of a prevailing squishiness underfoot.

It is twelve more kilometers down the road from the former line of demarcation to the village of Grenade-sur-l'Adour, population two thousand, where Laporterie still lives with his wife, Laure. Even as the average *landais* village goes, this one is high on a kind of charm which Laporterie himself sums up as "coquette." The few streets amble into the village square. In the middle of the square is a fountain which, despite various tiers of geysers and pools, manages to look merely playful rather than formal. Though this square has not escaped the auto any more than that of the remotest village of Europe, at least it is planted with young trees. A barnlike nineteenth-century church dominates the east side of the square, and it is the least charming building in the town. It faces an arcade whose columns were hewn, long ago, from the whole trunks of big oaks. They stand firm even as the buildings above have begun to sag. Behind those oak columns and sagging buildings flows the river Adour. It is a middling-sized stream that takes a lazy route to the Atlantic past flat pinelands and farms where big white geese waddle, presumably with no notion that their fame and fate rest securely in their swollen livers. In delicacy shops from Place Madeleine to Broadway, only caviar will fetch more. Along the banks of the Adour here in Grenade, in spring, the prize flowers are the cow lilies. When it rains and the river rises, they sway in the current—big, dumb, waxy. Overhead, starlings wheel and dive and chatter like wind in wires. They do it when it rains as well as when the sky is blue.

Laporterie lives on a corner of this square in the rear portion of the original Petite Maison. The front is a general store. It may seem minuscule compared with the sprawling discount emporiums that American suburbanites now grow up shopping in. But the stock here would give those places a good run for their money. You can find an alarm clock, a pair of pajamas, a bicycle inner tube, every sort of cosmetic, a meat thermometer. The difference is that you need one of the proprietors, Laure Laporterie or her daughter Irène, to extract what you want from high and low cubbyholes, closets, cabinets, and mahogany drawers. They can probably even find a few items which remain unavailable back home at K-Mart or Caldor with their acres of aisles and their long overhead fluorescents which, put end to end, would stretch to the moon. Just ask.

This is not actually Laporterie's town but his wife's town. She was born here, and before the couple established La Petite Maison, her parents kept a clothing store down the street from the square. She and her daughter are small women, solid and erect, with grey hair pulled back over full, handsome features. Both are grandmothers now, one a great-grandmother. When I arrive at four o'clock on a May afternoon, Laure Laporterie goes to the rear door leading to the residence to call her husband.

"Ra-ool," she sings out. The name casts off at a normal pitch and sails up from there—high, clear, sweet, and seamless. It is as startling to hear such a sound out of this small grey woman as it is to see a fat person dance lightly.

"Ra-ooool . . ."

It has not been easy to get this appointment with Laporterie. Not that he was unwilling. But his schedule, as he explained when I finally got him on the phone from Paris earlier in the week, is full almost every day. This week alone, he has gone to meetings of the Cancer Society, the Tuberculosis Society, and several committees responsible for planning the Fêtes de Mont-de-Marsan, a kind of ten-day-long Mardi gras-cum-bullfights that occurs each July and is clearly the joy of his life. He has been its mainstay for decades, and now that the time is approaching he is especially busy. But on this Friday he has cleared away a few late afternoon hours during which he will be glad to be of service.★

Laporterie appears suddenly at the door, so suddenly you can't be sure if he came from the rear or just materialized on the spot.

★Translating at this and future meetings with Laporterie was Violet Hellman, my mother.

He is a good mate for his wife—not tall, but compact and solid, with good carriage. His thinning grey hair is combed back immaculately. His eyes are pale brown. He wears a flawlessly tailored grey suit. Nothing about the man suggests that in three months, as he is quick to point out with pride, he will be an *octogénaire*. Certainly he does not look within fifteen, maybe even twenty, years of that age. But it is more than looks that throws you off. Old people who are as immaculately preserved as Laporterie tend to handle themselves as cautiously as one would handle antique china that is intact but fragile. But he is as fast as a rabbit. When a paper drops, he swoops down to pick it up with a movement which in a less limber man would have rattled the vertebrae.

Laporterie's study, at the back of his living quarters, is a dark room full of trophies and memorabilia and civic appreciations. Not only does Laporterie speak at high velocity but he speaks with an odd accent. It sounds as though it might be Basque, but he says it is Landaise. Despite the proximity of that region of Spain, he speaks no Basque because, as he explains, "It is crazily hard and you have to be born speaking it." But he does speak the *landais patois* very well. It was spoken in every home when he was a child, and even in the classroom. He took a little Spanish in school but stayed away from English because it had too many "irregular verbs." These are the only two English words we ever hear Laporterie speak. He pronounces "verbs" like "wherebs."

"Since we are near the border," he says, "I speak more Spanish than English. And," he adds with a fast smile, "more English than Hebrew."

Whatever he was able to do to help people pass between the two Frances, he explains now, was thanks to three lucky strokes of geography. The first was that he owned the store in Mont-de-Marsan, just inside the Occupied Zone. The second was that he lived here in Grenade-sur-l'Adour, just inside the Free Zone. The third was that he was mayor of Bascons, also here in the Free Zone. Together, the three added up to more than the sum of their parts. Since he was a trans-zonal commuter, the Germans granted him an *Ausweis*. As a mayor, he was granted the right to apply for *Ausweise* for the storekeepers and other little businesses of his community who could not be denied the regional marketplace of Mont-de-Marsan.

Laporterie's own *Ausweis* authorized him to cross the line of demarcation only on route 462 and restricted his movements to within ten kilometers of each side of the line. Laporterie points out with a shrug, however, that from the beginning he regarded this limitation as *élastique*. He violated it constantly, though not necessarily out of need. Whatever the Germans ordered, he did the opposite "as a matter of principle." In any case, for travel to distant cities he had other identification cards and other *Ausweise*. The *Ausweis* of others—particularly those he had acquired for the dead of Bascons—Laporterie regarded as even more *élastique* than his own.

Laporterie started his career as a *passeur* by carrying letters and small parcels for friends, for friends of friends, and, as the word inevitably spread, for strangers. At first it was a simple matter of finding hiding places in his Renault and trusting to luck and charm. Soon he was passing the people themselves, using his newly developed technique of resuscitating a variety of late citizens of Bascons.

"If you needed to cross the line of demarcation," explains Laporterie, "I picked someone of your age and description from among those who no longer needed an ID card or an *Ausweis* of their own. To this I would add your photo and the seal of the town. Validating these papers was my job as mayor. However, since I passed almost two thousand people and Bascons had a population of only six hundred, sometimes I had to make myself the mayor of another town. If you were from Gironde, I became the mayor of a town in that province. Or, rather, I had a seal which said I was the mayor. Out of my own pocket I also paid fifteen francs for the tax stamp for the *Ausweis*. I gave you a receipt for money and property, which I always passed separately. If you were just catching a ride with me back to Bascons, after all, you should only be carrying pocket money. At the frontier the doyens would examine your papers.

They would search you in one of their little cabins. Then they would say, 'Go!'

"'And that,'" sums up Laporterie, "is all I did for two years."

It seems astonishing, in retrospect, that Laporterie was able to wrap the rigid German border regulations around his finger for so long. Didn't the frontier guards grow suspicious of the man and his daily entourage? "They did not put the greatest German patriots in these little places," answers Laporterie with a shrug and a dry smile. "And we little Frenchmen—we had the reputation for being very crafty. I had my tricks. If passengers were in the car, for example, I always arrived at the frontier at exactly seven-fifty in the evening, ten minutes before the doyens were to be relieved. They didn't want to waste too much time with us. They wanted their dinner. Besides, I kept them more interested in what I had in my shop waiting for them than in my passengers. I spoiled them a little.

"The main point, of course, is that when these doyens said, '*Papiers*'"—here Laporterie gives the word a mocking, robotlike inflection—"my passengers handed over the correct papers. They might not have been more than a few hours old, but they were always correct. I never failed them in that."

Now that the basics of his regimen in the war have been almost airily disposed of, Laporterie has moved to the edge of his chair. It is apparent that he has meant the explanation so far to be only a preamble to something else on his mind.

"After the war, suddenly you heard from so many people how courageously they had worked against the enemy. Everybody had a story to tell. Well, I don't have stories. I don't have embroideries. I have the proofs. They are in the form of all the letters of thanks that came from those who had need of my services. In more than thirty years, I have shown them to almost nobody until today."

With that, Laporterie leaps up and darts to the door of a walk-in pantry. Most of the shelves in this neat little windowless room are lined with sealed bottles of jams, jellies, preserved fruits, and pickled vegetables prepared by his wife and daughter. The top shelf is lined with the tallest bottles. They are filled with extraordinarily long, unblemished, ivory-toned asparagus. If famine comes, this family will continue to eat well for a long time. But Laporterie does not even glance at this trove. He is busy in the right side of the pantry, clearly a separate domain, going through two long rows of bound black scrapbooks. They are as neatly kept as those wonderful bottles. In them are his proofs.

Laporterie lugs a stack of the scrapbooks back to the table. He opens the first to a frayed green leatherette folder containing a two-part ID card and *Ausweis*, printed in German and in French. It contains a photo, a fingerprint, and a precise description of his facial structure, against which the border guards could compare the photo. Laporterie's hair is black in this photo, his eyes dark and sparkling. Though most men are prone to look like dullards in official photos, Laporterie is smiling a gentle, even alluring smile. At one corner this picture is unglued. Behind it is a small portrait of a Jesus with downcast eyes.

"*Ça c'est le Christ qui m'a protégé* [That is the Christ who protected me]," he says with matter-of-fact assurance.

This first ID card was the one Laporterie used for his daily business and border crossings on route 462. It turns out to be only one of several such precious documents which he refers to simply as *les pièces*. It also happens to be the only one which contains a true statement of his identity. For other purposes, he had other *pièces*.

"Look here," he says, slipping to the next page, "in this one I am a *Bauführer*—a construction foreman. I was supposed to be in charge of building concrete blockhouses all the way down the Atlantic coast to Biarritz. That's why, according to this ID, it says I lived at the Hôtel Saint-Jean in Biarritz, which would normally have been reserved for quartering German officers. I have never set foot there. Not then and not now. But this ID gave me great freedom of movement because, when the Germans saw that I was a *Bauführer*, helping them to fortify the beaches against the invasion they were expecting eventually, they were very pleased. Here was one Frenchman, they thought, on their side. But while I seemed to be doing them a service, as usual, I was rolling them for all I could."

Laporterie flips the pages next to identification papers in the name of Paul Casunard. His profession is entered as traveling salesman based in Pau, a city to the southeast of Grenade. Then comes another complete ID, including ration cards, for Edgar Lamanière, another salesman, this time from the city of Dax. Each bears the same photo of Laporterie. It seems as if these additional ID's are purely superfluous. But he explains that along with his stores and his commuting chores between Grenade-sur-l'Adour and Mont-de-Marsan, he was also a faithful and busy soldier in the Gaullist underground army. "When I had a delicate mission to perform, I always used one of these other names," he says. "That way, if I was caught they could send me to Dachau, but I'd know that my family would not also be taken."

It looks as if there must be another tiny image of Jesus tucked beneath the loosened edge of the photo on the ID of Paul Casunard. But this time a sere and brittle leaf flutters to the floor. "It's the blessed laurel of the Catholics," Laporterie explains, stooping quicker than I, as usual, to pick it up. "I always carried something like that close to me."

The next album is devoted to letters from persons who needed mail or parcels forwarded across the frontier during the first months after France was cut in two. "I got your address from a friend this afternoon," writes Mademoiselle Alsberge from the town of Tourcoing. "I dare to believe that you will excuse me for taking the liberty to ask a service which isn't without danger for you. If you think you can get this [enclosed] letter delivered, you'll make me very happy, because my fiancé is without news of me for a month. . . ."

Since food is as serious a concern as love in a French heart, there is also a request from one Jean Maître to forward a small parcel to his mother-in-law at Clamart. "It contains a packet of grains for her garden. By this same mail I am expediting to you a box containing seeds of peas, beans, carrots, and so on, and a bit of string. The whole batch should not be too encumbering. . . ."

Another letter is from a woman named Madame Breton, the mother of a soldier who lives near Bucy-le-Long in l'Aisne.

Monsieur,

It's me, Madame "Old" Breton, the mama of Corporal Charles Breton, who sent me your address so that you might be able to pass his letters. I have sent this little package. It is letter-writing paper and, if you wish, I will send you a money order for him also. But first I'll wait for you to answer, because, believe me, it is hard for a mother to know that her son is without money.

I count on you, and if you could ask him if he has need of underwear, I'll make you up a package. I count on you. . . .

Such letters as the one above may not seem to fall in the category of forbidden communiqués. But, in fact, the Germans had forbidden all mail between the zones in the summer after the line of demarcation was drawn. In September, mindful of the torments as well as the simple inconveniences such a vacuum produced, the Germans relented in their own fashion. They authorized a new standard postcard. All the bench marks of life could now be reduced, with a certain genius, to a fixed, fill-in-the-blank, fourteen-line format:

. . . of . . . . 194 . . .

. . . . is in good health . . . . tired . . . .

. . . . is slightly, gravely sick, wounded . . . .

. . . . is killed . . . . prisoner . . . .

. . . . dead . . . . without news since . . . .

The family . . . . is well . . . .

. . . . needs provisions . . . . money . . . .

. . . . news, baggage . . . . will return on . . . .

. . . . works . . . . will return to school on . . . .

. . . . has been received . . . . going to . . . . . . on . . . . . .

. . . .

. . . .

. . . .

Fondest thoughts. Kisses . . . . Signature

Laporterie now opens a curious scrapbook filled exclusively with envelopes in which thank-you notes have been sent incorrectly addressed. He has long ago thrown away most of the notes themselves but has pasted in these envelopes by the dozen. "Look here," he says with surprise as fresh as if the postman had just delivered the letter, "it's addressed to Monsieur La Portage. . . . Here's one to Lapatrière . . . Portaneux . . . La Porte. And here's one to Monsieur *de* la Porterie. *Voilà!* I've become a nobleman! Look where they've addressed this one to La Maison Blanche, like your President Carter lives in. Here is La Maison Grande . . . La Maison Elégante . . . La Maison Française . . ."

Grateful as they are, it is obvious that many of these writers are even hazier about the address than about the name of their benefactor. They have sent their letters of thanks simply to some variant of "Laporterie" in the Province of Landes, or to Adour—a river lined with many towns, as Laporterie points out—or to Gironde, which is the wrong province. Yet they have all arrived. Astonishingly, there is even a writer who, having gotten the name of this village only slightly wrong, seems to think he has been passed directly across an international frontier. His letter is addressed to "La Petite Maison, Granada, Espagne." The fact that it arrived at this door gives Laporterie a new rush of delight. This whole album, in fact, gives him the joy of a stamp collector who has assembled an album of stamps printed with mistakes like upside-down airplanes.

"But all this is amusing only to me," he says, putting the album aside. "What interests you is Jewish matters." He brings out the next album, but for a moment leaves it closed. "It is true that I helped Jews," he says, speaking without smiling now. "But often I didn't know they were Jews until after they arrived in the Zone Libre or even until they wrote to me after the war was over. This was because when people asked for help I never asked them if they were Jews or anything else. If I could help, I did so gladly—the more so if their trouble was greater. But it didn't matter to me who they were."

From the tone of some early letters in this album, it hardly seems to be a matter of concern to the writers themselves that they are Jews. A certain Monsieur D. Schinazi, a broker at 199, rue Achard in Bordeaux, writes diffidently that "having need for business purposes to get into the non-occupied zone, I would be very much obliged if you would give me any useful information on this subject. As my mother has already had recourse to your service, I have thought to write to you. Let me know what day, as soon as possible, that I could come to Mont-de-Marsan."

Is this Schinazi only being cagey, or is he ignorant of the fact that it is for life rather than business he needs to get into the non-occupied zone? And is it in charming or pitiable innocence that he goes on to ask, "Would you advise me to come in an everyday suit or a dress suit? . . ."

Laporterie has thrown away most of the early letters asking for his help. But if any of them shared the diffidence, real or feigned, of Schinazi's request, it has been erased, naturally, from the letters of thanks that Laporterie has saved from the end of the war. Back home in Bordeaux, four years after the February evening on which Nessim Yaeche loaded his family into the Renault, for example, he wrote a long letter to Laporterie.

> . . . after the terrible torment we went through, in which so many of our co-religionists met an atrocious death, I would be the most ungrateful person on earth if I did not remember that it is to you that I and all my family owe our safety.
>
> Yes, M. Laporterie, the point of departure for our liberation goes back to February 24, 1941. On that day you opened the door of this prison that was the Occupied Zone and passed us across the line of demarcation of sad memory. Without this generous help from you—as pure in motive as it was bold—we would have remained in Bordeaux at the mercy of those ferocious beasts who were the Germans and their ignoble collaborators. We would have been deported with the others.

I am not the only one in your debt. Hundreds of people
of all categories owe you as much. . . .

"His wife wrote to me only a few months ago that he had died,"
says Laporterie, riffling a bit disconsolately through a sheaf of letters
from Yaeche. "He wrote to me each year, right up to the end."

In another letter, Yaeche marvels at how, in an age when *passeurs*
commonly extracted fortunes from people desperate for their lives,
Laporterie resolutely refused to accept—much less ask for—a
penny. "If you had taken a percentage on each valuable and ten
francs [the going rate] on each letter," writes Yaeche, "you would
have made a large fortune. For me alone, in addition to jewels and
money, you passed sixteen large packages."

Laporterie is indeed aware not only of what he missed out on,
but of what he lost that had been his own. Of the five stores he
operated before the war, he had to close down all but two, including the main store in Mont-de-Marsan.

The most he would accept was a gift here and there, offered in
thanks. On the wall of this study, for example, hangs a handsome
watercolor portrait of a Spanish dancer in a dress that is by turns
sinuous and billowy. The inscription to this painting is now pasted
into his album:

To Monsieur Laporterie
    With deepest thanks to a generous man of great heart
who helped me during a tragic period of my life.
                                        H. Halfer
Toulouse, 14 September, 1945

Another gift has come with a short note in a flowing hand
from a woman named Sarah Wisner. Laporterie believes she was
associated with the Rothschilds of Bordeaux. Her letter comes
from somewhere in the unoccupied zone soon after Laporterie
passed her through in 1941. She is a woman who knows that it is
harder for a man like Laporterie to accept a gift than to give one.

So she has framed her offering with a most delicate and thoughtful consideration.

> Dear Sir,
>
> I want very much for you to know of and be assured of all my thanks—though it is impossible to find the words for this. Would your daughter be kind enough to accept this ring, which comes to me from my husband? For me it has the great value of his memory. Being so dear to me, it would be with great joy that I will think that your daughter is wearing it.
>
> With infinite thanks,
S. Wisner

At the top of this note Laporterie has attached the small photo from the *Ausweis* he prepared for this woman. She is perhaps sixty years old, and she seems to have drawn a black, round-collared sweater tightly around her. Her face is fine, luminous, and sad. Her lips are slightly parted, as if the photographer has told her to smile but she has no heart for it. It looks, in fact, as if the full force of what was happening to her had hit at the moment the camera flashed—that a normal life was switching to abnormal, that a home had to be boarded up and abandoned, perhaps to squatters, that at this stage of her life she was trading a true name for a false name, that she was becoming a fugitive, hunted, and that she was suddenly depending on the wiles and decency of a stranger, albeit a charming and self-assured one, for survival.

It seems from a passage in one of Nessim Yaeche's letters that not everyone has responded to being rescued by Laporterie with uniform grace. ". . . I am scandalized," writes Yaeche, "by the conduct of one of 'ours' in your regard after the particularly great service you rendered him. This person is one of those black sheep who, unfortunately, are part of all groups. . . . We disapprove of and censure this ignoble attitude. In the middle of the recognition and gratitude our community owes you he makes a black stain. . . ."

Provocative as this passage is, Laporterie shows not the least interest in discussing it. But, seeing my curiosity, he stares ahead stonily after a deep breath and says, "This was a furrier named Angel from Bordeaux. I passed him across the line along with all his family, stocks of furs, his daughter's trousseau, cash, and many boxes of clothing. And as I refused money, he said, 'Here are two coats of Persian-lamb's wool—keep one for Yaeche and give one to your wife as a gift from me.' I was willing to keep the coat for Yaeche. But I didn't want the other one. But he insisted. Well, Yaeche picked up his coat without any problem. Then, after the Liberation, Angel came back here and said, 'Give me back the coat which I gave your wife.' As if I'm a thief. I said I'd throw him out the door. When the Jewish community heard about this, they were ready to support me in a suit against him. But it never came to that. Angel came back here again, this time to beg me not to go through with the suit. It is not a pretty story."

It is also, apparently, not the whole story. Laporterie skims past an entire fat file whose label is all I have time to see. It says "The Affair of the Coat." In his entire rich repository, that is the only file he does not offer to open. Just the same, I have the feeling that, as with any can of worms, bits of this story are sooner or later bound to find their way out.

Laporterie was formally and publicly given thanks by various parties on November 25, 1946, eighteen months after the war in Europe ended, at the biggest banquet ever held before or since in the town hall of his hometown of Bascons. High government officials came from Alsace-Lorraine on behalf of uprooted Alsatians who were helped by Laporterie when they arrived in Landes in 1940, having fled the invader's thoroughgoing effort to "Germanize" them. A committee of Jews arrived from Bordeaux. The noted wind band of Mont-de-Marsan came to play. Even the flag of the 52nd Battalion of Indo-Chinese Machine Gunners was carried all the way from its resting place at Les Invalides in Paris by a special honor guard. It was the same flag that Laporterie had rescued by stealth and daring from the attic of the tightly guarded German headquarters at the Hôtel de France in Arcachon, where it had been "accidentally" left behind when the enemy took over the premises.

"One was given three weeks to carry out a mission assigned by the Resistance," explains Laporterie. "If you failed, it was given to someone else. I was the third to try to get this flag back. If I had been caught, it would have been the end."

Hearing this, the translator looks at Laporterie in wide-eyed astonishment. "I can understand that you risked your life to save other people, but for a flag?"

Laporterie stares back, equally astonished. "*Le drapeau, c'est sacré,*" he says. ("The flag is sacred.") In order to prove he isn't crazy, reckless, or holding a belief unique among Frenchmen, Laporterie pulls out a letter handwritten to him by no less than Marshal Pétain, Chief of State of the Vichy regime, to whom the flag was directly delivered by a high member of the Resistance. ". . . Upon returning the flag of the 52nd Battalion of Indo-Chinese Machine Gunners," writes the ancient Marshal in a cramped but clear hand, "he [Laporterie's superior] told me what precious assistance he found in you in saving this precious emblem by rescuing it from the hands of the occupant. I congratulate you for the cleverness and coolness you used in this patriotic initiative, and I want to tell you of all my emotions. . . ."

"Doing this came naturally, you see," says Laporterie. "It was done prudently but with assurance. I don't know where it came from, this assurance, but in the face of danger, I had it. Certainly, if I had reflected more before I acted, I would have grown afraid."

Laporterie went about ensuring the total success of this banquet with his usual amalgam of thoroughness and unfettered enthusiasm. Besides the official contingents, he did not neglect to invite almost anyone touched, in a happy way, by the full range of his wartime activities. He invited the woman who gave him the key to the attic of the Hotel de France in Arcachon and he invited Sarah Wisner, whose ring his daughter still keeps. He invited practically everyone except Monsieur Angel. He has also preserved anything connected with this banquet that could be filed. The smallest are cards of regrets and the largest is the oversized menu which begins with foie gras and ends with a special reserve of Armagnac, the elixir of Landes. It is crested with drawings of the medals he was to receive. Copies of all the speeches that were given are here. Laporterie neither hides his own pleasure in these speeches nor expects anyone else to share it. "Here's all that was said," he says, holding up a sheaf of papers. "It's magnificent to read . . . but only for me."

Laporterie comes from a family which, he makes clear, was "very, very modest." His father was born in Mont-de-Marsan, where his grandfather was keeper of the gate at the offices of the regional prefecture. His mother's family owned a small grocery-and-tobacco store in Bascons. Upon their marriage, his parents took over the store. In 1914, at age seventeen, Laporterie went to Mont-de-Marsan to study accounting, in hopes of securing a job in the African colonies. But with his father off to war, his mother called him home. He left behind not only his studies but, by his reckoning, memberships in no less than eight student societies, his favorite among them being the drama troupe. A year later, at eighteen, Laporterie went off to war himself. He ended up as a prisoner of war in Germany.

"One fine day soon after my return," says Laporterie, "the director of our local theater, the Moderne Cinéma, suddenly died. His wife begged me to take over the management until her daughter was older. It was natural for her to ask me, since I was always haunting the theater. At this time the theaters presented both stage shows and movies, which were still a curiosity. So I took charge of booking the acts. Each Thursday, I brought in a troupe from Paris—comedies, musicals, operettas, the circus. Up there they called me 'Monsieur le Directeur des Arènes de Mont-de-Marsan.' I had an introduction into *le tout Paris*—the milieu of artists, that is. I adored that. And then I had to go sell suits."

Laporterie fell into selling suits as casually as he had found himself in the role of impresario. "A friend owned a vacant building in Mont-de-Marsan, well placed near the post office," he explains. "He said, 'Raoul, you take it and put in a little boutique.'" For fifteen years Laporterie handled both jobs, until the daughter of the late director of the Moderne Cinéma took over bookings herself. But that did not put him altogether out of show business. He has been in the midst of planning his beloved *course landaise*—if any blood spills in this humane version of the bullfight, it will be the toreador's—ever since. "But the theater," he says, "that was in truth my first love."

If not for that store so well placed near the post office, I suggest, Laporterie would never have qualified for the special *Ausweis* that allowed him to write and perform bits of theater each day for two years of the war.

"I suppose that's true," he admits, brightening a bit. "And I did work *sans filet*—without a net."

We left Laporterie that evening through the store portion of La Petite Maison as his wife and daughter laid dust covers neatly over their displays and other members of the family arrived for the dinner hour. They included his son-in-law, an Armagnac salesman, all three of his granddaughters, and—the youngest leaf on the family tree—a twenty-month-old great-granddaughter. Like many French women at the extremes of age, she is put together with chic—a well-cut dress, short blonde hair, and a minute pair of gold earrings. On the subject of this tiny creature, Laporterie said, with a dry but not unhappy smile, "My wife and I had hoped that our granddaughter would give us a great-grandson. But, alas, she proved just as maladroit as we."

Watching the rain come down that afternoon, Laporterie's wife and daughter had talked about the awful flood of 1953, which had brought the Adour into their store to a depth of over two feet. That evening, after dinner, I borrowed an umbrella and walked over to look at the river myself. It surged under the town bridge with the smooth energy you see in the flex of a powerful snake. The water level had risen enough to float the rowboats that had been dragged up on the lawns of the homes along its banks. Now the boats yanked and swayed at their moorings. All the bankside flowers had been submerged except for those oversized cow lilies. They also swayed in the current, creamy white and vaguely luminous.

I walked back to the square, hopping the puddles, and turned down the tiny street running behind the residential portion of La Petite Maison. There I came upon the large, frosted window of what I realized must be the dining room. Nearly a dozen well-blurred family figures sat around the table. Laporterie had mentioned that most evenings they gathered together like this in some combination of the four generations. I had asked if such togetherness was typical here. Laporterie hesitated before he answered. Clearly, this was a question which he found to be just a bit *gênant*—embarrassing—requiring, as it did, a favorable self-commentary. "People do say," he finally admitted, "'Look how close the Laporterie family is. They are an example of the way a family should be.'"

I did not want to be a voyeur, but I paused for the barest few seconds in front of that window. Blurred as the scene was by the frosted glass and the sheet of rain, there issued from that table an unmistakable feeling of harmony, kinship, and the relaxed satisfaction that comes from having eaten well. I could not make out which figure was Laporterie. But if all at the table had risen, I'm sure there would have been no mistake about it. He would have been the one who was up the quickest.

Among the few to write Laporterie faithfully after the war was the former Bordeaux merchant Isaac Levy. Laporterie himself, of course, was never one to let a letter go unanswered. Thanking the mayor of Bascons for a photo packet Laporterie had sent him and his wife, Levy had written from Jerusalem in 1966 that

...these photos took us back thirty years and we thought once again that without your greatness of soul we would have perhaps been deported with the six million Jews and the few million non-Jews who were exterminated. This heroic gesture on your part we have not forgotten and will never forget. Our only regret is not to have the material possibilities to invite you to this country to show our gratitude and thanks. But we would be happy to receive you at our house and to show you the rebirth of our old/new country, realized in such a short time despite the fanatic hostility of our neighbors. In this hope and in the pleasure of your good health, we leave you. . . .

This was the last in the long string of letters from Isaac Levy. It was almost ten years old. Laporterie had looked up from it with a cheerless smile and said, "I only hope that he's still of this world."

Isaac Levy had indeed left this world in 1969. But, according to the files at Yad Vashem, his widow still lived nearby, at 85 Avenue Herzl. When I was in Jerusalem some two weeks after visiting Laporterie, I decided to walk over there one evening. Since there was no telephone listing, I had to do it unannounced. Though it was just after six o'clock, the hour brought no relief from the baking wind, called *hamseen*, that blasts out of the eastern deserts. Worse than being simply enervating, it is a wind that is offensive to Jerusalemites. They believe, deeply and immovably in their hearts, that the *hamseen* is suited only to the desert or else to a secular—not to say craven— city like Tel Aviv and that the only air appropriate to their pristine City of Seven Gates is the kind that is so crisp, scintillating, and heady that it can seem, when inhaled on a fine morning, that somebody has sprayed champagne out of an aerosol.

Eighty-five Avenue Herzl turned out to be a modest three-story apartment house. On a first-floor balcony, facing the winding avenue, two elderly women were playing cards. They were not the type to play silently. They were speaking French, a language not heard so often here. I asked from the stoop if they knew where I might find Madame Levy.

"Who?" They looked at each other, puzzled.

"Madame Levy."

Again they looked confused. So was I. Speaking slowly, I tried once more. "I'm looking for Madame Isaac Levy."

"Ah, Madame *Levy*," one of them said, pronouncing it "Leh*vee*" to my "*Lee*-vee." I had forgotten that French precision doesn't give much leeway for American pronunciation. Getting the name right, however, did little to loosen up these two faces tight with suspicion. And then I mentioned—or, rather, invoked—the name of Raoul Laporterie.

If there had been any lingering bit of doubt that somehow all was not as it seemed—as there ought to be in any man's account of his own deeds, no matter how scrupulously documented—it now evaporated along with the suspicions of these two women. Those faded letters of gratitude closeted away for so long in Grenade-sur-l'Adour came alive in their suddenly open and beaming faces.

"*Ah, Monsieur Laporterie—c'est un homme formidable!*" said one of the two women, who introduced herself as Esther Levy. "If you only knew what he did for us. And not just for us but for all who came to ask him for help. . . ."

Now, amid a torrent of benedictions on Laporterie, I was ushered into the doorway that, just a moment ago, had been blocked. In no time at all, ice cream and coffee appeared on the table where the women had been playing cards. Here, with interjections and commentary by her sister Rivka Cassuto, Esther Levy told her story.

She and her husband had come to France from Turkey just before the First World War to escape the bloodletting between Greeks and Turks. Having served as a volunteer in the French army, Isaac Levy was granted citizenship after the war. For twenty years—until the next German occupation—they kept a small fabric store on rue Sainte-Catherine in Bordeaux. Like their friends the Yaeches, they sensed early that they had better get away from the Germans. Neither family knew Laporterie, seventy miles away in Mont-de-Marsan. To the provincial-minded French, seventy miles can be like seven thousand. But Yaeche had heard of this seller of suits from Parisian friends who had already used his services. When Yaeche traveled down to Mont-de-Marsan to inquire about passing his family across the frontier, Levy asked him to check the possibilities for his family as well. Laporterie's unhesitating answer was that they should come themselves for an interview.

"So one day we presented ourselves," says Madame Levy. "And he said, 'I'll pass you all.' That meant my husband and me, as well as his sister, her husband, and their young daughter. He told us then to go home. When the right time came, he would let us know. Then he got word to my husband that he would come up to Bordeaux to collect us and all our belongings just as soon as he could get some gas for his car. In those days you couldn't get gas except on the black market. My husband said, 'Don't worry, I'll see to it.' He knew a *garagiste* who sold him the gas. Then he sent a message back—phones were forbidden—that said, '*Monsieur Laporterie, votre vin est prêt*'—your wine is ready."

On the following evening, a familiar scene was enacted in the office of La Petite Maison. "We gave M. Laporterie our luggage and all our money except for ten francs," says Madame Levy. "He gave us ID and ration cards in the names of his townspeople to which our photos were attached. As long as we acted naturally and confidently at the border, he counseled, all would go well."

But Laporterie did not let his own breezy confidence push aside caution. He decided at the last minute, in fact, not to send over the Levy family as planned—perhaps because the border guards on duty were not to his liking. Instead the family was put up for the night in a hotel owned by a fellow *résistant*. In the morning, they were on the way. They were driven in the Renault by Laporterie's own chauffeur, whom they were flabbergasted to learn was, secretly, also a Jew. At the frontier, they presented themselves as just another family of merchants who, courtesy of Raoul Laporterie, were catching a ride home to Mont-de-Marsan.

"'Open your purse,' ordered the doyens," says Esther Levy. "They saw it contained only ten francs. As we had no other luggage, the guards said, 'Go.' As long as we weren't Jews, they weren't too concerned."

The two families arrived in Grenade-sur-l'Adour to be put up, as Laporterie's guests still are, a few doors down from La Petite Maison at the Hotel de France. That evening, Laporterie arrived home from his day at the store with all their money. Eight days later, he brought all their belongings—"boxes and boxes packed full." Furnished with new ID and ration cards that converted them all into good citizens of Bascons, the Levys and the Cassutos remained safe for the rest of the war. Afterward, like other Bordeaux families passed by Laporterie, they went back to tending their store.

"Then we got older," says Madame Levy, "and we didn't care so much to work anymore. So my husband said, 'What do we have to do here? We'll go to Israel.' That was fifteen years ago. Life wasn't so easy as it was in France, back then. Now we don't lack for anything. But even when we did, we were happy. This is a pays des rêves—a country of dreams."

Both women continue to be appalled, so many years after the event, at how Laporterie was finally tripped up as a *passeur*. They spill out the story, in fact, like a bulletin. "He gave this woman who caused the trouble his cousin's name, but still she didn't want to trust him," says Mrs. Levy. "Like us, she was supposed to keep only ten francs in her purse. But she had it filled with jewels. She didn't have *confiance*. At the frontier, naturally, she was ordered to open the bag. The jewels spilled out. The guards allowed the chauffeur to go back to his *patron*, but they held the woman until M. Laporterie crossed the line on his way home that evening. Then they pounced on him.

"'So, Monsieur, you are rich,' said the captain of the guard.

" 'Far from it,' answered Laporterie.

" 'Then you must have a rich cousin.' And the captain spread out the jewels from the bag on the table.

" 'The woman is not my cousin,' he said—it was all that he could say. Somehow, he talked his way out of it that night. They let him go home. But on the next day the Gestapo was looking for him. He had to close his store and hide until the end of the war. They took all that he had. My husband saw him when he was on the run in Pau. He had nothing. He was like a mendicant. And in the meanwhile other men became rich as *passeurs*. They were greedy, yet they were not the worst. They were deceitful men who took your money—sometimes all your money—and then disappeared. You were left alone. And there were men even worse than this. They were the ones who took your money and delivered you not to the Zone Libre but direct to the Germans. Today they are still spending the money they took then. But M. Laporterie, this *grand homme* who never took a sou, was himself betrayed by one of those he tried to help. My husband could never get over this. But then he would also say, 'I'm glad, at least, that the one who betrayed him, even inadvertently, was not a Jew.' "

Passeurs certainly did come in colors other than shining white. The chronicler of wartime France, Henri Amouroux, reports the story★ of five Jews from Paris who went to a French border town in November 1942, to get passage to Spain. The price demanded by a go-between was 35,000 francs. It was an exorbitant sum but the men had no choice. Still, that was not the end of the charges. Along the way, the *passeur* himself demanded yet another 25,000 francs from each. None of the men carried that much, but after they had turned over all they had, the *passeur* consented to take a signed note for the balance.

★Told in *La Vie des Français sous l'Occupation* (Paris: Librarie Artheme Fayard, 1961).

The most fragile of the four was named Jacques Grumbach. As they began the ascent of the Pyrenees, he was able to keep up. But then, in the rocks above the timber line, his feet became so swollen that he could not go on. Afraid that a German patrol would spot them, the *passeur* ordered the group to leave Grumbach behind. When they refused, he promised to return for their friend as soon as he had delivered the others into Spain. He did indeed return.

He found Grumbach propped against a rock, his shoes off, feet still swollen. The *passeur* leaned close to Grumbach. Drawing a revolver, he shot him dead. The bones lay on the rocks, alternately baked by the sun and buried by snow until they were found eight years later. At his trial, the *passeur* claimed in his defense that an officer of the Resistance, known only as Papa Noël, had given orders to kill anyone who could not make it, so that, in the event of capture, the security of the *passeurs* would not be breached. Papa Noël could not be located. On May 29, 1953, the *passeur* was acquitted.

The sisters Levy and Cassuto do not need to hear such stories. They know all too well that even an honest *passeur*, lacking the wiles of a Laporterie, could bring grief on himself as well as on his clients. "We have a third sister, who still lives in Bordeaux," explains Madame Levy. "When the Germans came, she had one son who was training to be a sailor, another who was in high school. These two boys decided they would go to England or North Africa to join the army that de Gaulle was building in exile. So, with three other boys, they went with a *passeur* through the mountains on their way to Spain. They were all taken by a German patrol. The two Jewish boys were sent to the camp at Drancy. Then to Auschwitz. Since then, my sister has been . . ."

A bus grinds by on Avenue Herzl and the word she whispers is lost. The room is left in silence. The name Auschwitz is almost certain, among those with no direct connection to it, to ignite strong opinions, theories, polemics. But among those whose connection is in blood, the word just as often leaves a silence like this, even as it fills the room with emotions as sudden and as strong as if a speeding train were noiseless.

. . .

Today, rue Sainte-Catherine in Bordeaux is one of those central city streets which have been converted to an autoless mall. At No. 47, the widow of Nessim Yaeche and her daughter still own a fabric shop called Niss. It is a narrow, teeming place stuffed high and low with bolts of cloth. Madame Yaeche was behind the cash register when I walked into the store. It would not have been a surprise for me to see a woman beset by age. But this was a handsome woman, hair white and eyes ice blue, who had a forceful and even imperious manner.

While a clerk kept the register ringing for the bustling late afternoon traffic, Madame Yaeche told how, one day in 1941, the couple had entrusted this store to her parents and fled. After Laporterie had taken them across the frontier, they had even lived for three months in his hamlet of Bascons. Then, with their new family name Grenier impeccably documented for generations back in the town hall, they moved on to Limoges. When the Germans occupied the former Free Zone a year later, the family moved on from one town to another, settling finally in a village in the Pyrenees. There, for two years, they lived the life of a decent French Catholic family.

"My daughter was named Huguette," says Madame Yaeche. "She lived in a pension kept by nuns. Every day they had to recite the Stations of the Cross." Pointing to her five-year-old grandson, who has just appeared behind the counter, she says, "My son Roger was the same age as this one. He was in school taught by the priest. My husband and I went to mass, of course. The only thing I didn't do was . . . *this*—" She makes a sign of the cross. "Others went to mass every morning of the week. We only went on Sundays. People said, 'The Greniers are very nice people. But why don't they go more often to mass?'

"So this was how we lived until the end of the war. On the surface, life was *tranquille*. But we suffered from such tensions! What if Roger, who was at such a delicate age, said the wrong thing in the wrong place? We kept drumming it into him: 'Whatever you do, *never* say you are a Yaeche. Or they'll kill you, they'll kill you. And us!'

"He was so frightened. But he and all the children kept the secret. We kept it so well that we were able to hide a Jew who had fled from being arrested in the middle of the night. He came to us because he had a feeling that we might be sympathetic to a wretched Jew. We took him right in. *He* certainly thought the Greniers were good Catholics."

A completely happy ending to the wartime story of this family was precluded by the loss of Madame Yaeche's parents—a loss that was almost certainly preventable. But even the intercession of Raoul Laporterie could not save them from their own certainty that the Germans would not bother them.

"Shortly after they went back to Bordeaux, they were taken," she says. "It wasn't the Germans who took them, either. It was the collaborators—Frenchmen. First they came and took all the furniture away. Then they came back for my parents. They were old people. They were trusting. But they should never have opened the door. They should have taken a cue from the action of the Grand Rabbi of Bordeaux, Joseph Cohen, when the French collaborators came to take him away from the Temple. He told them that he needed a few minutes in his upstairs office to collect his affairs. They were hesitant to let him go.

"'I give you my sacred word as a rabbi that I'll be right down,' he said.

"But obviously this was no time for honor. So the rabbi ran out the back door. And that was the last they ever saw of him. He stayed in hiding for the rest of the war.

"So why did my parents have to be so trusting? If they hadn't opened the door, perhaps the collaborators would have gone away. Why didn't they stay in Bascons with us? . . ." Though Madame Yaeche seems never to have ceased asking herself these same questions for thirty-five years, she persists in asking them now, ignoring the customers lined up before the cash register, as if from a stranger an answer might finally be at hand.

I sensed, even from this brief interview, that Madame Yaeche was a woman of fiery and perhaps vengeful temperament, and that she would hold a grudge well. So I did not want to leave without asking her if she could shed any light, or heat, on the small but intense scandal which, in Laporterie's dossier, had been called "the Affair of the Coat." At the mere mention of it, she fixed her eyes on me as sharply as an eagle which has just caught sight of a rabbit.

"I will tell you exactly how this furrier Angel repaid Monsieur Laporterie for his services," she said. "And I will tell you how I repaid Angel. This was a man who was more desperate than any of us to find a way into the Zone Libre. Because, you see, he had already been thrown into prison almost as soon as the Germans came. It was my father, Monsieur Haim, who arranged to get him out. Angel came home trembling like a leaf. There was nothing he wouldn't have given then to get across the line. So when he heard about this Monsieur Laporterie from other Jews, he rushed down to Mont-de-Marsan and begged for help. Of course, Monsieur Laporterie never turned anyone down. But it was not enough for this Angel that Monsieur Laporterie agreed to pass him, his wife, and his children into the Zone Libre. It was not enough that Laporterie agreed to pass all their money, jewels, and heaps of clothing. Angel even insisted on having his daughter's trousseau passed—a huge thing fit only for a princess. Laporterie had to come up here to Bordeaux three or four times to get it all. Of course, he would never accept a penny for himself for all this. So Angel pushed off this coat on him for his wife. That's how grateful he was. But then, at the end of the war, it was a different story. You'd think that Laporterie had wronged him like an extortionist. If you can imagine it, Angel was ready to sue the man who had saved him and all his family! Was there ever such an ingrate?"

Madame Yaeche leaned forward now across the counter. "I'll tell you a secret now that I kept even from my husband for as long as he lived. Since Monsieur Laporterie wanted no part of Angel anymore, it fell to me to be the intermediary who gave him back his coat. It was a handsome garment, covered with lovely long curls of Persian lamb. I gave it back to him all right. But first I took scissors and cut off all those curls. Every one. And when I handed it over to Angel, I said, 'Here's how you get your coat back!'

"He didn't deserve to have it back any other way. He deserved to be killed. Now he's an old man and very sick. I say *laissez le crever*—let him croak!"

In Grenade-sur-l'Adour on the following morning, the *landais* sky was a flawless blue and the Adour, so swift and greedy before, now flowed benignly. Those oversized cow lilies which it had previously engulfed now stood on banks of shaded grass, dumb and waxy as ever. Commencing at eleven o'clock, Laporterie had promised to devote the rest of the day to a guided tour of the two towns that, along with this one, have figured at the center of his life—Bascons, his *village natal*, where he was mayor for twenty-six years, and Mont-de-Marsan, where he worked as impresario, clothier, and *passeur*. But he is not about to go anywhere without a quick (everything in Laporterie's life is quick) stop at the bar of the Hôtel de France, a few doors down from La Petite Maison. He orders Noilly, an apéritif he admits to drinking, at precise intervals, five times each day.

"It aids the digestion," he explains. "Usually, I sit down with a bunch of fellows. On certain days we meet here, on other days at other places. But always on the same schedule. These other fellows are all half my age or less. But somehow I end up living with young people. That's why everybody wonders why I don't have the air of an old man."

Laporterie flashes one of his driest smiles before adding, "All of that gives me pleasure—but it doesn't console me."

When I delivered to him a package containing a gift for his wife from Madame Levy in Jerusalem, he nodded his head approvingly. "She deserves it," he said. "She was the one who had to open all the bags of mail that I brought home each night."

I had thought we would use my rented car to save him the effort of driving on this tour. "As you wish," he said politely, but it was clear that he preferred to chauffeur as well as to guide. With the barest prompting he opened the door of his car, a Peugeot sedan, and was ready to go. On the center of the dashboard, where many

Frenchmen keep religious medals, is a snapshot of a dog. Like all the others, this case is documented. "*Mon bon ami Bob*," it says in neat hand lettering. "Born August 8, 1962, died February 16, 1973." The dog is a mongrel, its eyes glinting red the way animal eyes often do when hit by headlights or flashbulbs. Laporterie has nothing to offer but the inevitable and heartfelt truisms of anyone who has ever loved a dog. "He sat here beside me, *mon Bob*. I talked to him like a man. He looked at me with an air of comprehension. When he died, it grieved me as much as if he had been human."

Laporterie spins along the country road to Bascons with one hand on the wheel, the other out the window. He is a quick and effortless driver and, in any case, he tells us that he knows this road "by heart." The road winds through land that is slightly rolling and more fertile than the flat pineland you see, mile upon mile, from the windows of the short red train that comes down the spur from Bordeaux to Mont-de-Marsan. We pass an old man, working in his garden in front of his house. "That's my *frère de lait*—brother of milk," he says. "When I was born, my mother didn't have enough milk for me. I almost died of starvation. This fellow was born at the same time, and since his mother had plenty of milk, she nursed me too." Seeing this slightly bent-over fellow, his face gaunt with age, is a little startling. He forces you to remember that Laporterie is also an old man.

Until he got hold of it, Laporterie tells us, Bascons was a *village perdu*—a lost village. The town church had been abandoned, the graveyard was overgrown, the streets were in disrepair, the already small population was falling off. The village was not only lost but dying. As mayor, Laporterie fixed all that. By 1959, in fact, the prestigious Touring Club of France had awarded it a diploma as a "Model Village." It won first prize nationally for villages "in flower." In 1968, it won the silver medal in the contest called "Village That I Love." Coming into town now, we pass an inn, built at his instigation. We ask Laporterie who stays there. "People seeking serenity and tranquillity," he answers. Bascons certainly has that. We do not see our first sign of local life until we pull up to the church in the center of town. And then it is only a ground hog, waddling fast for a hole in the lawn.

The pride of Bascons is this thirteenth-century church. Diplomas and silver medals are for today, but it is a rugged testament to the ancient standing of the town. The façade is asymmetric, with a triangular bell tower rising above the front portals and, to the right of that, a single tower shaped like a silo. The rough-hewn walls are windowless. "The first thing I did as mayor was to restore this church," says Laporterie. "I found paintings, figurines, sacred pieces lying in grime and dust. It was all cleaned, painted, and renewed. The town didn't have a budget for all the work. But I got people to do it *à l'oeil*—for nothing."

Going inside, we leave the warm late-May day behind. Here it is cool, almost chilly. It is not a coolness left over from winter, but the coolness that issues out of an enclosure of rocks, the coolness of ages. Statues and paintings are everywhere, most of them direct and unrefined. The vaulted ceiling is brightly and freely painted in a pattern that would suit a set of high-spirited provincial earthenware plates. Laporterie guides us over to a side chapel. "This room had been walled and sealed up for nobody knows how long," he says. "It was forgotten. Then, one day, I saw bees flying in and out of a tiny hole in the side of the church. I calculated the spot from inside and had a hole broken through. Here was the forgotten chapel. I got an altar for it and now it is the Chapel of Saint Joseph."

Laporterie invites me to climb up to the bell tower. I stare up at the spiral stairway, which is built like an overscale corkscrew, ascending twist by twist straight up and out of sight. Thinking that an old man ought to be spared this expedition, I volunteer to climb up myself. But before the words are out, he is already on his way up, going round and round, feet and coattails flying. I keep up as best I can until we arrive in a cavernous room that seems far too large to be contained in this church. In olden days, he explains, it served as both granary, in case of siege, and magazine. I asked who were the enemies.

"It was *les tribus sauvages*, then the English," he answers in one breath. Though no malice is intended, it is obvious that he considers them as one and the same.

We continue up the corkscrew stairway until, at last, we are on the bell-tower platform. Below it had been calm, but here a gentle wind blows. Laporterie takes a brief, critical look at the little town spread below, its clusters of tile-roofed buildings trailing into vineyards and open fields. I mention that his fervor for the renewal of this village is akin to that of the master builder Robert Moses, who had built and restructured vast portions of New York City. From the way he looks at me, it is obvious that Laporterie has never heard of Moses. But as we drive away from the church, he unwittingly confirms his kinship to that other intrepid doer and bulldozer of whatever stood in the way of his vision.

"Look back," he says. "Do you see how nicely you can see the church from all sides?" The church does indeed command its space unimpeded. "Well, when I took over, you could hardly see the church at all, because a lot of miserable, decrepit buildings were packed all around it. So I had them condemned. Then I tore them down, every one."

At the next stop, Laporterie shows that his instincts for reordering do not stop even at the town graveyard. The row upon row of neatly tended tombstones were not always this way, he explains. The stones had been cracked, overturned, taken over by weeds. Digging up coffins as necessary, he rearranged them along neat paths—promenades, really—giving easy access to all parts of the graveyard. It all worked out so well that nobody wanted to be buried anymore in the rear portion.

"I fixed that," says Laporterie. "Back here, I had a new monument built to make the rear section more desirable." The natural choice would have been a monument to the sons of Bascons who died in the last war. But Laporterie had already commissioned such a monument from his friend the noted *landais* sculptor Cel de Gaucher. So this time he built a memorial to the veterans who did not die until *after* the war. It stands there now, a handsome obelisk, commanding the rear of the cemetery. "After I built that," he says with satisfaction, "we had no more problems with people wanting to be buried only in the front."

The one structure which nearly everyone in town would just as soon have seen demolished, incidentally, is the one which Laporterie insisted on preserving. It is the public laundering station, consisting of several deep troughs set under a heavily tiled, handsome mansard roof supported by twelve stout pillars. Certainly it is archaic enough, standing there in the road behind the town arena. Anyone raised in the age of major appliances would not have much notion of its purpose. "I conserved it expressly because it was a part of our past," he explains. "People said it was outmoded. They thought I was crazy. Now they are themselves crazy for everything that reminds them of the past, so they are glad."

Laporterie has put two new chapels on the map of Bascons during his tenure as mayor. The first is a dark-framed, simple, white stucco building, dedicated to Saint Amand, a priest from Maestricht who arrived in these parts about 670, following his exile from the court of King Dagobert. In his usual fashion, Laporterie had whipped up this chapel "*à l'oeil*"—for free. "These were valiant people who helped me," he explains. "But they didn't have a soul. Some donated trees, others lumber, some just work. I found the altar in a corner somewhere. Do you see that Crucifixion piece overhead? It was lying in a warehouse. I said, 'You're not doing anything with that Christ—I'm taking it.' This old lantern I found in the bell tower. The other one I got somebody to give me. . . ."

With the waters from the spring in front of this chapel, Laporterie tells us, Saint Amand cured lepers. Though it is still said to be helpful to victims of eczema, in these days the water looks dark and dank enough to give a disease.

Though he does not say so directly, it is clear that the last chapel Laporterie takes us to see is closest to his heart. He has dedicated it expressly to Sainte Madeleine, patron of the *course landaise*. It stands in a field at the edge of the village, the original site of a chapel that looks more ancient than the central church. "It was in ruins," says Laporterie. "Nobody came out here anymore. I even had to build the road." Onto the original structure Laporterie has grafted a new front portion in Spanish style, simple and dazzling white. Above it rises the ancient rough stone façade, a pair of bells in its triangular tower. Inside there is no doubt about the theme of this chapel. The altar, which Laporterie had made in Spain, rests on four huge bull horns, and above the chapel doors is a portrait of a wild-eyed bull, its nose flaring and steaming, while the toreador kneels in prayer.

The *course landaise* is not the same as the true Spanish *corrida*, of course, since the bull which finds itself pushed into the local arena will, after discharging its duty by trying to impale the toreador, live for another day. Just the same, Laporterie feels that he must defend the *corrida*. As we drive away from the Chapelle Notre-Dame de la *course landaise*, as it is formally named, he says, "I have friends from Paris who came down here and spoke out against the *corrida*. So we argued amicably. I pointed out that these bulls are savage animals just like lions, like tigers that are hunted in Africa. Yet under no circumstances are they allowed to suffer for more than a quarter of an hour. Then I asked my friends if they liked to eat lobster. '*Ah, oui,*' they answered. And I said, 'And do you think it's courageous to pierce the animal and throw it alive into boiling water? And then you would make me a lesson of the *taureau sauvage*? This is combat—combat between a man and a *taureau*. That's all.' Then I said what about hunting? That's not combat at all, because the deer has no defense. The Germans have their cockfights. It goes on for much more than a quarter hour and they suffer. And what about in the hunt when the hunter hits the beast but only wounds it? Then it escapes into the woods and the poor beast suffers? . . ."

Until now Laporterie has always been ready to dismiss even the most dire subjects with a quick smile or a dry Gallic aside. But it is now not the war or even the loss of his fortune that is the topic at hand. This is the *course landaise*. The words spill out in the jumble that intensity brings. If that argument with his Parisian friends had indeed been "amicable," it hardly shows now. Later I came across an article he had written about the *course landaise* in a local tourist handbook. It helped to explain his feelings about the sport. Just as certain wine lovers believe, with firmest conviction, that the elements of beauty can be abstracted in a bottle of claret, Laporterie sees the potential in the proper execution of his beloved sport for elevated moral conduct to be demonstrated by both participants in the allegory at the center of the ring.

> . . . during a *course landaise* in which the adversaries
> approach perfection, one is forced to state that, as in the
> *corrida*, it is the qualities of nobility, of combativity, and
> of bravery on the part of the beasts, as well as courage,
> stoicism, and scorn of danger on the part of the men,
> which predominate and are, moreover, obligatory for
> obtaining the desired result.

In the days when Laporterie still operated La Petite Maison in Mont-de-Marsan, it was an elegant store. Now it is rented out to a men's-clothing discounter whose tables, on the narrow sidewalk in front, are heaped with blue jeans. Above the store, Laporterie still keeps his old office. The dark, massive desk, the big chairs, even the safe in the corner, are just as they were during the war. "Nothing," says Laporterie, "has budged." On the walls are photos of his *maison natale* and the church in his beloved Bascons, and also of boats in the streets of Grenade during the terrible flood of 1953. A nicely drawn caricature of Laporterie dominates one wall. It is dedicated to him with "cordial homage" by the late sculptor Cel de Gaucher.

"To me," says Laporterie, gesturing around a bit wistfully, "all this is *l'epoque*." By this phrase he seems to mean not merely the war years but also the time when he was last able to make full use of his energy, courage, and wiles.

"This office is where the Jews and all the rest passed through," he says. "Some fell to their knees. They knew they were fleeing death. Here I gave them their new ID cards, furnished them with clothing if they needed it, wrote receipts for the money and jewels that I would pass across the frontier for them later. It all came through this office. Even the Persian-lamb coat."

Off the hall is a windowless room hardly larger than a closet, with a pair of small desks still crammed in, side by side. "This is where I kept two secretaries working day and night processing the mail," explains Laporterie.

"Employees of the store?" I ask.

"Not exactly. They were hidden."

That was perplexing. Why should he have to hide the secretaries?

"Because they were also Jews," answers Laporterie. "One of them had been the secretary of the Chamber of Deputies of the French Parliament in Paris."

Back in his study in Grenade-sur-l'Adour, Laporterie had already explained exactly what went on here on the second floor of this store. It had all seemed remarkable enough then. But now, peering around this constructed space myself, it seemed absolutely unbelievable that such activity could be carried out under the very nose of the Germans. "Don't forget," explains Laporterie, "this was a store open to the public. It was normal for people to come and go all day long. If German soldiers came upstairs, they would find people looking at merchandise. I would go right over to them and say, 'May I show you something in particular, please?' And when the Jews left, I made sure they were always carrying a box that said 'La Petite Maison.'"

We go across the street now for a drink at the same Café du Sport which was a favorite of both Laporterie and the German officers during the war. "I drank with them—oh, did I drink with them! Once an officer looked at me carefully over his glass. 'It seems to me,' he said, 'that you have a Jewish face—*ein jüdisches Gesicht.*' I laughed at him. It was this assurance that gave me the air of having nothing to be reproached for when, in truth, I had everything to be reproached for—"

Unexpectedly, Laporterie lowers his head. "But there I go, boasting again. I don't like myself for that. . . ."

With the gentlest of encouragement, however, he is soon remembering, with relish, his most exotic client from those days—a young woman from Martinique, "black as coal." She wanted, no less, to be passed from the Free Zone to the Occupied Zone so that she could visit her sister who was a pharmacy student in Bordeaux.

"I told her right away that I could make up papers for her," he says, "but not, obviously, with a photo. We just didn't have any blacks in Bascons. Then I told her maybe we could whitewash her face and then take the photo. It was a joke, of course. But when I saw how anxious she was to visit her sister, I knew I'd better think of something. So I put her down flat on her back in the rear of my car and covered her with about a dozen suits and coats. I just left a little hole for her nose. Then we set off. I didn't worry much that the doyens would search through the suits as long as we were going from the Free Zone to the Occupied Zone. They were pleased to see nice merchandise going over to their side. It meant better pickings for them in my store. Once we got over to Mont-de-Marsan, I took her to a restaurant not far from here frequented mainly by German soldiers of the female corps. We were the object of many curious stares and smiles." The thought of that meal sends a smile streaking across Laporterie's own face, though this one is strictly mischievous.

He refers to those female soldiers at the restaurant, incidentally, as *les souris grises*, as in *gris de souris*, or mouse grey—the color of their uniforms. In the same way, the French today refer to the "meter maids" who patrol the sidewalks of Paris, writing tickets in their purple uniforms, as les aubergines. There is a derisive edge to both nicknames, of course. No Parisian woman finds it desirable to be compared to the bulbous-bottomed eggplant and no German, presumably, ever cared to be nicknamed for the color of rodents.

Laporterie's days of drinking and playing games with the

enemy, as well as his business at La Petite Maison itself, ended abruptly over the woman who would not trust him with her jewels. On the morning after he had been forced to disown her at the frontier, Laporterie decided not to appear at the store as early as usual. It was a prudent decision. When he did arrive, shortly after ten o'clock, he found his elderly saleslady, Madame Denais, in a state of agitation.

"You just missed three gentlemen who did not inspire my confidence," she said. "They want to see you back here at noon."

Telling this story, Laporterie had led us down a narrow street from the café to the post office square. Now, pointing to a handsome limestone building to the side of the post office, he says, "I was just getting that place in shape to be my annex when all this happened. It was on a day in the dead of August. The annex was to be named Erelli—the 'Er' for Raoul, the 'el' for my wife, Laure, and the 'i' for our daughter Irène."

Laporterie had known that his operations could not escape notice by the enemy forever. Now that the hour had come, he could only be grateful that he had just enough time to deal with the necessities. First came the morning mail—a typical haul of some two hundred letters in two bags. Laporterie and his chauffeur carried them over to Erelli, where the plasterers at work there sealed them into a hole in the wall until such time as they could be processed. Next came the all-important collection of ID cards, ration cards, and valuables in the office safe. These were loaded into bags normally used to haul coal, dumped in the back of the delivery truck, and buried under hastily piled on suits and coats. Laporterie ordered his driver to pull the truck around to a spot where it could not be seen and to wait. Then he went himself up to the second-floor balcony of Erelli to see what would happen.

Standing there calmly at the stroke of the shadowless noon, he watched three agents of the Gestapo round the corner and walk toward La Petite Maison. Though they wore suits rather than uniforms and carried briefcases like businessmen, Laporterie knew their faces, as he says, "by heart." They stayed only briefly. When they had gone, he dispatched his chauffeur to find out what had happened. He was startled to learn that not three but five agents had appeared in the store. Two of them had come from the rear, in case he had tried to slip out that way. That fact was disquieting, not only because he had failed to spot them himself, but because it was a sign that the Germans meant business. They wanted him badly enough to allot five agents to the task. They had been angered, obviously, not to find him in the store. They would be back just once more, at four o'clock. If the proprietor was not there, they warned Madame Denais, they might decide to take her instead.

"Foreseeing the worst," says Laporterie, "I had prepared as much as possible for this day. Still, I found that I had to stop and think of what to do next. How should we make our escape? My *Ausweis* allowed travel only on the direct route to Grenade.

" 'They know we can go back only one way,' I said to my chauffeur. 'No doubt these "smart" Germans' "—Laporterie curls the edges of the word with Gallic scorn—" 'will be waiting for us at the frontier.'

"Instead of going that way, we took the route that went around to Bascons. This choice took some nerve, since we had no *Ausweis* for the frontier there. Just before four o'clock, with all our papers and a fortune in cash and jewels under the suits, we set off. Needless to say, that day I did not eat my lunch!" Though Laporterie tosses off that last remark with his flashing smile, it is not to be taken lightly. In the orderly and meal-oriented life of a Frenchman, missing lunch is not such a minor privation.

On the road to Bascons, it seemed to Laporterie that there were more soldiers and more police dogs than was normal. But they were not stopped, and at the frontier itself he was relieved, initially, to see two soldiers whom he knew on duty. "They were surprised to see me twice over," he says. "First, because I never used this route and, second, because when they saw me on the road to Grenade on my way home, it was always exactly at seven-fifty— just before they were due to be relieved. The time now was four-thirty. Still, I could have dealt with these fellows. But they were not the problem. Unexpectedly, I saw behind them an officer I did not know. He wore leather boots up to his knees. He walked over to us as grandly as if he were Hitler himself.

"'*C'est cuit*'—we're cooked—I whispered to my chauffeur.

"'*Papiers*,' intoned the officer.

"I handed him my *Ausweis*. It was inspected with a frown.

"'*Strasse nach Grenade? . . . Dies ist nicht die Strasse nacht Grenade.*'"

"'Look,' I said, trying to sound neither disrespectful nor cowed, 'do you see those suits in the back? I have to deliver them to customers just down the road in Bascons. Be kind enough to let us make the delivery and I'll come right back. Otherwise, I'll have to go all the way around the other way for nothing.'

"'Who is this man?' asked the officer, turning to the two guards.

"'He sells suits in Mont-de-Marsan.'

"The officer fixed his gaze on me and I returned it just as steadily. 'You are the proprietor of La Petite Maison?'

"'Yes.'"

"'Then tell me, Monsieur Laporterie, could you make a nice suit for me?'

"'*Avec plaisir*. If you wish, come in tomorrow.'"

Since the Nazis still observed, as of that August 1942, the sovereignty of the Vichy state they had created, it was not likely that the Gestapo would chase Laporterie to Grenade. Still, to be safe, he slept for the next three nights in ditches in the fields. Then he slipped away to Pau, the nearby city where Isaac Levy saw him looking as bereft as a "mendicant." He lived there in a small room over a café owned by another member of the Resistance. With his usual attention to detail, Laporterie had selected the room because it had a rear door out of which he could slip if he did not want to greet the party knocking at the front door. "*Croyez-moi*," he says, "*j'étais catalogué*." ("Believe me, I was in their book.")

If that German officer in knee boots had indeed visited La Petite Maison on the day following Laporterie's invitation at the Bascons frontier, he would have found a sign on the door saying "Closed for Vacation." The proprietor would not return to his store, except for a few times in mufti, until the enemy left the region two years later. But he never stopped "circulating," as he puts it, on behalf of the Resistance movement between cities like Lyons, Toulouse, Biarritz, and even Paris. Somehow, he managed to continue operations, including the saving of Jews, even from his own home in Grenade. Even after the Germans occupied the former Free Zone late in 1942, he did this as often as not under his own name. He was, in fact, arrested one morning in April 1944, and it should have cost him his life. It was on the road to Pau, where the Germans unexpectedly threw a net over hundreds of Frenchmen taken at random, with the intent of finding members of the ever more troublesome Resistance movement.

"The officer who interrogated me spoke French as well as I," says Laporterie. "He wanted to know where I was coming from, where I was going, and why."

"'I am coming from Grenade-sur-l'Adour,' I answered him, 'and I am going to the prefecture at Pau because you burned down my village. I am the mayor of Grenade.'

"That was two lies I told. I was not the mayor of Grenade and they did not burn down the village. But I spoke right up like that to make him feel uncomfortable. I spoke with confidence. If this officer thought I had something to feel guilty about, it would have been over.

"'If it's true you have an appointment with the prefect,' this officer says, 'then he must be waiting for you now at his office.' He put a hand on the phone and motioned me to an extension.

"'I believe the prefect is absent. It is his assistant who is waiting for me.' I didn't tell him that the reason the prefect was absent was that he was a *grand résistant* who had been sent to Dachau.

"He looks me in the eyes as he dials.

" 'Allô, Monsieur le Préfet? I have here a Monsieur Laporterie who says you are expecting him.'

"There was a pause at the other end. Then I heard his voice crackle over the line. 'Why . . . yes . . . I expected him here already.' Then, to me, over the extension, he said in the *landais patois*, 'What are you doing there?' I answered that this officer had a few questions for me.

" 'Pardon this inconvenience,' said the officer. And he sent me on my way. Outside, there were many more waiting to be interrogated. In the morning they shot ten of them. The good Lord was with me, because nobody deserved it more than I."

Since he was himself a fugitive in these times, Laporterie might well have been expected to suspend or at least cut back his efforts to help people, particularly Jews, even as their plight grew more desperate. But in his "Jewish" file is a clipping of a letter to an unnamed newspaper, headed "Homage to Our Christian Compatriots" and signed by one Albert Elias, which shows that during this period he was more active than ever. "Though sought himself by the Gestapo because of his Gaullist and Judeophile actions," writes Elias, "he continued with all his heart to help our unfortunate compatriots. He intervened with local authorities to free them from local internment camps, he delivered them the necessary (if apocryphal) papers drawn up under his responsibility. Numerous are those whom he safeguarded in his own house at Bascons. . . ."

Elias does not say if he was among them, but it was the foreign-born Jews who, as the result of a calculated decision by the French authorities, were hunted most implacably in France. Faced with German demands to deliver any and all Jews for deportation, they decided in effect to cut back on the kill by sacrificing only the foreign-born Jews while refusing to deliver those born French. Just a few weeks before Laporterie had fled Mont-de-Marsan, that campaign went into high gear with the infamous impoundment at the Vélodrome d'Hiver. Of almost thirteen thousand foreign-born Jews rousted from their beds that night of July 16–17, 1942, about nine thousand adults were sent directly to Auschwitz. Only thirty adults resumed after the war. Of the four thousand children deported a few weeks later, not one survived. It seems especially cruel—although the outcome would not have changed—that the French authorities separated these children from their mothers and sent each group alone to their fate.

Four months later, the Germans answered the Allied invasion of North Africa by moving into the Free Zone. From then on it did not matter where a Jew was born. If caught, he or she faced extermination. At least six special camps for Jews had been established in the Free Zone. There they could be held until there were enough of them for a full train to be sent to the north and on to Auschwitz. The largest camp was at Gers and well before the deportations began, staying alive right there on French soil was a problem. The Acting Grand Rabbi of France, Jacob Kaplan, reported that at this camp Jews "lived in crowded barracks, sleeping on the ground, devoured by vermin, suffering from hunger and cold in a damp, muddy region. During the one winter of 1940–41, they suffered eight hundred deaths."

As Albert Elias gets down to a *"cas concret"* in his letter, it turns out that he was no stranger to Gers.

> The author of this letter, himself a Jew, feared deportation. Escaping from the camp at Gers in March, 1943, he went to Laporterie, who unhesitatingly offered him asylum in his own house at Bascons. Denounced here [to the gendarmerie] . . . Elias and his wife were sent to a camp at Muret [Haute-Garonne], while Laporterie undertook efforts—crowned by success—to keep Mme. Marie Elias from being sent back for internment at Gers.
>
> Moreover, M. Laporterie persuaded the captain of the gendarmerie, Collinet, to intervene on behalf of Monsieur E. Thanks to this intervention, he was again freed. On October 12, 1943, however, at six o'clock in the morning, the gendarmes again banged on the door of M. Laporterie's

house, this time with deportation in mind. Monsieur E. managed to jump from a second-floor window and flee.

M. Dumartin, town secretary at Bascons, seconded by his friends, then hid the couple in a nearby chateau for nine days. This property belonged to M. Mespleight and M. Gourdon, bakers at Bascons. Meanwhile, M. Laporterie procured the essential papers and, on October 21st, he personally drove them to the Haute-Garonne, thereby allowing the couple to be delivered from certain deportation and an atrocious death.

A city of thirty-one thousand ought to be large enough to give anonymity to an old man showing off its streets, the more so since the days of his storekeeping here are decades past. But in Mont-de-Marsan, Laporterie is known to all. The usual pleasantries, moreover, do not always suffice. This tour would have been shorter if he were not forever slipping aside for brief but intensive private conversations with everyone from the owner of the Café du Sport to the doctor whose parking space he wanted. Not all these contacts were initiated by Laporterie. As we stood on the post office square, for example, a pleasant-faced, large woman suddenly rushed up and enveloped Laporterie in her ample arms in the most enthusiastic greeting possible.

"That's an Alsatian woman," he explained after she had returned to her errands. "She was among those who fled here as refugees after the Germans occupied Alsace-Lorraine in 1940. They were homeless but, to tell the truth, not many people here wanted to help them. So I found them homes myself. This woman got so well established here that after the war she never went back. But those who did return remembered that I'd lent them a hand. Two years ago they made a celebration for me in Strasbourg. I was received like a prince—with bands, honor guards, a special mass in the cathedral. It went on like that for four days without a stop."

If, as a stranger, this retired proprietor of the little store around the corner had offered such an explanation of why a woman should greet him so warmly, I would have been skeptical. But it doesn't take long in Laporterie's company before such explanations become inevitable. If honors can flow from Jerusalem, they can just as well flow from Strasbourg.

On the way back to Grenade, Laporterie pulls the car over for a moment at the dip in the road where the line of demarcation once divided not only the nation but, sometimes, those who would die from those who would live. But the French are happy to forget all that and have left the spot unmarked. In any case, there is nothing to see and, with the trucks roaring by, meditation is not encouraged.

Laporterie keeps one more office in the aging building across the street from La Petite Maison. It is our last stop. The ground floor is used for grain storage by his brother. Old, hand-hewn tools lie around here, and there is the aroma of fermenting grain, piercing and sour. The floor is dirt. Upstairs is the office. More than the one across the street, more than the one above the store in Mont-de-Marsan, this office seems of another age. From one wall to the other, the room is lined with boxes of dusty and yellowed papers.

"This is my personal reserve of municipal records—all that I did in Bascons for fifty years," he says. Surveying it all, he shakes his head slowly and adds, "I'm just an old maniac, salting away things like this. . . ."

On one wall hangs a small but ornately framed certificate from a commercial academy in Mont-de-Marsan which attests that Laporterie has completed a course in *sténodactylo*, or shorthand, with the notation "*très bien*."

"You can take shorthand?" I ask.

"Check the date," he fires back, looking at me as if I were crazy. The date, now well faded, is June 1914.

Laporterie motions to his old desk by the window where the warm afternoon light floods in. "I come up here sometimes and I sit over there alone and in quiet. And I ask myself, 'What can I do now? What's the next thing?'"

He had meant this last comment to be a sort of self-deprecating addendum to his self-portrait as an "old maniac." But the comment also seemed, inadvertently, to explain why he could have so effortlessly conceived and conducted large-scale operations at the Vichy line and why he never did retreat from the endless requests for help. It was because he is a compulsive doer. The old maniac was then merely a young maniac. Doing what he did came to him as naturally as it comes to others to sing on perfect pitch. He had ripped up Bascons right down to its graveyard and put it back together again because he could not help doing it. If, as he intended when a student, he'd gone to work in one of the African colonies, Laporterie might well have saved—instead of Jews—sufferers of famine, disease and homelessness. He'd have become the prototype of the whirlwind Peace Corps volunteer.

The procedure for admitting guests to the ceremony honoring Raoul Laporterie as one of the Righteous of Nations, held in Paris at the Israeli Embassy on rue Rabelais at noon of May 14, 1977, was both grim and apt. You do not enter this eighteenth-century mansion by ascending its wide front stairway, but through a high gate to the side courtyard. You state your business to a metal box. A buzzer opens the gate lock. Fifteen steps take you to an armored door. While cameras peer down at you from the eaves, you state your business into a box once more. It is several minutes before a young, casually dressed Israeli guard opens the door. You enter an armor-plated anteroom where other guards view you through a bulletproof glass window.

"We apologize very much for this inconvenience, but we must search you," says the guard. "You know, we have this problem. . . ." The words trail off with eye-rolling surprise that life has forced upon him this cumbersome and wasteful procedure. It is the same in every Israeli Embassy in the world.

Your passport is handed through the small window. You remove coat and jacket. Your body is patted up and down everywhere, not excluding the crotch. Your belt comes off. Maybe a shoe. Then the guard goes to work with a pair of metal-detecting wands. In this steel room, the whine of these instruments is nasty. Even the voice from the booth, which has to travel only across the bulletproof glass panel, comes out crackly, metallic, and in a hardly more human timbre than the metal detectors.

So here, thirty-two years after the war, just a quick walk from the Place de l'Etoile, splendid now with fountains, flags, and spring flowers, is another rigorously guarded and charmless frontier. This one is meant to keep out the terror against the Jews, of course, but being a Jew does not make it any easier to pass through. Like anyone else, you submit to the armed powers that ask you to take off your belt, your shoe, your jacket. With all his adroitness, it is not a crossing that even Laporterie could talk his way through. Today he does not have to try. Picked up by embassy car at his hotel, he is one of the chosen few outsiders who are whisked through security without so much as a check of an ID or even a wave of the wand that detects knives, guns, and bombs.

The ceremony is held in a handsome salon that was handsomer before it was cut into smaller spaces. But for all its balustrades, columns, and cornices, the Israelis have managed to bring to this very French space a touch of home. On the table are bottles of juice, paper cups, and cookies, not from one of the elegant local bakeries but out of a package, all of which could just as well has been laid out for a party to celebrate the purchase of a new tractor on a kibbutz in the Negev Desert. These refreshments may not seem odd to Americans any more than to Israelis. But there are residents of Paris, particularly this part of Paris, who have never seen either a paper cup or a cookie that came out of a cellophane bag.

Laporterie, immaculate as usual in a brown suit, mixes among the two dozen guests until the Consul General, Aryeh Lapide, taps the table for quiet and calls him forward. Lapide himself is a small, slender man who is unexpectedly shy as he offers Laporterie formal thanks. He draws close to the older man almost as if for protection as he reads the official "Attestation" printed in French and Hebrew:

> "...The Committee on the Righteous of Nations of the Martyrs and Heroes Commemorative Institute has decided, on the faith of witnesses it has gathered, to render homage to
>
> Raoul Laporterie
>
> who, at the peril of his life, saved Jews during the time of extermination, to award him the Medal of the Righteous, and to authorize him to plant a tree on the Avenue of the Righteous of Nations on the Mount of Remembrance at Jerusalem.
>
> Done at Jerusalem,
> November 30, 1976."

With this certificate, Lapide hands Laporterie an olive-wood box containing the medallion.

Standing erect, reading without glasses in a soft voice, Laporterie begins his short speech of acceptance: "How can I translate into simple words the sentiments I feel at finding myself at the center of this ceremony and my joy at receiving the Medal of the Righteous...."

At home, Laporterie had been more than happy to explain what he had done in the war and how he had done it. But he had been less anxious to explain why he did it. He seemed to be a man who steers away from philosophy. Now, still speaking softly, he shows that beneath the breezy charm in which he likes to bathe his exploits runs a subcurrent of pure, fierce, and highly focused feeling for his obligations to others and to himself. Laporterie makes sure that his motives for helping Jews more than thirty years ago are understood by the people gathered here.

> "... If I was able to help numerous Jews to pass through the holes of the net that was set for them and to find them refuges which put them out of the reach-

es of the Germans, my action was dictated above all by humane sentiments for beings worse off than I—followed, as they were, by the implacable and monstrous hate of the Occupant—but also by my absolute refusal to submit to and accept the conditions of life which were imposed on us, and by a desire, a biting need, for revenge and struggle against despotism and tyranny."

After the ceremony I bumped into Laporterie on Rue Rabelais. He had in tow a friend who had come from London for the ceremony. He apologized for having not a free moment to spend with me all day. He was doubly apologetic, actually, since he had told me over the phone from his hotel on the previous morning—his first full day in Paris in sixteen years—that he had a day that was "*très chargé*" (very busy). Now, standing here under a sky that was turning sunny, he seemed like a horse ready to be let out to romp. So, after warm but brief courtesies, he streaked off, weaving through the slower-moving Parisians on their lunch hour, his companion barely able to keep up.

In the week following the ceremony, again with my mother as translator, I spent one more day in Grenade-sur-l'Adour with Laporterie. It would be at the moment of our departure the next morning that an unexpected gesture from her and an unexpected response by its recipient would, abruptly, help to place the old man in a context which until then had eluded me.

But first, as the evening began, we had all sunk down into the deep, crackled leather chairs of Laporterie's study in La Petite Maison for a drink. Our choice was an Armagnac laced with essence of orange. Laporterie hastens to point out that, good as this drink might taste, the classic Armagnac is best appreciated straight. And, just as a certain ritual applies to salting a tequila glass or even to chugging down six-packs of beer at a fraternity party, Laporterie explains that Armagnac has its own ritual.

"You sit down with friends, light up a cigar, perhaps, and talk.

While the discussion progresses, you warm the bowl of the glass with your hands. When the drink is all gone to the last drop, you continue to warm the glass. Then you inhale from the glass—empty. At this moment you will catch the aroma of plums. It will last for a quarter-hour or more. This aroma is your guarantee that the drink isn't made artificially. It has been properly aged in the barrel. There are other brandies, like cognac, which are made in the same fashion, of course. But they are much more commercialized. A real Armagnac, which can be fifty years old or more, will never do you any harm, never tire you out, on account of the purity of the product. It is the soil which gives Armagnac its particular flavor, of course. On some labels you'll see the appellation 'bas-Armagnac.' You might think this is inferior to just plain Armagnac. In fact, it is superior, because of the soil. . . ."

Like all true Frenchmen, Laporterie is pleased to discourse tirelessly on his particular fondnesses in food and drink. But I want to try once more to get an answer to a question from which, on my first trip here, Laporterie had shied away. I want to know who in his family, if anyone, might have been the model for the man who would earn the Yad Vashem medal. But he finds it "*gênant*" to speculate on why he is the way he is. I tell him I am not asking about himself. I am asking only about the sources which, like the soil of Armagnac, nurtured him to be what he is now.

Given that rationale, Laporterie allows, warily, that any artistic leanings he may have come down from his father, who was director of the municipal orchestra of Mont-de-Marsan. From his mother's side came more remarkable qualities, though the family on this side was, as he puts it, "almost peasants." His aunt, for example, was a nun who rose to be the Mother Superior of a topflight school in La Plata, Argentina. His own mother never strayed far from her father and her storekeeping duties in tiny Bascons. But within those confines, says Laporterie, "She was an agreeable and sainted woman who gave service to everyone. After she died, I found in her ledgers that many people had owed her money for years back. These were poor people who had nothing. And since they could not pay their debts, she did not ask for it. That's how she was. She'd give a service without asking for a thing in return."

Laporterie sits silent a moment, an eighty-year-old son thinking about his mother. It is not clear if he realizes that he has described her according to the same standard and even with the same words that he has applied, with fierce pride rather than reverence, to the conduct of his own business during the war. Except, of course, that for him matters went well beyond being left with uncalled debts on the books of the store. He was so busy "giving service" that in three out of five cases, he lost the stores themselves.

In the morning, before heading on to Bordeaux, we load up the car and then walk over from the Hôtel de France to La Petite Maison to say goodbye. It should be a quick courtesy, but Laporterie is seized with a sudden worry. Apart from the stack of letters and documents from the war with which he has plied me, do I have enough reference material on the locality itself? So we end this visit the way I had begun the first—standing with Laure Laporterie in the doorway between the store and the living quarters of La Petite Maison, waiting for her husband. She rolls her eyes very slightly, as if to say she has no more control of him than of a streaking deer. Then she calls out again in that unexpected voice—clear, soaring, and unstrained—which on an acoustic frequency chart must look like a perfect ascending curve.

"Raoul . . . Ra-oooooul . . ."

In his own time Laporterie materializes, carrying a neat stack of particulars: a set of postcard scenes of Bascons, a group of guidebooks to Landes and area maps. Finally, he has included copies of newspaper clippings about the ceremony in Paris and of the Certificate of Attestation in French and Hebrew.

Laporterie puts on his hat to see us off. A veil of haze has yet to burn off the square of Grenade. The mobile fishmonger has taken his station in front of the Hôtel de France, his sidegate thrown open to display black mussels, gleaming red and silver fish, as well as flounder looking like mud splats on the ice. We say our goodbyes in front of the rented car. To my surprise my mother, who has a goodly store of reserve as well as warmth, reaches up impulsively on tiptoe to give Laporterie a kiss. It happens fast, so fast that for once the old man is left standing in a puddle of his own surprise. For some reason that is as yet unclear, he is flustered. Shaking hands with me, he whispers, "I am afraid that with your mother I lost my *galanterie*."

It took a moment for me to understand what had left him so chagrined. For all his zest, Laporterie is still one of those old-fashioned types who would always and automatically remove their hat as soon as a woman entered an elevator. Failing at that elementary courtesy would have been bad enough. But allowing a woman to kiss him while his hat remained on his head? That came close to humiliation.

But this tiny catastrophe is also for me the key to completing a particular portrait whose subject I should have recognized much sooner. Like most schoolboys, I had been taught, long ago, that in the unlikely event I was ever to meet the figure in question, he could be identified by certain requisite qualities. He would be modest. His interest in personal wealth would be next to nil. He would be devoutly religious. His courage would be unfailing. He would be a doer of noble deeds, a rescuer of those in distress.

Now, catching a glimpse of Laporterie's face—still slightly crestfallen—in the rear-view mirror as the car pulls away, I remember the last essential attribute. He would hold to absolute courtesy with a woman. Then it all clicks. This *landais* village is home to an exemplar of what, long ago and across the Channel, Chaucer called a "parfit gentil knight."

As the first edition of this book was nearing press time, Raoul Laporterie went by invitation to Israel to visit the Holy Places and to plant his tree on the Avenue of the Righteous. At age eighty-three, he had never left France except, briefly, as a prisoner of the Germans in the First World War. Neither had he been on an air-plane. His wife, Laure, never one stricken by wanderlust, was more than content to stay home and, with her daughter, go on minding La Petite Maison. During his visit of a week, Laporterie squinted against the white desert sun, but his three suits remained the most immaculate in the land. He did not fail to notice, of course, that most Israeli men never wear a suit—even at their own weddings. But he did not relent. "What can I do?" he asked. "It's how I've dressed my whole life."

Ever the total archivist, Laporterie had arrived with a map on which he had precisely traced in red ink his voyage from Grenade-sur-l'Adour to Bordeaux to Paris to Tel Aviv. Now he kept an ongoing log of his travels in the Holy Land—through Jerusalem, including the Stations of the Cross, down into the Jordan Valley and north through Jericho to the Sea of Galilee. On these shores he showed particular interest in the ruins of the synagogue at Capernaum where Jesus spoke and in the pumping station that supplies water to much of Israel. He went up into the hills to Bethlehem where, in a grottolike space hardly larger than a dressing closet, he stood before the spot where Jesus was born to Mary. Then on to Haifa where in the early evening, from the heights of Mount Carmel, the city lay bathed in creamy light. Asked later by a stranger what he thought of Israel, Laporterie answered, "I'm struck by all that is ancient and all that is new."

The only two problems on this trip had to do, not surprisingly, with the exacting demands of a Frenchman's stomach and palate. The first problem was that nobody had thought to advise Laporterie to bring from home, in bottles, the various apéritifs—principally Noilly—that he drinks five times each day and which he believes are essential to his digestion. He soon adapted nicely, however, to the dry white wine made in the hills behind Haifa, in vineyards established by no less than the Rothschilds of France. The other problem was that no restaurant in Israel seemed able to create an omelette that was buttery and *baveuse*—runny. This dish, he said wistfully, his wife makes for him each day to perfection. As no solution to this problem could be found, Laporterie ate his eggs soft-boiled.

The central event was, of course, the ceremony at Yad Vashem.

It was held at eleven o'clock on Sunday, June 8, 1980. On the Avenue of the Righteous, a vigorous breeze ruffled the carob trees and spread a faint brown veil of dust on the distant hills. Grasping a hoe as cameras clicked and passersby gawked, Laporterie energetically planted his own small tree. At his side were three women, now from Jerusalem, who long ago he had passed across the line of demarcation, supplied with false IDs and given lodging. Two of the women were nearly his own age. The other, still young, had been only seven years old at the time. The fact that Laporterie did not recognize them was the result not simply of time elapsed but of the almost assembly-line volume at which he processed those who arrived in need of help at La Petite Maison.

In the days before this ceremony, Laporterie had been worried that, in the short speech he would give, he might fail to acknowledge one or another attending dignitary or commit some other "gaffe." Despite assurances that Israel was not as obsessively formal as his own country in ceremonial matters, his anxiety was hardly eased until the speech had been faultlessly delivered. In it, he noted that a French fabulist had once said that at his age "it is no longer time to build but to plant." This particular planting, he continued, symbolized the "rebirth of a nation finding its own deepest roots. My own satisfaction, no doubt like that of others who have helped you, is the greater because the fall of the forces that would have destroyed you corresponded to your resurrection." Laporterie ended by saying that this voyage and this occasion had "illuminated the last days of my life."

There were no signs during this week, however, to indicate that Laporterie's last days were at hand. At the airport for the trip home, he was tanned and vigorous and his eyes, accustomed now to the hard light, took in everything. Sitting at an outdoor café while waiting to board the plane for home, he observed a slender, fetching young policewoman dressed in a close-fitting khaki uniform. She had, he noted, quite a nice "coiffure."

"What's below the coiffure is also quite nice," said one of his new friends at the table.

"At my age," shot back the old man solemnly, "I no longer have the right to look below the coiffure." Then, flashing his dry and inimitably Gallic smile, he added, "At least, not after I'm home with my Laure at seven o'clock tonight."

EPILOGUE, 1999

Even the supercharged Raoul Laporterie could not go on forever. When I traveled to Grenade-sur-l'Adour to visit him in 1991, after a hiatus of ten years, his family told me that only a week earlier he'd sunk into a deep coma—the terminal phase of a long life, said his doctor. But Raoul wasn't ready. He revived suddenly and smartly on the day of my arrival. Reaching up to me from his bed, he took my hands with a firm grip and kissed my cheeks. Even in his pajamas, Laporterie was dapper. It was the last time I would see him. He died soon after at age ninety-four.

In his old age, Laporterie revealed one more surprise. A Canadian writer named James Bacque, in researching a biography of Laporterie, came across warm letters in his subject's archive from a former Wehrmacht soldier, Hans Goertz. Laporterie explained to a puzzled Bacque that, rather than being repatriated, Goertz had been enslaved in France after the Nazi defeat. A tailor in civilian life, the emaciated Goertz had been assigned to Laporterie's struggling haberdashery in Mont-de-Marsan after Liberation. Goertz was treated courteously and fed well until he could go home. In Germany, Bacque sought out Goertz, who said, "As soon as I saw that man, I knew my troubles were over. . . . He saved my life."

*Bacque quotes Laporterie's response: "*Comme ça, on a pas des enemies.*" ("That way, one has no enemies.")*

Raoul Laporterie commenced the war by helping Alsatian refugees. During the war, he helped Jews and others to cross the Vichy line. After the war ended, he helped his former enemy.

Dervis and Servet Korkut

It was only a piece of paper. As Lamija and Vllaznim Jaha were being expelled from their home in Kosovo for no sin other than having been born ethnic Albanian Muslims, so many things seemed more important to pack up than a piece of paper, and a photocopy at that. Written in English on the left and Hebrew on the right, it honored an act of rescue by Lamija's parents sixty years earlier. Few people had direct knowledge of what they had done. As parents themselves, Lamija and Vllazhim had not even spoken of it to their own children. Of what use could its telling be now? Lamija grabbed it anyway.

Her instinct was accurate. That piece of paper would shortly reveal the latent power of a courageous deed marked and remembered. It would enable the Jahas and their two teenagers to start life afresh. Like that piece of paper, their new life would be sourced in Jerusalem.

Not since that morning of April 2, 1999, has the Jaha family returned to their eighth-floor apartment in Pristina, provincial capital of Kosovo in the former Yugoslavia. Serbian militiamen, flowing into town from strongholds in the hills, ordered all ethnic Albanians of Muslim background to vacate their buildings. The grim process was called "ethnic cleansing." Because a Serb kingdom had existed in Kosovo long ago, the attacking Serbs believed that it was still historically and culturally theirs. Ethnic Albanians who comprised 90 percent of the population of Kosovo, were, in their eyes, trespassers.

A few weeks earlier, as the Serb threat loomed, the Jahas had sent their daughter Fitore, twenty, and son Fatos, seventeen, under assumed names to the safety of Budapest, Hungary. Until their own final week in Pristina, Vllaznim still worked as an electrical engineer, Lamija as an economist. But then the electricity was cut off. Then the telephone. The couple listened to their portable radio until the batteries went dead. That was the end of their contact with the outside world. "The amazing thing is that next door we had Serb neighbors who had already left," says Lamija. "Yet their phone kept ringing with nobody to answer it. Somehow, the Serbs knew how to cut off only the phones of us Albanians."

Thousands of Kosovars were killed during that winter and spring. Other victims suffered a fate which for them may have been worse than death. Dr. Bogdan Denitch, an American sociologist born in the region, reports that Serbs raped young women not by dragging them into the shadows but by doing it as a public act on village squares. For families of the victims, the defiling was an irreparable shame. "Villagers told me that if their homes were burnt down, they would rebuild them on the same spot," says Denitch. "But if their women were publicly raped, they felt their only choice was to leave. That was the desired effect." Denitch tells of visiting a young woman in the hospital who had been raped multiple times. "She had been there more than a week," he says, "but not one member of her family had visited her. They were too ashamed."

In the last week of March 1999, NATO bombers started hitting Serb positions. But that did not stop the ethnic cleansing.

From their window, the Jahas watched ragged columns of ethnic Albanians streaming toward the Pristina railroad station. Now their turn came. At mid-morning, Serb militia men entered their lobby and ordered the building to be cleared. Carrying what they could, the Jahas headed for the station. "We were lucky," says Lamija. "We managed to get on a train." Packed with refugees, it rolled south all day, arriving at dusk at the Macedonian border. In the bustle of being pushed off the train, the Jahas lost two bags containing family memorabilia. But Lamija held on to that piece of paper.

At the sight of thousands more refugees already massed in a broad field, Vllaznim says simply, "We felt lost."

With nowhere else to go, nothing else to do, the Jahas joined the aimless crowd. Some had been waiting for a week for a passage to refugee camps being hastily prepared by the UN in Macedonia. Several refugees, it was rumored, had been fatally stricken with infectious meningitis. A bad smell hung over the field. Nora Lee Baron, an American volunteer in the Kosovar refugee camps, was struck by "the unnatural silence in the air." It was the silence of resignation. With darkness came a cold drizzle. "When food packs were given out, everyone came running," says Lamija. "People grabbed from each other. I took two packs, but then an old woman came crying that she had none, so I gave her one of ours."

Rejecting a wait of "three or four days" until the refugees could be moved as a group into Macedonia, the Jahas crossed the border on their own late that night. A taxi took them to Kumanovo, a city where an aunt of Lamija lived. Their plan was to apply for visas to Sweden, where Vllaznim had a brother, or France, where Lamija's brother lived. But both countries "closed their doors on us," says Vllaznim. "They said we couldn't be admitted as individuals, only as part of organized groups through relief agencies."

Over a week passed. Although Lamija's aunt was not pressuring her guests to leave, Vllaznim felt uncomfortable, saying, "I don't like to disturb people." But where to go? Not to the war zone back home. And not, if they could help it, to a refugee camp in Macedonia or Albania. Vllaznim called the situation "a vacuum." Lamija wasn't so sure.

"What about this certificate my parents got?" she asked. Perhaps it could be helpful in reapplying for Swedish or French visas if it were shown to the Israeli consulate in nearby Skopje, capital of Macedonia. The couple contacted Victor Mizrahi, head of the local Jewish community. Lamija handed him the piece of paper, which said:

> *This is to certify that in its session of December 14, 1994,*
> *the commission for the designation of the Righteous,*
> *established by Yad Vashem, the Holocaust Heroes &*
> *Martyrs Remembrance Authority, on the basis of*
> *evidence presented before it, decided to honour*
>
> *Dervis & Servet Korkut*
>
> *who, during the Holocaust period in Europe risked their life*
> *to save persecuted Jews.*
>
> *The Commission, therefore, has accorded them the Medal*
> *of the Righteous Among Nations. Their name shall be for-*
> *ever engraved on the Honour Wall in the Garden of the*
> *Righteous, at Yad Vashem, Jerusalem.*
>
> *Jerusalem, Israel*
> *February 23, 1995*

"You are the daughter of Dervis Korkut?" asked Mizrahi, after he had scanned the certificate. "It's an honor to meet you."

Mizrahi already was familiar with the story of how, during the Nazi Occupation of Sarajevo in 1942, the Korkuts hid a young Jewish woman named Mira Papo in their home. He also knew that, as a curator of the Sarajevo Museum, Dervis Korkut hid the renowned "Sarajevo Haggadah" from a German officer who had come in search of it. The superbly illuminated fourteenth-century volume is the best known and most admired of all haggadahs, which are used as guides to the Exodus story recounted at the Passover table. Thanks to Korkut's action, the Sarajevo Haggadah did not become a Nazi artifact. The medal awarded by Yad Vashem, however, was for saving a life, not a book.

Mira Papo was born in Sarajevo in 1922. She was the only child of a family whose forbearers had been driven out of Spain by the Inquisition in 1492 (as were, probably, the original owners of the Sarajevo Haggadah). Surrounded by Balkan hills, Sarajevo lies on a cultural fault line between East and West. The Israeli journalist Amira Hass writes in her book, *Drinking the Sea at Gaza*, of her mother's growing up in "tolerant" Sarajevo before the Second World War: "The Muezzin's call to prayer, the church bells, and the Sabbath psalms sung in Ladino [a mixture of Spanish and Hebrew] were the melodies of her childhood.... Muslims, Christians, and Jews lived together, studied in the same classrooms, went together to university, together became atheists and joined the Communist underground." That harmony was destroyed during the Nazi occupation and again between 1992 and 1995 when Sarajevo was gripped by nationalistic warfare. Thousands of adults and children, mostly ethnic Albanian Muslims, were killed by Serbian forces shelling the city from the surrounding hills.

Solomon Papo, Mira's father, worked as a janitor in the city's ministry of finance. Her maternal grandfather had sold seeds in an outdoor market. As in most Sephardic Jewish homes, the Papos spoke both Ladino and Serbo-Croatian. "Simple and poor," is how the younger of Mira's two sons, Davor Bakovic, describes the family. "They neither traveled nor read books. They lived in a harsh climate, and it took all their energy to survive. The family was not religious, but my mother told me that as a young girl she was always excited before the Hanukkah holiday, because her aunts would bring her a new dress."

Davor describes his mother as "upbeat and full of life." As a teenager, Mira joined the Young Guardians (Hashomer Haza'ir in Hebrew), a group that provided training for Jewish youths who wanted to emigrate to Israel. Mira attended meetings twice a week in Sarajevo, but that fact was kept from her father, because he would not have approved of a secular Zionist group. The issue became moot when Yugoslavia was overrun by Germany in April 1941.

Before the year ended, Jewish men, including Solomon Papo, were arrested and taken away. Then the women were ordered to assemble at the community's social hall called La Benevolencia. Mira, then nineteen, did not obey. But she did sneak into the hall through a rear window and located her mother and two of her aunts. "My mom wanted to lead them to safety," Davor says. "When they refused, she insisted that she would stay with them. But they convinced her that she had to survive." From hiding, Mira watched the Jewish women being loaded onto trucks. She never again saw her mother or father or those aunts. They were murdered by Germans or by the vicious Croatian fascist militia called the *Ustashe* ("Uprising"). The anti-Nazi Serbs suffered the same treatment by the *Ustashe*.

Along with thirty other teenagers from the Young Guardians, Mira joined the Yugoslavian partisans, communists allied to the Soviet Union who organized to fight the Nazis from the forests after their country was overrun by Hitler. The Young Guardians stressed physical discipline that was helpful to partisan recruits. Winter was brutal in the Balkan forests, and partisan units had to keep moving. They were being hunted by Germans and their henchmen, the Ustashe. Mira, who had attended lectures on public health as a Young Guardian, was appointed medical officer of her partisan unit. She was also keeper of the unit's mule, which carried ammunition and medical supplies. Except for their own backs, the partisans had no other means of transporting supplies.

"My mom told me that she once fell asleep on the mule as her unit was on a night march. As her comrades turned, the mule kept going straight. When her buddies realized what had happened, they doubled back and found my mom. That was lucky for her. She knew of another unit in which the mule got lost. That was so serious to the entire unit that the person in charge of the mule was shot."

During the winter of 1942, the partisans fought in parallel against the Germans with Yugoslavian royalists called Chetniks. In March 1942, the rightist Chetniks turned against the leftist Partisans. That was "a heavy blow and our fighters began to desert their units," according to Mira's testimony to Yad Vashem in 1994. The partisan high command ordered the remaining units to reorganize into smaller, elite squadrons. "We were told that these units would have to be highly mobile," says Mira. "They would have to get rid of their ballast. Our group of Jewish students from Sarajevo were told we were too weak for the task before the remaining partisans. We were ordered to return to Sarajevo. And they took away our weapons."

Mira's group was warned to wait half a day before moving out of the field where they had been assembled, even though they were vulnerable to attack. If they tried to leave earlier, their former comrades would shoot them. "The Germans were using dogs to hunt lost partisans day and night," says Mira. "Most of my friends got caught and killed." Her fate would be the same if she stayed in the forest. But barring a miracle, it would be the same in her German-occupied hometown.

"I entered occupied Sarajevo before dawn of that early spring day," according to her testimony. "In my hand were a few eggs tied up in a cloth that had been given to me by the mother of a friend who lived in the countryside. We had survived together. The streets were empty. I was trying to think of what to do, where to go. I reached the center of the city and found myself in front of the finance ministry where my father had worked. My feet carried me to the entrance of the building. Nothing moved at that hour. But I heard footsteps. From out of the shadows came a man.

At that moment, my heart pounding in fear, I recognized him as a porter who had worked with my father. An honest man named Sava.

"Out of the silence, I called him by his name and offered him the traditional Serbo-Croatian greeting: 'May God help us.' Sava came closer and peered closely at me.

"'Aren't you the daughter of Salomon Papo?' he asked.

"I nodded and started to cry. He took me to the janitor's dressing room where I told him how we had been exiled from our partisan unit and how, after much suffering, I had reached Sarajevo. Then I asked him, 'Can you do anything to save me? If not, then just deliver me directly to the Ustashe and get it over with.'

"Sava stared at me and thought for a long time without speaking. Then he took me by the hand and led me out of the dressing room and locked the entrance door to the building. We walked a few blocks to the Sarajevo Museum, still not exchanging a word. There in the porter's room, he motioned me to wait. That time was an eternity. Finally, Sava returned with a gentleman wearing a fez [a traditional Turkish hat, usually red with a black tassel, worn by Muslim men]. Then Sava vanished. I never saw him again.

"The gentleman motioned me to follow him. At the rear of the museum, we got into his car and only then did he ask me a few questions about where I'd been and for how long. He had a plan for me: I would stay with his family in their apartment on the ground floor of a two-story building. My name would now be Amira, a Muslim name. He and his wife, married for two years, had just had their first child, a son named Munib. The family spoke Albanian at home. If anyone was curious as to why I had suddenly shown up in his household, the explanation was that I had been hired to help take care of the baby. But I was not to speak to anyone except the family."

"Amira" remained a member of the Korkut household until August 1942. German officers who sometimes visited the house would have had no reason to be suspicious of the young, so-called "servant" who was fully robed in traditional Muslim fashion. In her four months with the family, Mira never left the house. Early one morning, she answered a knock on the door. She was handed an envelope by a young man. "It's for you," he whispered, and was gone. Mira waited until she was alone in her room that night before opening the envelope. It contained false identity papers for her and a railroad ticket.

"One of my mother's sisters, Aunt Matilda, was married to a Catholic," according to Mira's testimony. "She had arranged for me to go to a house on the Dalmatian coast belonging to her husband's family. No Germans were in that region and I would be safe. Above the Korkut home lived a high officer in the Ustashe. He had a Jewish wife! I was instructed that after midnight on a certain day, I was to climb the stairs to this officer's apartment. From there, two soldiers who guarded him would escort me to the Sarajevo train station. As I left, Dervis Korkut told me to take care of myself. That is how I parted from his family. I never managed to contact them for the rest of the war."

In that same year that the Korkut family rescued Mira from the Germans, Dervis Korkut did the same for the Sarajevo Haggadah, composed of 109 bleached calfskin pages. Legend has it that that the Haggadah was a wedding gift to a Jewish couple married in Spain in the fourteenth century. It may have been taken to Italy after the expulsion of Jews from Iberia in 1492, and from there to Sarajevo. It was sold to the museum in 1894 by a boy whose father had recently died, leaving the family in desperate straits. There is no more beautiful haggadah than this one. It was regarded as the crown jewel of the national museum and was exactly the sort of artifact that Hitler wanted to preserve after he had killed all the Jews. According to research by Kemal Bakaršić, former chief librarian of Sarajevo's national library, a Nazi general, Johann Hans Fortner, arrived with a retinue at the museum in 1942. After being given a tour, General Fortner confronted the museum director, Dr. Petrovic:

"*Und jetz, bitte, übergeben Sie mir die Haggadah.*" ("And now, please give me the Haggadah.").

"That's not possible, General," said Dr. Petrovic. "Just two hours ago, one of your lieutenants came to the Museum and demanded the Haggadah. Of course, we complied."

"Who was this officer?" shouted the general.

"He didn't identify himself."

Fortner left in a huff. Dr. Petrovic had lied to protect the Haggadah. As he dissembled to the general, the Haggadah was actually elsewhere in the museum, in the hands of Dervis Korkut, the museum's curator of books and manuscripts. Korkut slipped out of the museum with the treasure and entrusted it to a Muslim friend who lived in an isolated farmhouse deep in the hills. The Haggadah remained there for the duration of the war. It had another close call fifty years later when the Serb bombardment of Sarajevo began in 1992. Cultural institutions, including the national museum, were a particular target of the Serbs. Again, museum officials removed the Haggadah for safekeeping, this time to a vault in the national bank. Then, in 2002, the Haggadah was returned to the museum, where it was put on permanent display. For Bosnians, the Haggadah is more than an ancient and ceremonial object. Venerated by Jews, protected by Muslims and Croats, it is a symbol of Sarajevo's traditional multi-ethnic harmony.

Instead of honoring Dervis Korkut as an antifascist hero after the war, Yugoslavia's new communist government accused him of having been a collaborator with the Nazis. Why would such a man be targeted as an enemy of the state? The Germans, it seems, had hoped to create an elite Muslim SS-like unit in Bosnia. A fraternal organization, the "Young Muslims," was to furnish its members. As a leading Muslim figure, Korkut was asked by the Germans to be a leader of the unit. He refused. Even so, and without his permission, Korkut's name was put on a list of the Young Muslim volunteers.

After the war, the new Yugoslav communist government began a clean-up of political enemies. It was also determined to smother religion in the new secular society which was to be built. Muslims were a special target, many having sided with Hitler. The Grand

Mufti of Jerusalem had set the pro-Nazi example by spending the war years in Berlin as Hitler's honored guest. Now that it was payback time in Yugoslavia, Dervis Korkut was a high-visibility scapegoat. "If my father hadn't been such a big intellectual, and very independent, they wouldn't have bothered with him," says Lamija.

Long before the war, the Jewish community knew Korkut as a friend. In the early 1920's, the rising young scholar had defended the Jewish community when the government was preparing anti-Jewish laws. Korkut did important ethnological research on the eclectic history of the local Jewish community, including translation of old documents in Turkish. As the Nazi Occupation began in 1941, Korkut could have jumped on the anti-Semitic bandwagon. Instead, he courageously sent a position paper to the government titled "Anti-Semitism Is Foreign to the Muslims of Bosnia and Herzegovina." In it, he pinpointed anti-Semitism as being "only the lightning rod used to draw the people's attention away from their real problems."

In his position paper that instead of enacting anti-Jewish measures, Korkut urged it would be better to "provide help to the poor Jewish population . . . the number of which is higher than we think." Korkut ended the paper by noting that "the most beautiful proof of religious tolerance in Bosnia is that [in Sarajevo] all four domestic religious houses of worship [Catholic, Orthodox, Muslim, and Jewish] were exactly one beside the other."

Dervis Korkut's idealism did not count with the post-war government. His situation as a defendant charged with anti-communist activities in 1946 was dire. Once the government decided to hold a political trial, conviction was all but certain. The only question was whether the punishment would be prison or execution.

Mira Papo, meanwhile, had fared better than her rescuer in the aftermath of the war, although her own life would soon take a turn for the worse. Commissioned as an officer in the army medical corps, she became engaged to marry Bozidar Bakovic, also a former partisan and now an army officer.

Since being spirited out of the Korkut household that night in

1942, Mira had not been in contact with her rescuers. Then, in June 1946, she suddenly was confronted by that chapter in her life in which she was a hunted Jew. Mira was walking on Sarajevo's main street when, she says, "an unknown veiled woman with a young boy dropped to her knees before me. I almost fell over her." As Mira helped the woman to her feet, she begged Mira to testify on behalf of her husband. She was babbling, but Mira gathered that he was being tried as leading member of the Young Muslims. His life was in the balance.

"Who are you?" asked Mira.

The weeping woman lifted her veil. Mira saw the tear-stained face of Servet Korkut. The boy, who had been an infant when she last saw him, was Munib, now a four-year-old.

"I firmly told Servet that I would be a witness for her husband in court," Mira later wrote in her testimony to Yad Vashem. "But I was a military person, and my superiors prohibited me from appearing at the trial." According to her son Davor, Mira's fiancé also forbid her to testify since Korkut's trial was a political event and her testimony could only harm both their careers. He even posted a guard in case she tried to disobey.

Mira's failure to step forward on behalf of her rescuer, a secret kept from her children until her old age, would haunt her always. She long assumed that Dervis Korkut, like many other declared enemies of the new communist state, had faced a firing squad.

In 1947, Mira was wedded to Bozidar Bakovic. Two years later, Bozidar died, apparently due to complications from war wounds. Mira, then twenty-seven, was left with two young sons, Daniel and Davor, and no job, since the army had recently demobilized her. "Since my mother had lost her only remaining link to the army, she had to give up our government-sponsored apartments," says Davor, who was then three months old. "Yugoslavia was still in ruins, and nothing was well organized. She had no pension, no social services to help us. We were put out on the street with our furniture."

Mira and her brood were lent a room with a family that had known her parents. "Great pressure to help my mom was put on the authorities by army officers who knew us," says Davor. "After a long struggle, the army agreed to take her back. She was put in charge of medical affairs for the Dalmatian coast and its islands. So my brother and I grew up as the sons of an officer. I remember that we'd get to go with her on a boat as she did her duties. Other times, we'd have soldiers as babysitters. My mother told me and my brother that she would never again marry, because she didn't want to share us with anybody. And we were such naughty twerps!"

In the mid-1950's, Mira and her children settled in Rijeka, on the northern Dalmatian coast, where she worked at a hospital. "My mom was a devoted communist and Yugoslav," says Davor. "She believed in the rights of all people. But she believed in no gods. She wasn't anti-anything except anti-religious."

Mira did not, however, find it so easy to cast off her cultural links to the remnant of the Yugoslavian Jewish community. Of the 75,000 pre-war Jews in her land, 12,000 survived the war, many as partisans, including a number of commanders. As Mira in childhood had been nicely dressed by her aunts for Hanukkah, so she dressed her boys in special clothes when the holiday came around. As a twelve-year-old, Davor was taken for the first time to Rijeka's Jewish community center. "It was hidden behind a wall and a large grey gate," he remembers. "Within, the hall was lit by candles and was full of children." Feeling an "intuitive sense of belonging," Davor became a regular at the center. He even began to bring along his best friend, who was not Jewish.

Davor joined the army at age eighteen. Like his mother and the father he never knew, he experienced "long maneuvers under harsh circumstances." As he completed his service two years later, he sat around a campfire with his fellow soldiers as they talked about themselves. "I said I'm a Jew," Davor says, "and the other guys asked what that meant, exactly. Their question forced me to ask myself where I really belonged. My officer, a wonderful guy, asked what I planned to do after the army. And I answered that I was going to visit this land of mine, Israel."

At the harbor in Rijeka, Davor struck up a conversation with the captain of an Israeli freighter. In three hours, said the captain, the ship would sail for Israel. Davor called his mother and asked her to pack his suitcase. When the freighter departed, Davor was aboard. "That was in 1969, and Yugoslavia was much more advanced than Israel," he says. "Even the buses were far more modern." To Davor, that wasn't what mattered. "In the deepest and most profound way," he says, "I felt at home. It was clear that I was going back to Yugoslavia to collect the bits and pieces of my old life and then come to Israel for good."

Davor found a future wife as well as a life in Israel when he emigrated there in 1970. Her name was Grania. Born in India to a Swiss mother and Irish father who managed a British-owned tea plantation, she had come to Israel, like Davor, first as a visitor and then returned to make her life there. "Swiss and Brits are cold," says Grania. "Here, I felt warmth. When I came back for good, I felt I'd come home." The feeling was not reciprocal. When Grania tried to enroll in an intensive Hebrew language course meant for immigrants, she was at first rejected because she wasn't Jewish.

"I told them that was racist," she says. Her application was reconsidered and accepted. At that course, she met Davor.

Their marriage caused a rupture between Grania and her father. He did not want his daughter to wed a Jew raised in a communist country. His rejection was so absolute that, for years, Grania's mother begged her to address letters only to her, since her father rejected letters addressed to "Mr. and Mrs." On one visit, her father rejected her gift of a bottle of whiskey from the duty-free shop. Reconciliation came, but only after her father was felled by a stroke. By then, her parents had retired to England. Grania visited with her infant daughter, Smadar, the first of the couple's three adopted children.

"Everything will be all right now," her father said from his bed upon the arrival of his daughter and granddaughter. "Smadar loved to play at the foot of his bed as he lay there," says Grania. "She was there when he died. When my mother came to visit us after my father's death, for the first time, she wore slacks."

Mira's older son, Daniel, had gone to live in America. With no family left in Yugoslavia, and with diminished enthusiasm for communism, fifty-year-old Mira Bakovic emigrated to Israel in 1972, the same year that Grania and Davor were married. After several years on a kibbutz, she moved to Jerusalem. Davor and his family lived nearby in Neve Ilan, a cooperative community nestled in the Judean hills. Down the road from their home is Davor's sculpture and metal fabrication workshop.

Mira was happy in Israel. But she was shadowed by the memory of the kneeling Servet Korkut's unrequited plea that Mira testify at the trial of her husband. And by her assumption that Dervis had been executed as an enemy of the state. Then, in early 1994, Mira came across an old copy of a newspaper published in Serbo-Croatian by the Yugoslavian Jewish community. In it was an article commemorating the tenth anniversary of the death of Dervis Korkut. At his trial, Mira now learned, other Jews had testified on his behalf. Their testimony may have saved him. Instead of being shot, he was sentenced to six years in prison in harsh conditions. Released in 1953, Korkut returned to Sarajevo. In 1956, Lamija was born. Her father died an octogenarian in 1969.

Lamija attended college in Pristina, where she met Vllaznim, who was from an Albanian-speaking family like her own. His father, president of the Kosovo Red Cross, was a moral facsimile of hers. "If my father had one apple," says Vllaznim, "he would cut it up exactly into sixths for his six kids. You try to cut an apple into six equal parts—it's hard. And if my father had two apples, he would give one away." Vllaznim's father wrote a multi-volume Albanian cultural history, later published privately by Vllaznim and Lamija and given to interested readers at no cost. "I made each volume short," says Vllaznim, "because if you show an Albanian a thick book, he won't want to read it. But a thin book, he's willing to give it a try." While most ethnic Albanians were tradition bound, Vllaznim was always progressive. As a father in Pristina, he even did child care while Lamija was at work.

"The article in which Mira belatedly read about Dervis Korkut gave her the shock of her life," says Grania. "She was weeping and babbling in Serbo-Croatian. I didn't understand a word. This was the first time that Davor had heard about Dervis Korkut. And the first time Mira had talked about what had happened."

It had been twenty-five years since the death of Dervis Korkut. Not wishing to ask her son in Paris for money, Servet had done tailoring to earn a living. "At my father's funeral," says Lamija, "strangers came up to my mother and told her how generous my father had been in loaning them money when they needed it. My mother wasn't too happy to hear that because she was left with nothing." When Sarajevo was under siege in 1992, the Jewish community organized a bus convoy to bring people out of the city. A seat was reserved for Servet. She went to stay with Munib in Paris. "Mira talked to my mother by telephone soon after she read this article about my father," says Lamija. "She asked for forgiveness. My mother told Mira, 'What happened, happened. It is in the past.'"

Mira had failed to testify for her rescuer in 1946. But there was a way for her to testify for him a half-century later. Not far from Mira's home in Jerusalem, at Yad Vashem on Mount Herzl, was the Garden of the Righteous Among Nations. Mira was determined to see Dervis and Servet Korkut inscribed there. Direct testimony from the rescued person is the key to gaining that honor. That, Mira was able to provide to Yad Vashem in a three-page, single-spaced letter dated February 2, 1994. That testimony would also provide a way, after her death, to rescue the family of Lamija Jaha.

On March 27, 1996, a ceremony honoring the couple was held at the Israeli embassy in Paris. Servet attended with her son. Like his father, Munib had once been honorary French counsel in Sarajevo. They were presented with a bronze medallion, set in an olivewood case, and the certificate in Hebrew and English naming Dervis and Servet as Righteous Among Nations.

It was almost three years later when Lamija Jaha handed a copy of that certificate to Victor Mizrahi in Skopje, Macedonia. The plight of the Kosovar refugees had struck a chord with the Israeli public, which recalled how most of the world had once turned its back on Jewish refugees from Hitler. Israel had flown a seventy-five-bed field hospital, complete with doctors and nurses, to a Macedonian refugee camp. The small nation had also invited several hundred refugees to be its guests for six months. They could then either return to Kosovo or possibly resettle in Israel.

"Your parents once helped the Jews," Mizrahi told Lamija. "It's our turn to help you. If you and your husband want to be flown to Israel, it will be arranged."

"We agreed to go to Israel, but only if our children in Budapest could join us," says Vllaznim. That, too, would be arranged.

Walking back to the home of Lamija's aunt, the couple met a friend who was working for a relief agency. He offered to let them call their children on his wireless telephone to tell them the news.

"We're going to Israel," Vllaznim told his children in Budapest.

"Not Sweden? Not France?"

"Israel is the only country that agrees to take us."

"But we'll be together? Then it's okay."

Did the family feel fright at the prospect of going to a country where a bus could blow up anywhere, anytime? "We're from Kosovo," answered Vllaznim. "Enough said."

Ten days after being driven from their home in Pristina, Lamija and Vllaznim were on the three-hour flight to Tel Aviv. Before landing, an escort from the Jewish Agency asked each Kosovar to slip on a tee shirt emblazoned with a blue and white Israeli logo. Vllaznim, a fiercely proud man, prickled at that request. "I may have lost everything else," he said, "but I still have dignity. I don't want to look like a monkey. And I *will* look like a monkey if I put your tee shirt over my winter clothes."

"I also didn't like the idea," says Lamija. "But I don't like any kind of conflict. It's not good, but that's the way I am."

• • •

The word spread quickly among journalists covering the refugees in Macedonia that the daughter of a couple honored as rescuers by Yad Vashem was being brought to Israel with her family. On the evening before the arrival of the refugees, Davor had gone to bed early because he had to wake up for guard duty starting at midnight. When the phone rang at 10:00 P.M., one of his children answered. It was a reporter who wanted to know if Davor would be at the airport the next morning.

"My dad is fast asleep. Call back in the morning."

"No, no, I need to talk to him now."

Blearily, Davor took the phone and heard the reporter say, "This story is a scoop for Israel. The second generation of the rescued welcomes the second generation of the rescuers. You must be there. We'll pick you up and take you to the airport." Davor knew only vaguely that the Korkuts had a daughter born fifteen years after their son.

The Israeli government wasn't shy about its own willingness to host a plane full of Kosovars. Prime Minister Benjamin Netanyahu and his wife went directly aboard the plane to welcome them. He singled out Lamija Jaha, saying, "Today we are closing a circle by granting shelter to the daughter of those who saved Jews."

The press awaited the moment when that daughter met the son of the rescued woman. But airport security officers knew nothing about Davor Bakovic's special status. Without clearance, he was not admitted to the arrival hall. "The journalists were cross," says Grania. "They grabbed someone in Netanyahu's entourage who got Davor in at the last moment."

As the refugees, most of them wearing the blue-and-white tee shirts rejected by Vllaznim, entered the arrival hall from the tarmac, they were "highly stressed out," says Grania. Not least, the Jahas. As microphones were thrust in their faces, journalists asked if they were happy to be in Israel.

"Happy? shot back Vllaznim, his blue eyes blazing. "Of course, I'm not happy. I've lost everything. I'm a refugee. Why should I be happy?"

At that moment, Davor Bakovic, a small, wiry man, was pushed forward. Vllaznim was on the verge of shoving him away.

"I'm Davor, son of Mira," he said in Serbo-Croatian.

Instantly, Vllaznim's expression changed. Davor hugged Vllaznim but saved his most heartfelt embrace for Lamija. "He felt that he was hugging a sister," says Grania, "even though he had known nothing about her until the previous evening."

In his remarks, Netanyahu said, "When we see...lines of refugees, and the faces of frightened children and crying mothers, we feel a responsibility to get up and help.... We are children of Abraham, who taught us about being hospitable to strangers." Speaking directly to the Jahas, the prime minister promised them that they would be granted Israeli citizenship if they so desired. And he noted the symbolism of that day, April 12. At sundown would begin Holocaust Remembrance Day.

The refugees were bussed to a nature camp that had been prepared for them on Israel's northern Mediterranean coast. The camp was named for Gail Rubin, a photographer who had been killed by terrorists on the nearby beach. Israeli children were on hand to offer a warm welcome. Even cell phones were offered. A neighboring kibbutz, Ma'agan Michael, provided daily dining and other essential services. The refugees lived in simple cabins which Israeli volunteers had tried to cheer up with wall hangings, flowers, and knickknacks. "They gave us two rooms," says Vllaznim. "Lamija and I had one, the kids the other. After about a month, a teacher came and said that two brothers from Kosovo had arrived, and she needed a place to put them. None of the other Albanian families wanted to give up any space. I said, 'Listen, we're not here voluntarily and we're not paying for this housing, so I don't have the right to say no to you. We'll give you one room.' We stayed five more months at the camp, all four of us in one room."

Vllaznim and Lamija both took part-time jobs in a kibbutz plastics factory and also studied Hebrew. "I had never even been in a factory before," says Lamija, "but that didn't matter. We were suddenly so full of life and energy! One life had ended but another had begun."

A front-page story about the Jahas appeared in the *New York Times* on May 2, 1999, several weeks after their arrival in Israel. The story, by Joel Greenberg, noted that Fitore Jaha, then twenty, had studied one year of computer science at the University of Pristina before fleeing from Kosovo. It was read by June Walker, president of worldwide Jewish women's service organization Hadassah. Walker had an idea: Why not offer Fitore the chance to continue her studies at Hadassah College in Jerusalem?

"I got this call at the nature center," says Fitore. "It was the head of Hadassah College. He was offering me a scholarship in computer science if I qualified. He was sending a car to pick me up for an interview. I thought he was kidding, but it was for real." The rub was that classes were starting in the fall—in Hebrew. For the next five months, Fitore studied the language intensively. "The first year was hard," she says. "I didn't give myself the option to fail, because I knew that many hopes were invested in me." Fitore received her degree in computer science in 2003. In the college's courtyard, only a short walk from Yad Vashem, a memorial stone was dedicated to her maternal grandparents.

By the spring of 2004, nearly all the Kosovar refugees hosted by Israel had returned home. But the Jaha family put down steadily deeper roots. They sold their apartment in Pristina and moved to a small apartment near a park in the Old Katamon neighborhood of Jerusalem. They bought a used Kia sedan. Fitore got a job as webmaster for GuruNet, a Web search engine. Fatos was completing a dental technician's course. Vllaznim found the kind of work he had done in Kosovo, maintaining large electrical transformers. Lamija got a job in information technology with the Israeli justice department. "We adults had to take jobs that paid less than most Israelis were willing to accept," says Vllaznim. "But we're the new people on the block. We didn't have a choice if we wanted to work."

The family's path toward Israeli citizenship was not easy, despite the promise of the Israeli prime minister "We had really good friends helped us get through the bureaucracy," says Lamija.

Finally, on a Sunday morning in March 2004 a workday in Israel, the Jahas left their apartment at 7:45 and drove to Interior Ministry office in central Jerusalem. They ascended a shabby stairway to the third floor citizenship registry. Though prepared for a long wait in a crowded office, the family was quickly ushered into the office of Tzipora Benita, an immigration officer. After speaking briefly with each of the Jahas, she said, "I'm not always so pleased to give the citizenship oath as I am to you."

One by one, the Jahas stepped forward and faced a blue-and-white Israeli flag in the corner of the office. The oath in Hebrew was simple and did not mention God: "I swear to be faithful to the state of Israel."

As they left the office, Benita said, "National elections are coming up. Now that you are citizens, you have to decide who to vote for."

Next door to the ministry, the Jahas ducked into a studio to have photos taken for their new passports. How long had it been since anyone in the family had actual passports?

"Twelve years," answered Vllaznim.

The Jahas walked briskly along the busy street in the brilliant Jerusalem sunlight. They were now Israelis like any others, even if their story was one of a kind.

Timeline

	SCHIVO [ITALY]	HENRI & CHAUMAT [BELGIUM]	POSTMA [NETHERLANDS]
1930s	**'35:** Ushi and her mother leave Germany for Italy **11/38:** Italian racial laws, banning Jews from key professions **'39:** Ushi's father joins them; later arrested; U. and mother briefly imprisoned		
1940	**6/40:** Italy declares war on Great Britain and France; makes pact with Germany	**5/40:** Germany invades Belgium	**5/40:** Germany invades Holland **Fall '04:** anti-Jewish laws begin; Nurit loses job and begins nursing school
		10/40: anti-Jewish laws, including banning from key professions; Jewish registration required	
1941	**'41:** Ushi and her mother sent to Citta di Castello; Ushi introduces herself to Monsignior Schivo	**5/41:** "Aryanization" of Jewish property begins	**1/41:** Jewish registration required **2/41:** roundups begin; 425 young men deported
1942		**Spring '42:** yellow star required **Mid '42–Mid '44:** roundups and deportations of Jews **8/42:** first roundups of Jews in Antwerp **9/42:** Gestapo search Lipski household **Fall '42:** after others change their minds, Mme. Chaumat agrees to care for Raffi	**5/42:** Jews required to wear yellow star **6/42:** mass deportations began **7/42–9/43:** mass roundups and deportations

LAPORTERIE [FRANCE]	JAROMIRSKA [POLAND]	KORKUT [YUGOSLAVIA]	
	7/39: Germany invades Poland (beginning WWII)		1930s
6/40: Germany invades France; country divided into Occupied and Unoccupied (southern) zone, with French government in Vichy **7/40:** Laporterie receives "pass" from Germans to cross Demarcation line between home and work; after, begins fabricating passes for Jews **10/40:** Vichy begins French anti-Jewish laws; first internments of foreign Jews	**4/40:** Leokadia's husband Bolek is arrested by Germans as a Polish national		1940
5/41–8/41: massive roundups of Jews around Paris	**6/41:** Leokadia begins work in a German warehouse in Warsaw	**Spring '41:** Nazi Germany invades and conquers Yugoslavia **7/41:** Tito begins partisan uprising, fighting Germans and later Serb nationalists (chetniks) **Late '41:** Jewish men, including Mira Papo's father, rounded up in Sarajevo, capital of Bosnia and Herzegovina	1941
3/42: first deportation of Jews from France to Auschwitz **3/42–7/44:** roundups and deportations (8/42–first roundups for deportation of Jews in Unoccupied zone) **11/42:** German military takes over "Unoccupied" zone **Fall '42:** Gestapo come to look for Laporterie; he lives in hiding	**10/42:** Leokadia finds baby by the road, after nearby ghetto is "liquidated"	**Early '42:** Jewish women, including Mira's mother, are rounded up. Like the men, most were murdered. Mira escapes to join partisans in the forest **4/42:** Mira forced to return to occupied Sarajevo; she is hidden by Dervis and Servet Korkut **'42:** Dervis hides the Sarajevo Haggadah **8/42:** Mira escapes to the Dalmatian coast	1942

	SCHIVO [ITALY]	HENRI & CHAUMAT [BELGIUM]	POSTMA [NETHERLANDS]
1943	**9/43:** Allies land in southern Italy; German troops move in; Jews deported from Rome **10/43:** Ushi and parents imprisoned; temporarily released; Schivo hides Ushi and parents	**4/43:** Mme. Chaumat moves to small village with Raffi **8/43:** Raffi recognized on street; decision made to stay put	**3/43:** roundups at Jewish hospital where Nurit works **6/43:** Postma family takes in Nurit
1944	**Winter '44:** Germans move into area; Schivo finds new hiding places **7/44:** area is liberated by British (Germany holds northern Italy until the war's end); Ushi and parents are free	**8/44:** Brussels and Ghent liberated by British and American troops; Raffi and parents are free	**Spring '44:** Germans search Postma house for able-bodied men **9/44:** Allies liberate southern part of country; Germans continue to hold north
MID '40S–MID '50S			**4/45:** Germans retreat; Nurit is free
LATE '60S–PRESENT			
	Jewish toll: 8,000 of 57,000	Jewish toll: 40,000 of 65,000	Jewish toll: 105,000 of 140,000

LAPORTERIE [FRANCE]	JAROMIRSKA [POLAND]	KORKUT [YUGOSLAVIA]	
	'43: two incidents in which certain neighbors attempt to report on Leokadia		1943
8/44: France liberated	**Summer '44:** Russians move through Poland toward Warsaw **9/44:** Leokadia and Bogusha leave home to try to flee the fighting		1944
	1/45: Warsaw liberated by Russians **Summer '45:** Bolek returns **9/45:** Bogusha's father appears at Leokadia's door	**6/46:** Dervis is tried as anticommunist; Mira does not testify on his behalf and believes he has been executed **'47–'53:** Dervis is imprisoned **'56:** A daughter, Lamija, is born to Dervis and Servet	MID '40S–MID '50S
		'69: Dervis dies **'72:** Mira emigrates to Israel to join her son Davor **4/92:** Serbian siege of Sarajevo begins; Servet is evacuated from city **'94:** Mira, haunted by her failure to help Dervis, nominates him and Servet to be Rightous Among Nations. **3/97:** Servet and her late husband honored by Israel in Paris ceremony **'98:** Mira dies in Israel **3/99:** during the "ethnic cleansing" campaign, Serb militias order Albanian Moslems to leave Pristina, Kosovo; Lamija Jaha's family become refugees **4/99:** Jahas invited to Israel; welcomed by Davor **3/04:** Jahas become Israeli citizens	LATE '60S–PRESENT
Jewish toll: 76,000 of 300,000	**Jewish toll: 3 million of 3.3 million**	**Jewish toll: 60,000 of 76,000**	

Sources

This is primarily a work of reportage. I depended on the scholarship of others to establish what I hope is an reliable framework for each case. The following sources are of special interest on the topic of the Righteous Among Nations:

Bakaršić, Kemal, *Never-Ending Story of C-4436, A.K.A. The Sarajevo Haggada Codex*. Vienna: Wiener Slawistische Almanach, Sonderband 52, 2001 Wien/Munchen. pp. 267–289.

Bauminger, Arieh L. *The Righteous Among Nations*. Jerusalem: Yad Vashem, 1990.

Ceresnjes, Ivan: *Caught in the Winds of War* (Policy Study No. 17): Jerusalem: Institute of the World Jewish Congress, 1999.

Dinour, Ben-Zion: *Loi du Martyre et de l'Héroïsme Yad Vashem* (Martyrs and Heroes Remembrance Act Yad Vashem. Paris: Association Les Fils et Filles des Déportées de France, 2003.

Gilbert, Martin. *The Righteous*. New York: Henry Holt and Company, 2003.

Laqueur, Walter. *The Holocaust Encyclopedia*: New Haven and London: Yale University Press, 2001.

Paldiel, Morecai. *The Path of the Righteous*. Hoboken: KTAV Publishing House Inc., 1992.

Paldiel, Morecai. *Saving the Jews*. Rockville: Schreiber Publishers, 2000.